Information Choice in
Macroeconomics and Finance

Information Choice in Macroeconomics and Finance

Laura L. Veldkamp

PRINCETON UNIVERSITY PRESS

PRINCETON AND OXFORD

Library of Congress Cataloging-in-Publication Data

Veldkamp, Laura.

  Information choice in macroeconomics and finance / Laura L. Veldkamp.

      p. cm.

  Includes bibliographical references and index.

  ISBN 978-0-691-14220-3 (alk. paper)

  1. Macroeconomics–Decision making. 2. Finance–Decision making.
  3. Information resources. 4. Choice (Psychology) I. Title.

    HB172.5.V45 2011

    339.5–dc22

                          2011010183

British Library Cataloging-in-Publication Data is available

This book has been composed in Times

Printed on acid-free paper. ∞

Typeset by S R Nova Pvt Ltd, Bangalore, India

Printed in the United States of America

10 9 8 7 6 5 4 3 2 1

Contents

Acknowledgments

While working on this book, I received constructive suggestions and comments from many people. The book grew out of a set of notes that I had prepared for a Ph.D. symposium held at Humboldt University in Berlin and later expanded for a Ph.D. topics class in macroeconomics at New York University. The students in both classes read through drafts of the book and provided me with enormously useful feedback.

In addition, many colleagues and economists at other schools provided their input. In particular, I am grateful to Manuel Amador, Cosmin Ilut, Peter Kondor, Pierre-Olivier Weill, Mirko Wiederholt, and two anonymous reviewers for extensive comments. Anna Orlik provided invaluable editing and proofreading assistance and helped formulate and solve many of the exercises. Of course, I retain responsibility for any remaining errors. I appreciate being notified of errata. Please email comments to lveldkam@stern.nyu.edu. I will try to maintain a list of corrections on my homepage.

Last, but not least, I am indebted to my husband, Stijn Van Nieuwerburgh, for encouraging me to undertake and complete this project.

Information Choice in Macroeconomics and Finance

PART I
Preliminaries

Chapter One

Why Study Information Choice?

The developed world is becoming increasingly a knowledge-driven economy. Fewer and fewer workers are involved in producing goods. Instead, much of value added comes from activities such as consulting, forecasting, and financial analysis. Even traditional firms devote significant resources to activities such as managerial decision making, price-setting, and evaluating potential investments, each of which involves acquiring, processing, and synthesizing information. Most macroeconomic models focus on goods production. Similarly, most portfolio and asset-pricing theories derive the investment decisions that maximize investors' utility. Only a small body of research tells us about the information acquisition that regulates these production and investment decisions, even as the amount of resources devoted to information-related activities grows ever larger. This book examines macroeconomics and finance models where people choose what information they want to know.

Every expectation, mean, variance, and covariance, every moment of every random variable, is conditional on some information set. Typically, we think of that information set as consisting of all the past realizations of the variable. But what if people do not know the entire history of all the realizations? Or, alternatively, what if they have information in addition to the history? Which information set people have will typically change every moment of the random variable. The information does not affect what the future realizations of the random variable will be. It changes what people know about those realizations. Moments of a random variable summarize what someone knows about it.

Since means, variances, and covariances appear all over economics and finance, how people evaluate these moments affects how they behave in any environment where a random variable matters. The effect of random changes in productivity in a business cycle model, of changes in asset valuation in a portfolio problem, of shocks to endowments in a consumption/savings problem, of money-supply shocks in a price-setting problem, and of changes in the state in a coordination game all depend on what information people know.

This book describes both a narrow and a broad research area. It focuses narrowly on predicting what information agents have and how that information affects aggregate outcomes. It presents a tool kit for writing applied theories: it does not explore theory so much for its own sake but explores theories that provide explanations for the phenomena we see in the world around us. The applications are wide-ranging, from asset pricing to monetary economics to international economics to business cycles. This book covers both the mathematical structures necessary to work in this area and ways of thinking about the modeling choices that arise. My hope is that at the end, the reader will be at the frontier of applied theory research in information choice and might be inspired to contribute to it.

1.1 TYPES OF LEARNING MODELS

The literature on learning is expansive. Before delving into the material, let's review what kinds of subjects are covered here and what is omitted.

Learning is often used to refer to a literature in which agents do not use Bayes' law to form their expectations. One example is adaptive least-squares learning, where agents behave as econometricians, trying to discover the optimal linear forecasting rule for the next period's state. Evans and Honkapohja (2001) offer an exhaustive treatment of this literature. Information frictions also feature prominently in the literature on model misspecification. In these models, agents do not know the true model of the economy and choose actions that would produce good outcomes even if their model of the economy is not quite right (Hansen and Sargent 2003). This book focuses exclusively on Bayesian learning. It considers only environments where agents update their information sets using Bayes' law. They know the true model of the economy and are uncertain only about which realization of the state will be drawn by nature. Agents in this class of models are not uncertain about the distribution of outcomes from which nature draws that state. In other words, they have rational expectations. This focus creates a distinction between the study of the process through which agents learn and the information they acquire and learn from. It allows for a deeper understanding of what information agents observe by making simple assumptions about how learning takes place.

Among models with Bayesian learning, there are models of passive learning and models of active learning. In passive-learning models, agents are endowed with signals and/or learn as an unintended consequence of observing prices and quantities. One set of examples is models where information is exogenous. Information may be an endowment (Morris and Shin 1998), or it may arrive stochastically (Mankiw and Reis 2002). Even when information is endogenous, agents can still be passive learners. For example, information could be produced as a by-product of other activity, or information could be conveyed by market prices. This is still passive learning because agents are not exercising any control over the information they observe.

The other way people acquire information is intentionally, by choice. Acquiring information by choice is also called active learning. This choice might involve purchasing information, choosing how to allocate limited attention, or choosing an action, taking into account the information it will generate. Such models go beyond explaining the consequences of having information; they also predict what information agents will choose to have. Active learning is starting to play a more prominent role in macroeconomics and finance. In macroeconomics, it has been used to reexamine consumption savings problems (Sims 1998), price-setting frictions (Maćkowiak and Wiederholt 2009b; Reis 2006), and business-cycle dynamics (Veldkamp and Wolfers 2007). In finance, active learning has a long tradition in investment-allocation models (Grossman and Stiglitz 1980; Hellwig 1980) and has more recently been used in dynamic asset-pricing theories (Peng and Xiong 2006), models of mutual funds (Garcia and Vanden 2005; Kacperczyk, Van Nieuwerburgh, and Veldkamp 2010), and models of decentralized trade (Golosov, Lorenzoni, and Tsyvinski 2008).

The vast majority of models in dynamic macroeconomics and finance still employ passive learning. Beliefs change when agents observe new outcomes or when new signals arrive because the model assumes they do. While such models clarify the role of information in aggregate outcomes, they do not tell us what information we may or may not observe. Models of active learning complement this literature by predicting what information agents choose to observe. Because an active-learning model can predict information sets on the basis of observable features of the economic environment, pairing it with a passive-learning model where information predicts observable outcomes results in a model where observables predict observables. That is the kind of model that is empirically testable. If the goal is to write applied theories that explain observed phenomena, we need a testable theory to know if the proposed explanation is correct. Therefore, while this book devotes substantial attention to passive-learning models, which form the bulk of the literature, it systematically complements this coverage with a discussion of how information choice affects the predictions.

Bayesian learning models are also used prolifically in other literatures. While this book focuses on applications of interest to researchers in macroeconomics and macro-finance, others cover related topics: Vives (2008) and Brunnermeier (2001) focus on market microstructure and information aggregation in rational expectations markets; Chamley (2004) explores models of herding where agents move sequentially and learn from each other's actions. Each of these volumes would be a good complement to the material presented here.

1.2 THEMES THAT RUN THROUGH THE BOOK

Theme 1: Information choice bridges the gap between rational and behavioral approaches. The first theme is about the place information-based models occupy in the macroeconomics and finance literature. We look to incomplete-information models in situations where the standard full-information, rational models fail to explain some feature of the data. Since these are the same set of circumstances that motivate much of the work in behavioral economics, modeling incomplete information is an alternative to the behavioral economics approach. Both literatures take a small step away from the fully informed, ex post optimal decision making that characterizes classical macroeconomics and finance. This step is useful because adding incomplete information allows the standard models to explain a broader set of phenomena such as portfolio underdiversification, asset-price bubbles, inertia in asset allocation, and sticky prices.

The line between incomplete information and behavioral assumptions can be further blurred because some approaches to modeling incomplete information—for example, information-processing constraints—are a form of bounded rationality. Yet, there is a fundamental distinction between the two approaches.

At its core, information choice is a rational choice. Agents in information-choice models treat their information constraints just as agents in a standard model treat their budget constraints. Rather than attacking tenets of the rational framework, information choice seeks to extend it by enlarging the set of choice variables. The advantage of this approach is that requiring information sets to be a solution to a rational-choice problem disciplines the forms of information asymmetry one can consider in a given environment.

Theme 2: Information is different from physical goods because it is expensive to discover and cheap to replicate. Because information is expensive to discover and cheap to replicate, the more copies of it are sold, the lower the cost per copy. In other words, information has increasing returns to scale. That property often produces extreme solutions and complementarities that make the predictions of models with information choice fundamentally different from those without it (Wilson 1975).

The fact that the economics of producing information is so different from the economics of producing physical goods allows information-choice models to explain phenomena that pose a challenge to standard theory. This idea shows up in the discussion of information choice and investment, where investors value information about a larger asset more because one piece of information can be used to evaluate every dollar of the investment. It reappears in the section on information markets, where information has a market price that decreases in the quantity of information sold because it is free to replicate. That makes observing information that others observe a cost-effective strategy.

Theme 3: Correlated information or coordination motive? Many works in economics and finance study situations where many agents take similar actions at the same time. Examples include bank runs, speculative attacks, market bubbles, and fads. The most common explanation is the existence of a *coordination motive*: people want to behave similarly because acting like others directly increases their utility. Yet, in some settings, people appear to be acting as if they had a coordination motive when no such motive is apparent. An alternative explanation is that people observe *correlated information*, which leads them to behave similarly. One example is the theory of herds, which is based on the following parable (taken from Banerjee 1992). Suppose diners arrive sequentially at two adjacent restaurants, A and B. The first and second diners believe A to be the better restaurant. So, both dine there. The third diner believes that B is the better restaurant but sees no one there. He infers the two diners in restaurant A must have been told that A was better and chooses A over B. All subsequent diners make similar calculations and dine at restaurant A. Thus, sequential, publicly observable actions provide one reason that people could have similar information sets. An alternative reason why people may have similar information is based on information choice. In the language of the parable, all the diners might go to restaurant B because a reviewer on the evening news recommends it. A diner could acquire private information by trying each restaurant. But watching the evening news and seeing the information that everyone else sees is less costly.

Theme 4: The effect of introducing information choice depends on the strategic motives in actions and on whether the information being chosen is public or private. This theme governs the organization of the book. The first half considers settings with strategic complementarity, while the second half focuses on substitutability. Each half examines public and private information choice.

One example of the interaction between strategic motives and information choice is when the combination of coordination motives and heterogeneous (private) information creates powerful inertia. Because information is imperfect, people do not know what the state of the world is and cannot adjust their actions precisely whenever that state changes. Furthermore, people do not know what the average action of others is because they do not know what information others have. If information accumulates over time, all people know more about what happened in the past than about the present state of the world. Thus, to be better coordinated, people put more weight on past than on current signals. Being unresponsive to new information creates inertia in actions. They also choose to acquire little new information because the old information is much more useful. Since actions can only respond to the changes in the state that people know about, delayed learning slows reactions. This delay creates even more inertia. Researchers in monetary economics use this mechanism to generate price stickiness.

However, when people want to coordinate their actions and have access to public information, the result is typically multiple equilibria. Such an economy may exhibit very little inertia because changes in expectations could cause switches from one equilibrium to another.

In other settings, people do not want to coordinate but instead prefer to take actions that are different from those of other people. Such strategic substitutability makes people want to act based on information that others do not have. They prefer private information. Since information about recent events is scarcer, people give more weight to recent signals. Instead of inertia, this kind of model generates highly volatile actions. Since asset markets are settings where investors prefer to buy assets that others do not demand because their price is lower, this mechanism provides a rationale for the volatility of investment behavior and, in turn, the volatility of asset prices.

Even though people with strategic substitutability in actions prefer private information, they may acquire public information if it is substantially cheaper than private information. Because information is expensive to discover and cheap to replicate, public or partially public information that can be sold in volume is less expensive to produce and therefore to purchase. As explained in theme 3, people who observe common information typically make similar decisions. Even though people's strategic motives dictate they should take actions that differ, their similar information sets may lead them to take similar actions. The result is coordinated actions.

The following table summarizes the key model outcomes from the four types of models described in the four preceding paragraphs. Each has either complementarity or substitutability in actions. In addition, each model allows agents to choose either public or private signals. For example, models with complementarity and private information choice typically produce inertia in actions, while models with substitutability and private information typically generate actions that are dispersed and volatile.

Model Outcome	Private Signals	Public Signals
Complementarity	Inertia	Multiple equilibria
Substitutability	Dispersion and volatility	Coordinated actions

Theme 5: Information choice facilitates empirical testing of information-based theories. Writing models that predict what agents know is a way to get around the problem that information sets are not directly observable. If the theory predicts information sets on the basis of observable variables and then uses those information sets to predict actions of agents that are also observable, then the theory begins and ends with observable variables. A theory that begins and ends with observable variables is empirically verifiable. Therefore, an entire chapter is devoted to various ways of empirically evaluating information-based theories. It draws together ideas about what kinds of measurable fundamentals determine information sets, suggests proxy variables that others have used to measure information, and collects stylized facts that support a range of asymmetric information theories.

1.3 ORGANIZATION OF THE BOOK

This book is meant to be used as a guide or reference for researchers or as a textbook for a second-year Ph.D. course in economics or finance. One of the unusual features of this book is that it touches on many different topics, and yet it is not meant as an introductory text to macroeconomics, monetary economics, or finance. The reason for this approach is that each of these fields has developed insights about endogenous information that can and should be applied to other fields. Yet, since communication across research communities is often limited, opportunities for doing cutting-edge research are being lost because those who know the tools are not familiar with many of their potential applications and vice versa.

As a result, the text is filled with suggestions for how ideas in one field might be applied to another. This feature should make it a worthwhile read for graduate students searching for a dissertation topic. It also draws connections between literatures by illustrating, for example, that the driving force in a monetary-policy model is the same as that in a portfolio-choice model. These connections can help established researchers familiar with one area to quickly have a strong intuitive grasp of the logic behind the models in another area. This feature makes the chapters on monetary non-neutrality and business cycles perfectly appropriate for a class on asset pricing and the portfolio-choice chapter appropriate for a class on macroeconomics. The ideas about how information choice can generate inertia in prices are just as relevant for explaining inertia in portfolio choices and the mechanism by which news about future productivity affects current output can be used as the basis of an asset-pricing model. Likewise, ideas about how agents choose to trade financial securities can be used to explain puzzling features of cross-country trade in goods and services. By drawing together insights from various corners of macro-economics and finance, I hope this book might advance work in endogenous information by illuminating the possibilities for new applications of existing tools. Ultimately, such applications could generate new insights about the role of information in the aggregate economy.

Chapters 2 and 3 contain essential mathematical tools for understanding the material in chapters 4 through 9. Chapters 4 and 5 consider a strategic game with many players. Stripping away the details of any particular application makes the general themes that run through the later models more transparent. Chapter 4 shows that when agents can choose information to acquire before playing a strategic game, complementarity (substitutability) in actions typically generates complementarity (substitutability) in information choices. It also explains why heterogeneous information can deliver unique predictions out of a model with coordination motives where common knowledge would predict multiple equilibrium outcomes. Chapter 5 illustrates how changing the amount of public information agents know affects welfare differently than does changing the amount of private information.

Chapter 6 uses models from monetary economics to show how the combination of coordination motives in price-setting and heterogeneous information creates strong inertia in actions. When information choice is added to this setting, the coordination motive in information strengthens this inertia. Chapter 7 shows how the decision to invest in risky assets exhibits substitutability instead of complementarity. As a result, agents want to acquire information that is different from what other agents know. This different information leads them to hold different portfolios. Chapter 8 explores a setting where agents choose risky investments. But rather than focusing on the interaction between strategic motives in actions and information choices, it introduces the idea of increasing returns in information. Neither the monetary nor the investment models considered a production economy. Introducing an active role for information into such a general-equilibrium setting creates new challenges. Chapter 9 explores what model features allow information to act as an aggregate shock and create realistic business cycle fluctuations or realistic asset-price dynamics.

Each of the applied theory chapters (6 through 9) concludes with ideas about how its tools or insights might be applied to answer other questions. Each particular project may or may not be viable. The goal is to illustrate how the main concepts might be applied more broadly so that the reader might be better able to formulate his or her own research idea.

Of course, a work of applied theory is rarely considered complete without some empirical support for its hypothesis. Therefore, chapter 10 is devoted to the subject of testing information-based models. Chapter 11 offers some concluding thoughts.

As information technology makes it possible to access a vast array of knowledge, constraints on what one can and cannot observe become less relevant. Yet, having access to information is not the same as knowing it. Just as you can buy a textbook and not learn its material, agents with access to information might not really acquire it in their working memories. But putting information in our working memories— learning—is a choice. In other words, information constraints are systematically being replaced with information choices. It is such choices that this book seeks to understand.

Chapter Two

Bayesian Updating

The literature on Bayesian theory is extensive. This chapter does not attempt to be comprehensive. Rather, it provides only the minimum set of necessary tools to understand the material that follows. We begin with the simplest statement of Bayes' law.

Bayes' law 1. *The probability of event A occurring, given that event B occurred, is*

$$P(A|B) = \frac{P(B|A)P(A)}{P(B)}$$

as long as $P(B) \neq 0$.

This law comes from the definition of a conditional probability:

$$P(A|B) = \frac{P(A \cap B)}{P(B)}. \tag{2.1}$$

Likewise, $P(B|A) = P(A \cap B)/P(A)$. Rearranging both of these expressions yields

$$P(A|B)P(B) = P(A \cap B) = P(B|A)P(A). \tag{2.2}$$

Dividing through by $P(B)$ delivers Bayes' law. (See Elliott, Aggoun, and Moore 1995 or Lipster and Shiryaev's book 2001 for technical conditions and rigorous derivations of the various forms of Bayes' law.)

For continuous random variables with smooth distributions, the probability of any discrete realization is zero. However, Bayes' law can be applied to probability densities as well.

Bayes' law 2. *The probability density of event A, given that event B occurred, is*

$$f(A|B) = \frac{f(B|A)f(A)}{f(B)}.$$

Sometimes the term $f(B)$ in Bayes' law is replaced with the equivalent term $\int_{-\infty}^{\infty} f(B|A)f(A)dA$.

2.1 NORMAL RANDOM VARIABLES

For normal random variables, applying this version of Bayes' law can be computationally intensive. Luckily, there is a handy shortcut. Suppose there is an unknown random variable x and according to one's prior beliefs $x \sim N(A, \alpha^{-1})$. In other words, before observing any additional information, x was believed to be A on average, with a precision of α. Note that the precision is the inverse of the variance (not the standard deviation). We will work extensively with precisions because doing so generally makes the solutions simpler, as we will see shortly.

Suppose that an agent in a model or an econometrician sees a signal $B = x + e$, where $e \sim N(0, \beta^{-1})$. From here on, I will use the shorthand $B|x \sim N(x, \beta^{-1})$ to describe this signal. We assume that the signal is an unbiased piece of data about x with precision β. We also assume that B is *conditionally independent* of A. That means that B and A are related only because they are both pieces of information about x, but their signal errors are independent. Independence implies that $E[(A - x)(B - x)] = 0$.

Given the prior information and the signal, the agent forms a posterior belief, also called a conditional belief, about the value of x using Bayes' law:

$$E[x|B] = \frac{\alpha A + \beta B}{\alpha + \beta}. \tag{2.3}$$

This tells us that the posterior belief is simply a weighted average of the prior belief and the signal. Each is weighted by its relative precision. If a signal contains no information about x, it would have zero precision. In this case, the posterior belief would be the same as the prior belief.

The posterior variance (or conditional variance) that results from applying Bayes' law also has a simple form:

$$V[x|B] = (\alpha + \beta)^{-1}. \tag{2.4}$$

If we invert both sides, this expression says that the precision of the posterior is the precision of the prior, plus the precision of the signal. Every time we get another piece of independent information, we can simply add its precision onto what we had before.

The formulas also apply to multivariate normals, as long as the division is replaced with a matrix inverse. If x is an $N \times 1$ vector of random variables, A and B are $N \times 1$ vectors, and α^{-1} and β^{-1} are $N \times N$ variance-covariance matrices, then $E[x|B] = (\alpha + \beta)^{-1}(\alpha A + \beta B)$ and $V[x|B] = (\alpha + \beta)^{-1}$.

But what if A and B are not conditionally independent? If A and B have some common component to their errors, the common component must be removed and agents can form posterior beliefs over the independent piece. This may mean subtracting a known common piece of the signal or running a linear regression of one signal on the other and using the residual.

What if B is not an unbiased signal? Suppose that $B = cx + d + e$ where c and d are non-zero constants and $e \sim N(0, \beta^{-1})$. We could apply the previous formula to $(B - d)/c$, which would be an unbiased signal of x. In doing such a transformation, do not forget to transform the variance accordingly. In this case, the variance of the unbiased signal would be β^{-1}/c^2.

2.2 UNIFORM RANDOM VARIABLES

Occasionally, working with uniform variables makes a model more tractable. Updating with uniform variables is conceptually easy. But one needs to pay some attention to avoid problems at the bounds of the uniform intervals.

Suppose that the prior belief is that $x \sim \text{unif}[-b, b]$ and an agent observes a signal $k = x + \varepsilon$ where $\varepsilon \sim \text{unif}[-a, a]$. The simplest case is where $k - a \geq -b$ and $k + a \leq b$. This means that for every value of x that the signal assigns a positive probability density, the prior beliefs also assign a positive probability density to x. Under the prior beliefs, the probability densities of the x and the signal k are both $1/(2b)$. The probability density of the signal given the state x is $f(k|x) = 1/(2a)$. Applying Bayes' law, $f(x|k) = 1/(2a) \cdot 1/(2b)/(1/(2b)) = 1/(2a)$ for all $x \in [k - a, k + a]$. If x is outside that range, then $f(k|x) = 0$, thus Bayes' law dictates that $f(x|k) = 0$ as well. In other words, $x|k \sim \text{unif}[k - a, k + a]$.

What if the signal k is close to one of the bounds of the prior distribution? For example, suppose that $k - a < -b$. Then the set of values that both the prior and the signal place positive probability mass on is $[-b, k + a]$. The posterior will then be uniform over this smaller interval: $x|k \sim \text{unif}[-b, k + a]$. In sum,

$$x|k \sim \text{unif}\left[\max(-b, k - a), \min(b, k + a)\right]. \tag{2.5}$$

The diffuse prior. One way to specify uniform prior beliefs is the so-called diffuse prior. This assumption is used to represent an agent who knows absolutely nothing about the value of a random variable. A diffuse prior for a variable x is a uniform distribution over the entire real line: $x \sim \text{unif}[-\infty, +\infty]$. Since the probability density of a continuous uniform interval $[a, b]$ is $1/(b-a)$, the density of a variable with a diffuse prior is zero.

If an agent with a diffuse prior gets a signal, his posterior is the distribution of the random variable conditional on that signal. For example, suppose the signal is $k = x + \varepsilon$ where $\varepsilon \sim \text{unif}[-a, a]$. Applying Bayes' law for uniform variables (2.5) and taking the limit as $b \to \infty$ delivers $x|k \sim \text{unif}[k - a, k + a]$. In other words, the posterior probability density $f(x|k)$ is $1/(2a)$ over the interval $[k - a, k + a]$ and 0 everywhere else.

The fact that $f(x|k)$ and $f(k|x)$ take the same form when the prior belief is diffuse does not depend on the signal being uniform. If the prior is diffuse but the signal is normally distributed, this same result holds. One consequence of this property is that the following two modeling assumptions are equivalent: (1) agent i has a diffuse prior, observes signal k_i, and updates, and (2) agent i has a prior belief given by $f(x|k_i)$.

2.3 THE KALMAN FILTER

When applied in dynamic models, the formula for Bayesian updating with normal variables becomes the Kalman filter. The Kalman filtering formulas can be applied whenever there is a problem that can be written in the following form: an unknown state variable x_t has a known linear evolution over time:

$$x_{t+1} = Dx_t + Fe_{t+1}. \tag{2.6}$$

In each period t, there is a signal about x_t, which takes the form

$$y_t = Gx_t + H\eta_t. \tag{2.7}$$

The two shock sequences e_t and η_t are mutually independent, independent and identically distributed (i.i.d.) over time, standard normal variables.

While the dynamic problems we study in this book typically have an unknown state that is a scalar, in principle, the Kalman filtering formula can be applied to vectors as well. If x_t and y_t are $n \times 1$ and $m \times 1$ vectors, then D and F are $n \times n$ matrices, G is $m \times n$, H is $m \times m$, $e_t \sim N(0, I_n)$ is $n \times 1$, and $\eta_t \sim N(0, I_m)$ is $m \times 1$.

To start out, there must be prior beliefs. Suppose that $x_0 \sim N(\hat{x}_0, \Sigma_0)$. For all $t > 0$, let $\hat{x}_t$ denote the expectation of x_t conditional on all the signals y observed up to but excluding time t: $\hat{x}_t \equiv E[x_t|y_0, \ldots, y_{t-1}]$. Similarly, let Σ_t denote the conditional variance of x_t: $\Sigma_t \equiv Var[x_t|y_0, \ldots, y_{t-1}] = E[(x_t - \hat{x}_t)(x_t - \hat{x}_t)']$. Then the following three recursive formulas describe how to update beliefs $\hat{x}$ and Σ:

$$\hat{x}_{t+1} = (D - K_tG)\hat{x}_t + K_ty_t \tag{2.8}$$

$$K_t = D\Sigma_tG'(G\Sigma_tG' + HH')^{-1} \tag{2.9}$$

$$\Sigma_{t+1} = D\Sigma_tD' + FF' - D\Sigma_tG'(G\Sigma_tG' + HH')^{-1}G\Sigma_tD. \tag{2.10}$$

The term K_t is called the *Kalman gain*. It represents how much weight is put on the new information y_t, relative to the old information in the prior belief $\hat{x}_t$ when forming the posterior belief $\hat{x}_{t+1}$. The Kalman gain is the analog of the term $\beta/(\alpha + \beta)$ in (2.3) that dictates how much weight the signal is given relative to the prior belief. In that formula, this weight is written in terms of the precision of the prior α and the precision of the signal β. That same Bayesian weight can be written in terms of variances as $\alpha^{-1}/(\alpha^{-1} + \beta^{-1})$. This formula tells us that new information is weighted in proportion to the variance of the prior, divided by the sum of the prior and signal variances. Substituting the prior and signal variances from the Kalman problem into the Bayesian weight formula (and multiplying by D) produces the Kalman gain. In the Kalman system, the unbiased signal about x_t is $G^{-1}y_t$ (where G^{-1} denotes the left inverse). Conditional on x_t, that signal has variance $G^{-1}HH'(G')^{-1}$. The variance of the prior beliefs about x_t is Σ_t. Thus the weight given to the signal $G^{-1}y_t$ is $\Sigma_t(\Sigma_t + G^{-1}HH'(G')^{-1})^{-1}$. We can insert two identity matrices, $(G')^{-1}G'$ and GG^{-1}, just before and after the inverse term to get $D^{-1}K_tG$. Multiplying $D^{-1}K_tG$ by $G^{-1}y_t$ leaves $D^{-1}K_ty_t$. The Kalman gain is pre-multiplied by D because $E[x_{t+1}|\hat{x}_t] = D\hat{x}_t$. The Bayesian updating formula tells us how to form posterior beliefs about x_t, conditional on y_t. To convert those into beliefs about x_{t+1}, pre-multiply by D.

The conditional variance of $\hat{x}_{t+1}$ can be similarly interpreted as the recursive analog of the Bayesian updating formula for posterior variance of normal variables (2.4). The conditional variance Σ_t is the inverse of the posterior precision of beliefs about x_{t+1}. According to Bayes' law for normal variables (2.4), that precision is the sum of the prior precision and the signal precision. The prior precision comes from taking the variance of the left and right sides of equation (2.6). That delivers $Var[x_{t+1}|y_0, \ldots, y_{t-1}] = D\Sigma_t D' + FF'$. As shown above, the signal $G^{-1}y_t$ has precision $G(HH')^{-1}G'$. Combining these expressions and some algebraic manipulation delivers Σ_{t+1} in (2.10).

2.4 BAYESIAN UPDATING IN CONTINUOUS TIME

The key result for solving Bayesian updating problems in continuous time comes from theorem 12.1 in Lipster and Shiryaev's book (2001). Suppose there is an unobserved state process θ_t that is a continuous-time diffusion process:

$$d\theta_t = (a_0 + a_1\theta_t)dt + b_1 dW_1(t) + b_2 dW_2(t), \tag{2.11}$$

where W_1 and W_2 are standard Brownian motions. Thus, the drift is a linear function of the state variable's level. There are two random innovation terms because the signal will contain information about one of these innovations (W_2) but not the other (W_1). An agent observes the signal, which is also a continuous-time diffusion process:

$$ds_t = (A_0 + A_1\theta_t)dt + B dW_2(t). \tag{2.12}$$

The version of this problem presented in Lipster and Shiryaev is more general than this. It allows all the coefficients in both the state and the signal process to be deterministic functions of time and of the signal s_t, as long as these functions satisfy some integrability conditions.

Then, if the agent forms expectations that minimize the mean squared error of his forecast, those expectations will be normally distributed with a mean that follows a continuous-time diffusion process: $\theta_t|\{s'_t\}_{t'\leq t} \sim N(\hat{\theta}_t, \hat{\gamma}_t)$, where

$$d\hat{\theta}_t = (a_0 + a_1\hat{\theta}_t)dt + \frac{b_2 B + \hat{\gamma}_t A_1}{B^2}\left(ds_t - \left(A_0 + A_1\hat{\theta}_t\right)dt\right) \tag{2.13}$$

$$\frac{d\hat{\gamma}_t}{dt} = 2a_1\hat{\gamma}_t + b_1^2 + b_2^2 - \left(\frac{b_2 B + \hat{\gamma}_t A_1}{B}\right)^2. \tag{2.14}$$

Given some exogenous time-0 prior beliefs $\hat{\theta}_0$ and $\hat{\gamma}_0$, (2.13) and (2.14) describe the evolution of the mean and variance of beliefs.

In equation (2.13), the first term is just the expected drift of $\hat{\theta}$. The second term adjusts that drift for information incorporated in the signal s_t. The information that the agent wants to extract from s_t is knowledge of $W_2(t)$, because that enters in equation (2.11) for θ_t and information about θ_t directly. Thus, he constructs $dW_2(t) + A_1(\theta_t - \hat{\theta}_t)dt/B = (ds_t - (A_0 + A_1\hat{\theta}_t)dt)/B$. The term $b_2 + \hat{\gamma}_t A_1/B$ is the analog of the Kalman gain in discrete time. It is the weight that the agent puts on the new information. That weight is higher if b_2 is higher because the state is more sensitive to the shock W_2. The weight on the new signal is also higher if the agent has a more uncertain prior belief ($\hat{\gamma}_t$ is higher). The remaining term

A_1/B accounts for the fact that if $A_1 > 0$, then θ_t enters in s_t and thus s_t provides information about the level of θ_t, beyond just revealing its innovation dW_2.

2.5 MATHEMATICAL REFERENCES

This chapter has put forward many of the tools needed to work through the models in the rest of the book. It has also, I hope, given the reader some intuitive understanding of the formulas. But it has not derived them or explained the precise technical conditions under which each holds. To learn more about the foundations for the results in the chapter, turn to the following references: for derivations of Bayes' law and the Kalman filter, see Elliott, Aggoun, and Moore 1995; for the probability and measure theory underlying the expectations, variances, and covariances, see Billingsley 1995; and to learn more about working with continuous-time problems, see Karatzas and Shreve 1991 and Lipster and Shiryaev's book 2001.

2.6 EXERCISES

For problems 1–4, assume that all signals and prior beliefs are conditionally independent.

1. Suppose the prior belief is that $x \sim \mathcal{N}\left(A, \alpha^{-1}\right)$ and the signal is $B|x \sim \mathcal{N}\left(x, \beta^{-1}\right)$. Prove carefully that the posterior density is also normal, that is, that the mean $E[x|B]$ and variance $V[x|B]$ are, in fact, the mean and variance of a normal distribution.

2. Suppose the prior belief is that $x \sim N(A, \alpha^{-1})$ and the signal is $B|x \sim N(x, \beta^{-1})$. If instead the prior was $x \sim N(B, \beta^{-1})$ and the signal was $A|x \sim N(x, \alpha^{-1})$, would the posterior be the same or different? Show your work.

3. Suppose that the prior is diffuse, meaning that $x \sim N(z, \zeta^{-1})$, and take the limit as $\zeta \to 0$, but the agent then observes two signals, $A|x \sim N(x, \alpha^{-1})$ and $B|x \sim N(x, \beta^{-1})$. What is the posterior in this case? Are prior beliefs fundamentally different from signals?

4. Suppose the prior belief is that $x \sim N(A, \alpha^{-1})$ and two signals are observed: $B|x \sim N(x, \beta^{-1})$ and $C|x \sim (x, \chi^{-1})$. What is the posterior belief?

5. Suppose the prior belief is that $x \sim N(A, \alpha^{-1})$ and the signal is $B|x \sim N(x, \beta^{-1})$. If the agent has not yet observed the signal B, does not know x, and only has his prior beliefs to go on, what are $E[B]$ and $V[B]$?

6. Suppose that $x = a + b$. The agent has prior beliefs that a and b are independently distributed $a \sim N(\mu_a, \sigma_a)$, $b \sim N(\mu_b, \sigma_b)$. He observes one signal, y, where $y = a + \eta$ and $\eta \sim N(\mu_\eta, \sigma_\eta)$. What are $E[x|y]$ and $V[x|y]$?

Chapter Three

Measuring Information Flows

What is the feasible set of information choices? This is like asking, what is the feasible set of labor-consumption choices for a consumer in a production economy? In that setting, the budget set depends on the relative price of each of the goods and of labor. But information processing is something that individuals do for themselves. It has no market price.[1] Of course, we could just assign a price to each signal. But how do we do that? Should a signal that contains information about one risk be priced the same as a signal that contains some information about many risks? Should a signal with one unit less variance cost $1 more, or should a signal with one unit more precision cost $1 more, or neither? There is no right answer to these questions. They are very important for the predictions of models based on them. Any time you write down a model, you should think carefully about what its learning technology means and why you chose it. What follows are some examples of technologies that people use.

3.1 PRELIMINARIES

Why choose the variance instead of the mean? Investors can choose to see good or bad news only if the information they are seeing is biased. An unbiased signal about x is x plus mean-zero noise. The investor chooses how much information to get, not its content.

Consider the following analogy. Suppose there is an urn, one for each asset, that contains balls with numbers printed on them. Those numbers are the true payoff of the asset, with noise. The investor is choosing how many balls to draw from each urn. That determines the precision of his signal. But he does not get to choose what is printed on any given ball. That is the luck of the draw.

Choosing the signal variances is the same as choosing a variance of the posterior belief. Recall that one of the rules for Bayesian updating with normal variables is that the precision of the posterior belief is the sum of the precisions of the prior and the signals. In most models, there is one prior belief (with precision Σ^{-1}) but one or two signals. There is one signal the agent chooses to observe; suppose it has precision Σ_η^{-1}. In applications where equilibrium prices (or quantities) also convey noisy information, there is a second signal, which is the information contained in prices; suppose it has precision Σ_p^{-1}. The problem should be set up

---

[1] The idea that someone can process information for you and sell that service on a market is an idea we will return to at the end. Set that idea aside for now.

so that prices are linear functions of the true state with normally distributed noise. Otherwise, a non-linear filtering problem may render the problem intractable.

The precision of posterior beliefs is

$$\widehat{\Sigma}^{-1} = \Sigma^{-1} + \Sigma_p^{-1} + \Sigma_\eta^{-1}.$$

The first term is information the agent is endowed with. The second term depends on how much all other investors learn. Since the agent is typically one of a continuum, his actions alone do not affect prices. Therefore, for every choice of Σ_η, there is a unique $\widehat{\Sigma}$ that results. Because of this one-to-one mapping, we can model the agent as choosing $\widehat{\Sigma}$, instead of Σ_η, taking Σ and Σ_p as given.

3.2 ENTROPY AND RATIONAL INATTENTION

The standard measure of the quantity of information in information theory is entropy (Cover and Thomas 1991). It is frequently used in econometrics and statistics and has been used in economics to model limited information processing by individuals and to measure model uncertainty.[2] Entropy measures the amount of uncertainty in a random variable. It is also used to measure the complexity of information transmitted. Following Sims (2003), this section models the amount of information transmitted as the reduction in entropy achieved by conditioning on that additional information (mutual information). The idea that economic agents have limited ability to process information, or to pay attention, is often referred to as *rational inattention*.

Entropy is a measure of the uncertainty of a random variable. It answers the following question: How much information is required, on average, to describe x with probability density function $p(\cdot)$?

$$H(x) = -E[\ln(p(x))]$$
$$= -\sum_x [p(x)\ln(p(x))] \quad \text{if p discrete.}$$

For a multivariate continuous distribution f,

$$H(x) = -\int f(x_1, \ldots, x_n) \ln(f(x_1, \ldots, x_n)) dx_1, \ldots, dx_n.$$

To make the idea of entropy more concrete, here are some examples.

- Constant: $p(x) = 1 - \delta$ and $p(y) = \delta$ for all $y \neq x$. In the limit, as $\delta \to 0$, $p(x)\ln(p(x)) = 1 \cdot 0$ at x and by L'Hôpital's rule $p(y)\ln(p(x)) = 0$ everywhere else. This is a zero entropy variable because if the variable is equal to x with certainty, no information needs to be transmitted to know the value of the variable. I need a zero length code to tell me that $2 = 2$.

---

[2] This is also referred to as a Shannon measure of information (Shannon 1948). In econometrics, it is a log likelihood ratio. In statistics, it is a difference of the prior and posterior distributions' Kullback-Liebler distance from the truth. Mathematically, it is a Radon-Nikodym derivative. In robust control, it is the distance between two models (Cagetti et al. 2002). It has been previously used in economics to model limited mental-processing ability (Radner and Van Zandt 2001; Sims 2003).

- Binomial: 2 points each with equal probability.

$$H = -\left(\frac{1}{2}\ln\left(\frac{1}{2}\right) + \frac{1}{2}\ln\left(\frac{1}{2}\right)\right) = -\ln\left(\frac{1}{2}\right) = \ln(2)$$

Suppose we had a code that said if zero is observed, the variable takes on its first value; if one is observed, it takes on its second value. Then, one zero or one must be transmitted to reveal exactly the value of the variable. This is called one bit of information. Bits are information flows, measured in base 2.

- Uniform: If $x \sim \text{unif}[0, a]$, the probability density of x is $1/a$ between zero and a:

$$H(x) = -\int_0^a 1/a \ \ln(1/a)dx = -\ln(1/a) = \ln(a).$$

Mutual information. Mutual information answers the following question: How much do two variables x and y tell me about each other? How much does knowing one reduce the entropy of the other?

$$I(x, y) = H(x) - H(x|y) \tag{3.1}$$

The second term in the above expression is conditional entropy. It answers the following question: How much information is required to describe x if y is already known?

$$H(x|y) = H(x, y) - H(y)$$

A useful property of mutual information is that it is symmetric:

$$I(x, y) = I(y, x).$$

What x tells you about y, y tells you about x.

Entropy and mutual information of normal variables. Suppose that a variable x is normally distributed: $x \sim N(\mu, \sigma^2)$. Then it has entropy

$$H(x) = \frac{1}{2}\ln(2\pi e\sigma^2). \tag{3.2}$$

If x is an $n \times 1$ vector of normal variables, $x \sim N(\mu, \Sigma)$, then it has entropy

$$H(x) = \frac{1}{2}\ln[(2\pi e)^n|\Sigma|], \tag{3.3}$$

where $|\Sigma|$ denotes the matrix determinant of Σ.

Most models that use rational inattention in economics constrain the mutual information that a set of signals can provide about the true state. With multidimensional, normally distributed random variables, such a constraint takes the form

$$|\widehat{\Sigma}| = \exp(-2K)|\Sigma|, \tag{3.4}$$

where $\widehat{\Sigma}$ is the posterior variance-covariance matrix, Σ is the prior variance-covariance matrix, and K is a measure of mutual information, often called information capacity.

This constraint comes from the fact that an n-dimensional normal variable $x \sim N(\mu, \Sigma)$ has entropy $H(x) = n/2[(\ln(2\pi) + 1] + 1/2 \ln(|\Sigma|)$. Conditional on a set of normal signals y, the conditional entropy of x is the same, replacing the higher variance Σ with the lower conditional variance $\widehat{\Sigma}$. Capacity K measures the mutual information of a signal y. The mutual information of x and y is $H(x) - H(x|y)$. Taking the difference of the entropy and conditional entropy and then exponentiating yields the constraint (3.4).

A useful property of normal variables is that the normal distribution maximizes entropy over all distributions with a given variance.

Economic interpretation of rational inattention. This technology represents learning as a process of more and more refined searching. A capacity K is approximately the number of binary signals that partition states of the world.[3] A simple example is where a first signal tells the agent whether a random variable's realization is above or below the median outcome. The second signal tells the agent, conditional on being in the top half or the bottom half, what quartile of the state space the outcome is in. In conjunction with the first two signals, the third reveals what eighth of the sample space the outcome is in, and so forth. Notice that the interpretation of each signal depends on its predecessors. The second signal alone does not reveal the quartile an outcome is in. Since each signal refines the information conveyed by previous signals, this learning technology has the characteristics of an increasingly directed or refined search for an answer. This technology does not imply that an agent can dynamically reoptimize his learning choice based on signal realizations. Rather, imagine that in period 1, the agent tells the computer what information to download. In period 2, he reads the computer output written in binary code. When reading the binary code, the meaning of each 0 or 1 depends on the sequence of 0s and 1s that precede it.

3.3 ADDITIVE COST IN SIGNAL PRECISION

With this constraint, learning takes the form of a sequence of independent draws. Each independent draw of a normally distributed signal with mean f and variance σ adds σ^{-1} to the precision of posterior beliefs. If each signal draw requires equal resources to acquire, then resources devoted to information acquisition will depend on a sum of signal precisions. Thus, the entropy technology represents a process of more and more refined searching while the linear technology models search as a sequence of independent explorations.

To see the relationship between this technology and entropy, consider a case where all the risks are independent of each other and the signal about each risk has normally distributed errors that are uncorrelated with the other signals. In that case, the prior and posterior variances, Σ and $\widehat{\Sigma}$, are diagonal matrices. Since the entropy of a normal variable depends on the determinant of its variance (equation [3.3]) and the determinant of a diagonal matrix is the product of its diagonals, the

---

[3] See Cover and Thomas 1991, section 9.3, for a proof that the entropy of a random variable is an approximation of the number of binary signals needed to convey the same information.

entropy constraint takes the form

$$\prod_{i=1}^{N} \hat{\Sigma}_{ii}^{-1} \le \tilde{K},$$

while the linear precision constraint would be

$$\sum_{i=1}^{N} \hat{\Sigma}_{ii}^{-1} \le \tilde{K}'$$

for some constants $\tilde{K}$ and $\tilde{K}'$.

Entropy constrains the product of precisions, while the linear constraint bounds the sum of precisions. With entropy, it is easier to add a fixed amount of signal precision when the agent already has more precise information. If $\hat{\Sigma}_{ii}^{-1}$ is small, then adding one unit of precision to get $\hat{\Sigma}_{ii}^{-1} + 1$ is a large proportional increase and thus requires a large increase in $\tilde{K}$. But if $\hat{\Sigma}_{ii}^{-1}$ is already large, adding one unit of precision is a small proportional increase and requires only a small proportional increase in $\tilde{K}$. In this sense, it is less costly to learn more about risks that are already well understood. This lower cost represents a form of increasing returns to learning built into an entropy constraint. At the same time, one might argue that precision is not the right metric. Maybe we should be thinking about how difficult it is to reduce variance. As variance falls ($\hat{\Sigma}_{ii} \to 0$), further reducing variance by one unit results in larger and larger increases in precision and requires more and more capacity under either learning technology. Thus, with variance reduction, there are decreasing returns built into both measures.

3.4 DIMINISHING RETURNS TO LEARNING AND UNLEARNABLE RISK

Adding unlearnable risk is also a way of generating diminishing returns to learning, which has intuitive appeal. When all risk is learnable and capacity approaches infinity, the posterior variance of the random variables approaches zero. In many settings, achieving zero-variance outcomes is implausible. For example, in a portfolio investment problem, zero variance means that an arbitrage arises.

Unlearnable risk makes learning more and more about a single risk an increasing costly activity. To reduce an asset's learnable payoff variance to near zero costs an unbounded amount of information capacity and typically yields only a finite benefit. One way to build unlearnable risk into a model of rational inattention is as follows. Suppose that eliminating all learnable risk (reducing $\hat{\Sigma}$ to $\alpha\Sigma$ for $\alpha \in (0, 1)$) requires infinite capacity. When $\hat{\Sigma} = \Sigma$, the investor is not learning anything, and no capacity is required. Such a constraint would take the form

$$\frac{|\Sigma - \alpha\Sigma|}{|\hat{\Sigma} - \alpha\Sigma|} \le e^{2K}. \tag{3.5}$$

3.5 INATTENTIVENESS

Despite the fact that inattention and inattentiveness sound almost the same, they are completely different learning technologies. Rational inattention has a constant, noisy flow of information. With inattentiveness, the agent gets no information flow almost all of the time and then occasionally observes the current state perfectly.

What settings does this make sense in? In settings where an agent has to exert some effort to observe information, but that information can be easily interpreted, this technology makes sense. Examples include checking one's bank balance, looking up a sports score, or checking the current temperature.

The term "inattentiveness" was coined by Reis (2006), who used it to model the information constraints that price-setters face when learning about past money supply and consumer demand (see section 6.3). More recent work by Abel, Eberly, and Panageas (2007) uses this constraint in a model of portfolio choice. Their information friction is such that the investor has to pay a cost to see the true value of the risky asset portfolio. They combine this fixed cost of learning with tools from the literature on S-s models, which analyze fixed costs of capital adjustment. The results describe the dynamics of an optimal portfolio. In both works, small information costs generate long periods of inertia.

In each of the examples so far, there has been only one random variable for the agent to learn about. How might attentiveness govern the flow of information with multiple risky assets? There is no right answer to this, only some ideas. One possibility is that an agent pays a fixed cost to learn all past realizations of all risks. Another possibility is that learning about each risk happens independently. There could be a fixed cost of updating information about each risk.

3.6 RECOGNITION

Another form of incomplete information is that agents may not be aware of their choice set. For example, according to Merton (1987), investors pay a cost to know an asset exists. Once they recognize the asset, they can trade it costlessly. Merton calls this information "recognition." The concept is similar to that in search models where profitable trading opportunities exist but agents cannot exploit these opportunities unless they pay a cost to search for them. The difference is that recognition is cumulative. An investor who becomes aware of an asset can include it in his choice set forever after. An agent who searches can trade with counterparties that he encounters in that period. If he wants to trade in the next period, the agent must search again.

Barber and Odean (2008) argue that when a stock is mentioned in the news, investors become aware of it and that stock enters in their choice set. In other words, the market supply of information affects individual investors' attention allocation. They support this hypothesis using data on news coverage, trading volume, and asset-price changes.

Very little theoretical work has been done with this type of information constraint. In addition to its applications in portfolio choice, it could be relevant for finding a job or hiring workers, investing in or adopting a new technology, or building trade relationships with foreign importers or exporters.

3.7 INFORMATION-PROCESSING FRICTIONS

Another kind of information friction, similar to incomplete information, is the failure to process observed information. For example, Hirschleifer, Teoh, and Lin (2005) assume that all agents observe whether or not a firm discloses a signal. But only a fraction of agents who observe non-disclosure infer correctly that non-disclosing firms have bad news.

Such assumptions blur the line between information frictions and non-rational behavior. Yet, there is a close relationship between information flow constraints and computational complexity constraints. In particular, entropy can be interpreted as either kind of constraint. (See Cover and Thomas 1991 for more on measuring computational complexity; see Radner and Van Zandt 2001 for a model that uses an entropy-based complexity constraint to determine the optimal size of a firm.)

This kind of assumption may be useful in avoiding problems that arise in equilibrium models. For example, agents need to know prices to satisfy their budget constraints. Yet, prices may contain information that allows agents to infer what others know. In such a setting, an information-processing constraint can preserve belief heterogeneity by making it costly to use the price to infer others' information. In contrast, costly information acquisition might not preserve belief heterogeneity because once all agents see prices, using the price information to infer what others know is free.

3.8 LEARNING WHEN OUTCOMES ARE CORRELATED

Suppose asset A and asset B have payoffs that are unknown but positively correlated. An investor observes a signal about asset A, suggesting that its payoff is likely to be high. Knowing that the payoff of asset B is positively correlated, the investor infers that B's payoff is also likely to be high. How can we describe the information content of this signal? It is a signal about asset A's payoff that contains information about B's payoff as well. The first objective of this section is to put forth a language for describing the information content of signals when risks are correlated.

The second issue this section addresses is about how to model information choice. Should agents choose the entire covariance structure of the signals they observe, or should we restrict their choice set and allow them to obtain only signals about risks, with a given covariance structure? This question arises with many of the learning technologies we have described. Any problem where signal variances are chosen and multiple risks are present is confronted with this question.

Correlated outcomes and orthogonal risk factors. If a signal can pertain to multiple assets, we need a language to describe what information each signal has.

One way is to describe signals according to how much information they contain about each realization of each principal component.

Suppose we have an $N \times 1$ random variable $f \sim N(\mu, \Sigma)$, where Σ, the prior variance-covariance matrix, is not a diagonal matrix. Thus, the realizations of the N elements of f are correlated. An eigen-decomposition splits Σ into a diagonal eigenvalue matrix Λ and an eigenvector matrix Γ:

$$\Sigma = \Gamma \Lambda \Gamma'. \qquad (3.6)$$

(See section 3.10 for more information and rules about eigen-decompositions.) The Λ_i's are the variances of each principal component, or risk factor, i. The ith column of Γ (denoted Γ_i) gives the loadings of each random variable on the ith principal component. Since realizations of principal components $f'\Gamma_i$ are independent of each other, a signal that is about principal component i would contain no information about principal component j. This allows an unambiguous description of the information content of a signal.

What we are doing is taking some correlated random variables and forming linear combinations of those variables such that the linear combinations are independent of each other. Take an example where the variables are the payoffs of risky assets. The principal components would then be linear combinations of assets—call them portfolios or synthetic assets—that one can learn about, buy, and price, just as if they were the underlying assets. Such synthetic assets are also referred to as *Arrow-Debreu securities*. The reason we want to work with these synthetic assets is that their payoffs are independent of each other. Principal component analysis is frequently used in the portfolio literature (Ross 1976). Principal components could represent business cycle risk, industry-specific risk, or firm-specific risk. As long as there are no redundant assets (i.e., the variance-covariance matrix of payoffs is full-rank), rewriting the problem and solving it in terms of the independent synthetic assets can be done without loss of generality.

Thus, after transforming the problem with our eigen-decomposition, we can proceed and solve the model as if assets were independent. If you can solve the model with independent risks, you can just as easily solve the correlated risk version as well.

Should signals about independent risks be independent? An assumption that a signal about any principal component i does not contain information about any other principal components is not without loss of generality. To be clear, this assumption does not rule out learning about many risks. It does rule out signals with correlated information about risks that are independent. Here is a simple example of what the assumption prohibits: If rain in Delhi and the supply of Norwegian oil are independent risks, the investor cannot choose to observe a signal that is the difference between the millions of barrels of Norwegian oil pumped and the centimeters of rain in Delhi. He can learn about oil and rain separately and construct that difference. But he cannot learn the difference without knowing the separate components. If he learned the difference, such a signal would induce positive correlation between his beliefs about oil and rainfall. For example, if he believed that oil will be abundant and observed a signal that tells him that the difference between oil and rainfall is small, then he must believe that rainfall will be abundant as well. Since such a signal does not preserve independence of independent risks, the proposed assumption would prohibit an investor from choosing to observe it.

The mathematics of the independent signal assumption is as follows: for a normally distributed signal about f's principal components, $\eta_i \equiv \Gamma'_i f + \epsilon_i$, the signal noise ϵ_i must be uncorrelated across components i. In other words, the $n \times 1$ vector of noise terms for each principal component is distributed $\epsilon \sim N(0, \Lambda_\eta)$, where Λ_η is a diagonal matrix. The assumption that Λ_η is diagonal simplifies the problem greatly because it reduces its dimensionality. It allows us to only keep track of the n diagonal entries of Λ_η, rather than the $n(n+1)/2$ distinct entries of a symmetric variance covariance matrix. But the reduced number of choice variables is clearly a restriction on the problem.

Equivalently, the signal could be about the underlying random variable, as long as the signal noise has the same risk structure as the random variable itself. Define $\nu \equiv \Gamma \eta$. Then $\nu | f$ has mean $\Gamma E[\eta | f] = \Gamma \Gamma' f$. Since eigenvectors of symmetric matrices are idempotent by construction, $\Gamma \Gamma' = I$ and $E[\nu | f] = f$. Thus, ν is a signal about the variable f. Since multiplication by Γ is a linear operation, ν is normally distributed, $\nu | f \sim N(f, \Gamma \Lambda_\eta \Gamma')$. Notice that the variance of the signal noise in ν has the same eigenvectors (same risk structure) as the prior beliefs about f.

If we do make the assumption that signals about principal components are independent, then the variance of posterior beliefs has the same eigenvectors as prior beliefs. If $f | \eta \sim N(\hat{\mu}, \widehat{\Sigma})$, then $\widehat{\Sigma} = \Gamma \hat{\Lambda} \Gamma'$. (The proof of this is left as an exercise.) The diagonal matrix $\hat{\Lambda}$ contains the posterior variance of beliefs about each risk factor. Learning about risk i lowers $\hat{\Lambda}_i$ relative to the prior variance Λ_i. The decrease in risk factor variance $\Lambda_{i,i} - \hat{\Lambda}_{i,i}$ captures how much an agent learned about risk i.

In the asset example, if we assume that signal errors have the same risk structure (their variance has the same eigenvectors) as asset payoffs, then the synthetic asset payoffs are conditionally and unconditionally independent. In other words, the prior and posterior variance-covariance matrices of the synthetic asset payoffs are diagonal.

When using information flow measures to quantify information acquisition or research effort, uncorrelated signals may be a realistic assumption. Acquiring information about oil is a separate task from acquiring information about rainfall. Perhaps someone can learn about the difference of oil and rain, if someone else constructs that joint signal for them. But then who constructs the signal and how they price it become important questions and should be part of the model. Sims (2006) disagrees; he thinks of rational inattention as describing a setting where complete and perfect information is available for any agent to observe. The agent just cannot observe all the information and must choose the optimal information to observe. If optimized information flows involve constructing correlated signals about independent events, so be it. Which procedure most resembles how economic decision makers learn is an open question.

If you are willing to assume that signals about uncorrelated principal components have uncorrelated signal errors, then you can solve your problem as if all your assets and signals are independent. Once you have a solution for the independent (synthetic) asset and independent signal case, just pre-multiply the price and quantity vectors by the eigenvector matrix Γ' to get the price and quantity vectors for the underlying correlated assets.

3.9 WHAT IS THE RIGHT LEARNING TECHNOLOGY?

Does learning have increasing or decreasing returns? Does it have to apply to all the stochastic variables in the model? Are people like computers in their processing abilities? These are open questions in the literature. The answers probably depend on the context.

The following are three suggestions for how to evaluate a learning technology.

1. Collect experimental evidence. Decision-making experiments could reveal that some learning technologies are more realistic. They might at least tell us what descriptions of learning are most accurate in which contexts.
2. Adopt a standard within the field. For example, there are many ways one might represent goods production, yet the profession has settled on the Cobb-Douglas function as an industry standard. This literature may settle on a few key properties that a reasonable information production function should have. For goods production, that feature was a stable share of income paid to labor and to capital. One possible standard for information production is scale neutrality, discussed below.
3. Justify model assumptions with model results. If putting in a different learning technology would make the model predict unrealistic outcomes, then perhaps another learning technology is in order. The problem with this answer is that if one learning technology fails to explain a phenomenon, it could also be because learning is not a key part of the explanation. It is important to distinguish between facts that justify your assumptions and independent facts that you use to evaluate the model's explanation.

One of the drawbacks to using the additive precision measure of information is that it is not scale neutral. For example, the definition of what constitutes one share of an asset will change the feasible set of signals. Take a share of an asset with payoff $f \sim N(\mu, \sigma)$ and split it into two shares of a new asset, each with payoff $f/2$. The new asset has payoffs with one-half the standard deviation and one-fourth the variance. The prior precision of information about its payoff is therefore $4\sigma^{-1}$.

The additive learning technology allows the investor to add K units of precision to his information. If he adds K units of precision to his information about the new asset, the new precision is $4\sigma^{-1} + K$. Since the new asset always has four times the payoff precision of the old asset, this implies that the old asset has payoff precision $\sigma^{-1} + K/4$, after the investor learns. If the investor added K units of precision to his information about the old asset, the posterior precision would be $\sigma^{-1} + K$. The two posterior precisions are different. Thus, changing what constitutes a share of an asset changes the precision of the information an investor can acquire.

In contrast, the entropy learning technology allows the investor to multiply the precision of that information by K. Increasing the precision of information about the new asset by a factor of K will result in the precision of information about the old asset also being K times higher. This is the scale neutrality of entropy. The entropy technology in equation (3.4) is not the only scale-neutral learning technology. The diminishing returns technology in section 3.4 is scale neutral. Similarly, inattentiveness and recognition, which are based on fixed costs, are not sensitive to an asset's size.

3.10 APPENDIX: MATRIX ALGEBRA AND EIGEN-DECOMPOSITIONS

1. Any square, symmetric positive semi-definite matrix Σ can be decomposed into its eigenvalues and eigenvectors:

$$\Sigma = \Gamma \Lambda \Gamma'.$$

   The eigenvector matrix Λ is diagonal.

2. Eigenvector matrices are idempotent: $\Gamma'\Gamma = I$. This implies that for any columns i, j of the eigenvector matrix, $\Gamma_i'\Gamma_i = 1$ and $\Gamma_i'\Gamma_j = 0$ for $i \neq j$.

3. Sums of matrices with the same eigenvectors have the same eigenvectors: if $\Sigma = \Gamma \Lambda \Gamma'$ and $\tilde{\Sigma} = \Gamma \tilde{\Lambda} \Gamma'$ are eigen-decompositions, then $\Sigma + \tilde{\Sigma} = \Gamma (\Lambda + \tilde{\Lambda})\Gamma'$.

4. Products of matrices with the same eigenvectors have the same eigenvectors: if $\Sigma = \Gamma \Lambda \Gamma'$ and $\tilde{\Sigma} = \Gamma \tilde{\Lambda} \Gamma'$ are eigen-decompositions, then $\Sigma \tilde{\Sigma} = \Gamma (\Lambda \tilde{\Lambda})\Gamma'$.

5. Inverting a matrix preserves its eigenvectors: if $\Sigma = \Gamma \Lambda \Gamma'$ then $\Sigma^{-1} = \Gamma \Lambda^{-1}\Gamma'$.

6. The determinant of a square, positive semi-definite matrix Σ is the product of its eigenvalues:

$$|\Sigma| = \prod_i \Lambda_{ii}.$$

   This implies that $|\Sigma^{-1}| = |\Sigma|^{-1}$.

7. The trace of a matrix is defined as the sum of its diagonal elements. It is also equal to the sum of its eigenvalues:

$$Tr(\Sigma) = \sum_i \Lambda_{ii}.$$

3.11 EXERCISES

1. Using the definitions of mutual information and conditional entropy, prove that mutual information is symmetric: $I(x, y) = I(y, x)$.

2. Suppose a variable x takes on 4 possible values: 0 with probability 0.25, 1 with probability 0.3, 2 with probability 0.25, and 3 with probability 0.2. What is the entropy of x? What is the entropy of $2x^2$?

3.   Suppose there is an $n \times 1$ variable $x \sim N(\mu, \Sigma)$ and an $n \times 1$ signal $\eta \sim N(x, \Sigma_\eta)$, where Σ and Σ_η share common eigenvectors: $\Sigma = \Gamma \Lambda \Gamma'$ and $\Sigma_\eta = \Gamma \Lambda_\eta \Gamma'$. Express the mutual information of x and η as a function of the eigenvalues in Λ and Λ_η.

Hint: Recall that the determinant of a square matrix is the product of its eigenvalues.

4. Suppose that prior beliefs and signals have variance-covariance matrices that share the same eigenvectors. Show that posterior beliefs will have these same eigenvectors as well. (See section 3.10 for helpful rules about eigen-decompositions.)

5. Show that entropy is a scale-neutral learning technology. Suppose that one asset has a payoff $f \sim N(\mu, \sigma)$ and a second asset has a payoff that is exactly half of the first asset's payoff $f/2$. Show that using capacity K to acquire a normally distributed signal about the first asset is equivalent to using that capacity to acquire a signal about the second asset.

6. Consider a problem with a single random variable. Suppose the prior belief is that $x \sim \mathcal{N}\left(A, \alpha^{-1}\right)$ and the agent is using all his capacity K, defined as in equation (3.4) to observe x. What is the precision of that signal?

7. Suppose the prior belief is that $x \sim \mathcal{N}\left(A, \alpha^{-1}\right)$ and the agent has capacity K, which he uses to process (public) information contained in prices, p, and a private signal. It is common knowledge that $p|x \sim \mathcal{N}\left(x, \beta^{-1}\right)$. What fraction of his capacity does the agent have to use to process information contained in prices? How precise a private signal can he observe with the remaining capacity?

Chapter Four

Games with Heterogeneous Information

This is a large and rapidly growing literature that we will only touch on briefly so that we can then explore its interactions with information choice. The main idea is that while coordination games often have multiple equilibria, adding heterogeneous information can deliver a unique prediction. For example, if speculating on (short-selling) a fixed exchange rate currency is profitable only when many others speculate, then a full-information model would typically predict that there can be two Nash equilibria: either all speculate or no one speculates. But when the currency traders have heterogeneous information about the probability that a speculative attack will be successful, then each set of initial conditions has a unique equilibrium outcome. This type of model was labeled a "global game" by Carlsson and Van Damme (1993).

Uniqueness is a useful property for the model to have because it dictates a specific set of circumstances that will produce speculative attacks. Such a model is easier to evaluate empirically and to use for policy purposes. In contrast, a model with multiple equilibria is not very useful for forecasting. In the speculation example, it says only that a successful currency attack will occur when currency traders think it will occur. Thus, by showing that multiple equilibria in coordination games are quite fragile, this line of work has facilitated research progress on many questions where coordination motives play a role.

Why study strategic games in a book that is largely about information choice? One conclusion of the heterogeneous information models is that the outcomes depend a lot on what information agents have. Even whether or not the model has a unique prediction depends on this information. But typically, what agents know is an assumption. In other words, these models employ passive learning. If information determines outcomes, we ought to think about what information rational agents should have. Therefore, the end of this chapter introduces active learning. Agents choose what information or how much information to learn.

4.1 PRELIMINARY CONCEPTS

Before we examine a model of strategic interactions, it is useful to first define some vocabulary.

Definition 1. *An action a_i by agent i is a strategic complement if the optimal choice of a_i is increasing in the average action of other agents $\int a_j dj$.*

In other words, actions are strategic complements when agents prefer to take actions that are similar to each other. Examples of strategic complementarity include speculative attacks in financial markets, bank runs, price-setting in models of monopolistic competition, and investment in the presence of increasing returns. In models of information markets (chapter 8), information acquisition is a strategic complement. Investors want to buy information that others buy because that information will be cheap.

Definition 2. *An action a_i by agent i is a strategic substitute if the optimal choice of a_i is decreasing in the average action of other agents $\int a_j dj$.*

In other words, when actions are strategic substitutes, agents prefer actions that are different from others' actions. In standard portfolio choice models, investment is usually a strategic substitute because when other investors buy more of an asset, its price rises. The more expensive the asset is, the less of it investor i chooses to buy. Likewise, hiring labor is a strategic substitute in a standard production economy. When other firms hire, the wage rate rises, making hiring less attractive to other firms.

Higher-order beliefs. Suppose there are two players indexed by i. Each gets a signal x_i about a common fundamental θ:

$$x_i = \theta + \eta_i, \quad \eta_i \sim \text{unif}[-\epsilon, \epsilon] \quad \theta \sim \text{unif}(\Re).$$

Agent i's *first-order belief* is simply $E[\theta|x_i]$, the distribution of θ conditional on his information x_i. In this example, agent i knows that $x_i - \epsilon < \theta < x_i + \epsilon$. The *second-order belief* is $E[E[\theta|x_j]|x_i]$, what an agent believes about what others' beliefs are. In this case, another player's signal can differ from your own by, at most, 2ϵ: you might observe $\theta - \epsilon$ while the other player observes $\theta + \epsilon$ or vice versa. With a signal of $\theta + \epsilon$, the most extreme value of θ that the other player can put positive weight on is $\theta + 2\epsilon$, which is 3ϵ away from your signal. Thus, you know that the other player is certain that $\theta \geq \underline{\theta}$ if you observe a signal $x_i \geq \underline{\theta} + 3\epsilon$. By symmetry, you know that everyone knows that $x_i - 3\epsilon < \theta < x_i + 3\epsilon$. Extending this logic, *nth-order beliefs* answer the following question: When do you know that everyone knows that you know that ... (n times) that $\theta \in [\underline{\theta}, \bar{\theta}]$? As the order of beliefs grows, the size of the interval $[\underline{\theta}, \bar{\theta}]$ grows. In other words, higher-order beliefs are more uncertain.

Common knowledge is the limit of this process as $n \to \infty$. In other words, $\theta < \bar{\theta}$ (or $\theta > \bar{\theta}$) is common knowledge if it is in any agent's (and therefore in every agent's) infinite-order beliefs.

4.2 HETEROGENEOUS INFORMATION ELIMINATES MULTIPLE EQUILIBRIA

One of the key reasons that many now model games of strategic complementarity with heterogeneous beliefs is that the heterogeneity can make the model's equilibrium unique. The canonical model of this phenomenon is by Morris and Shin (1998). Its key features are that a player's payoff depends on his own action, the action of others, and an aggregate state. Crucially, information about the true state is heterogeneous. The model is written as a description of speculative currency attacks against fixed-exchange-rate currencies. But the impact of the results extends well beyond the realm of international finance, as we will see in later applications to monetary economics and business cycles.

A model of currency speculation. There is an unobserved state, uniformly distributed $\theta \sim \text{unif}[0, 1]$, which determines the likelihood of a successful speculative attack against a fixed-exchange-rate currency. The exchange rate is fixed to e^*. But if that peg is released, the currency will return to its market value, which is $f(\theta)$. The cost of speculating is t. Therefore, a successful speculative attack earns a speculator

$$e^* - f(\theta) - t$$

while an unsuccessful speculative attack results in a utility payoff of $-t$.

The government decides whether or not to devalue the currency, but it is not a strategic player. It just observes α, the fraction of investors who attack the currency, and mechanically devalues whenever the benefit of the currency peg is less than its cost. It gets a benefit v from defending the currency's fixed value but incurs a cost $c(\alpha, \theta)$, which depends positively on the size of an attack ($\partial c/\partial \alpha > 0$) and negatively on the unobserved state ($\partial c/\partial \theta < 0$). We can rewrite the condition for devaluation as a cutoff rule in the size of an attack α by defining a function a such that $c(\alpha, \theta) > v$, and thus the government devalues, whenever

$$\alpha > a(\theta).$$

The timing of the model is as follows:

1. Nature draws a θ from $[0, 1]$. This prior distribution of θ is common knowledge.
2. Each investor i draws signal x_i from an uniform distribution on $[\theta - \epsilon, \theta + \epsilon]$. Based on x_i, investors decide whether to speculate.
3. The government observes the attack size α and the true state θ and devalues if $\alpha > a(\theta)$.

There are three key parameter assumptions. These keep the problem from being trivial by ensuring that both beliefs about the state and beliefs about others' actions are used to predict whether the government will devalue. First, $c(0, 0) > v$; in the worst state, the government devalues, even with no speculators. Second, $c(1,1) > v$; in the best state, if all investors speculate, the government also devalues. Third, $e^* - f(1) - t < 0$; in the best state, the payoff to speculating is negative.

Symmetric Nash equilibrium. Agent i speculates if and only if the expected benefit of receiving speculation profit $e^* - f(\theta)$, in the case that the government devalues, is greater than the certain cost t. Define a strategy function $\pi(x)$ such that

$$\pi(x) = 1 \quad \text{if } E\left[\mathbf{1}_{[c(\alpha,\theta)>v]}(e^* - f(\theta)) \mid x_i\right] > t$$
$$\pi(x) = 0 \quad \text{otherwise.} \tag{4.1}$$

To describe aggregate behavior, let $\alpha(\theta, \pi) \equiv \int \pi(x_i)dx_i$ be the fraction of agents that speculates. This depends on the state θ, which determines the distribution of signals x_i, and the strategy function π. The fraction of speculators, along with the state θ, then determines the set of states A where devaluation occurs:

$$A(\pi) = \{\theta : \alpha(\theta, \pi) \geq a(\theta)\}.$$

Finally, the expected utility of attacking currency (4.1) can be rewritten as[1]

$$u(x, \pi) = \frac{1}{2\epsilon} \left[\int_{\theta \in A(\pi) \cap [x-\epsilon, x+\epsilon]} (e^* - f(\theta))d\theta \right] - t.$$

Solving the model. Most of Morris and Shin's work (1998) is devoted to proving that the equilibrium is unique. Instead of reproducing that argument, I refer the reader to their work and focus instead on the solution to their model and its properties. The approach is to guess and verify that the solution takes the form of a threshold rule where agents speculate on the currency if their signal is sufficiently low. Then, solve for the threshold value itself at the end.

Speculators' optimal policy follows a cutoff rule in their signals. There is a cutoff signal value k such that a speculator speculates if and only if $x < k$. Given this cutoff, the fraction α of agents who will speculate is $\alpha = P[x_i < k]$. Since x_i is uniformly distributed on the interval $[\theta - \epsilon, \theta + \epsilon]$, the probability of $x_i < k$ is $\frac{1}{2\epsilon}(k - \theta + \epsilon)$. Thus, devaluation occurs if $\frac{1}{2} + \frac{k-\theta}{2\epsilon} > a(\theta)$. Let θ^* be the highest state that produces a successful speculative attack. It is the solution to

$$\frac{1}{2} + \frac{k - \theta^*}{2\epsilon} = a(\theta^*). \tag{4.2}$$

Since the left side is decreasing in θ and a is increasing, there will be one solution θ^*. For all $\theta < \theta^*$, the speculative attack will be successful.

Given this rule for speculative attacks, solve for k as the signal of a speculator who is indifferent because the expected benefit of speculating equals the cost t:

$$P[\theta < \theta^* | x_i = k]E[e^* - f(\theta)|x_i = k, \theta < \theta^*] = t. \tag{4.3}$$

Conditional on the signal $x_i = k$, Bayes' law for uniform variables tells us that the state is distributed $\theta \sim \text{unif}[k - \epsilon, k + \epsilon]$.

To derive the conditional expectation of $e^* - f(\theta)$, integrate $e^* - f(\theta)$ times the density $1/(2\epsilon)$ over the interval $[k - \epsilon, \theta^*]$;[2] then divide by the probability that

---

[1] The expectation is computed as if the agent has posterior beliefs that are uniformly distributed on $[x - \epsilon, x + \epsilon]$. Bayes' law (2.5) says the posterior should be uniform on $[max(0, x - \epsilon), min(1, x + \epsilon)]$ because the prior belief is that $x \sim unif[0, 1]$. However, to avoid having to carry around the max and min operators, Morris and Shin consider states that are at least ϵ distance away from the bounds of prior beliefs. In other words, $x \in [\epsilon, 1 - \epsilon]$.

[2] Again, there is a question of whether these are the right bounds for the posterior distribution of θ. Bayes' law (2.5) says that the upper bound should be $min(\theta^*, k+\epsilon)$. However, if we make the additional assumption that $f(1) < e - t$, then $min(\theta^*, k + \epsilon) = \theta^*$. Suppose not. If $k + \epsilon < \theta^*$, then $P(\theta < \theta^*|k) = 1$: the indifferent speculator knows that the highest possible state is not sufficiently high to prevent a successful speculative attack. If a speculative attack will succeed with probability 1, then expected utility from speculating, $e - f(1) - t$, is strictly positive, which means that k cannot be the signal of an indifferent speculator, which is a contradiction.

θ is in the conditioning set, $P[\theta < \theta^*|x_i = k]$. That last step cancels out the $P[\theta < \theta^*|x_i = k]$ term that multiplies the conditional expectation in (4.3). The result is

$$\int_{k-\epsilon}^{\theta^*} (e^* - f(\theta)) \frac{1}{2\epsilon} d\theta = t. \tag{4.4}$$

Equations (4.2) and (4.4), both in k and θ^*, characterize the solution.

A simple example. Suppose the government's cost of defending the currency is $c(\alpha, \theta) = \alpha - \theta$ and the free-floating exchange rate is a known constant: $f(\theta) = F$. Then $c(\alpha, \theta) > v$ if and only if $\alpha > v + \theta$. That is $a(\theta)$, the size of an attack needed to cause a devaluation for state θ.

The cutoff level of the state variable θ^* that triggers a successful attack is determined by equating the size of the attack in (4.2) with critical size $a(\theta)$:

$$\frac{1}{2} + \frac{k - \theta^*}{2\epsilon} = v + \theta^*.$$

This tells us that whenever θ is greater than $\theta^* = (\epsilon + k - 2\epsilon v)/(1 + 2\epsilon)$, a successful speculative attack takes place.

Finally, the cutoff signal that makes an agent speculate comes from (4.4). Replacing the function $f(\theta)$ with the constant F and integrating over the uniformly distributed θ delivers $(e^* - F)\frac{\theta^* - k + \epsilon}{2\epsilon} = t$. Rearranging reveals the cutoff signal

$$\theta^* = \frac{2\epsilon t}{e^* - F} + k - \epsilon.$$

Thus an agent speculates if and only if his signal is $x_i \leq \theta^*$.

Comments on the solution. One of the challenges that previous work in this literature encountered was that expressing higher- and higher-order beliefs becomes more and more complicated (Townsend 1983). The solution here depended on the entire hierarchy of beliefs. The reason that hierarchy of beliefs stayed tractable is due to the symmetric nature of agents' strategies. The strategy function (4.1) was common knowledge. The interpretation is that agents are solving for their strategy and others' strategies simultaneously. Furthermore, expectations of others' signals depended only on the expectation of the state variable θ. This structure is essential to keeping the problem tractable.

4.3 INFORMATION AND COVARIANCE: A BEAUTY CONTEST MODEL

While the discrete choice model of the previous section is useful to illustrate the possibility of multiple equilibria and how information can eliminate them, in many situations, agents take continuous actions. A quadratic loss model is useful in these situations. Many more complicated environments can be quadratically approximated using second-order Taylor approximations. Popularized by Morris and Shin (2002), this game has been used as a static representation of many settings with incomplete information and strategic interaction including financial markets, investment decisions, and price adjustment with monopolistic competition.

Model setup. There is a continuum of agents indexed by i. Each agent chooses an action a_i to minimize the expected distance between their action and the average action $a = \int a_i di$, as well as the expected distance between their action and an unknown exogenous state variable $s \sim \mathcal{N}\left(y, \tau_y^{-1}\right)$:

$$EL\,(a_i, a, s) = E\left[(1 - r)\,(a_i - s)^2 + r\,(a_i - a)^2\right], \tag{4.5}$$

where EL stands for "expected loss." An agent's objective is $-EL$. The parameter r governs the type of strategic interaction between agents. There are three possibilities:

$r > 0$: strategic complements, optimal a_i increasing in a,

$r = 0$: no interaction, optimal a_i independent of a,

$r < 0$: strategic substitutes, optimal a_i decreasing in a.

The order of events is as follows. First, nature draws $s \sim N\left(y, \tau_y^{-1}\right)$. The mean and variance of the s distribution are common knowledge and summarize all prior public information. Second, each agent receives a public and a private signal containing additional information about the state s: $z|s \sim N\left(s, \tau_z^{-1}\right)$ and $w_i|s \sim N\left(s, \tau_w^{-1}\right)$. In other words, $z = s + \epsilon_z$ and $w_i = s + \epsilon_{w,i}$ where $\epsilon_z \sim N(0, \tau_z^{-1})$ and $\epsilon_{w,i} \sim N(0, \tau_w^{-1})$, independent of all other $\epsilon_{x,j}$ and of ϵ_z. Finally, agents choose their actions a_i and payoffs are realized. We look for a Nash equilibrium to solve the game.

Full-information solution. Before continuing, consider the full-information problem. This will be a useful benchmark for comparison to highlight the effect of heterogeneous, incomplete information:

$$\min_{a_i} (1 - r)\,(a_i - s)^2 + r\,(a_i - a)^2. \tag{4.6}$$

The first derivative of the objective, with respect to a_i, is $2(1 - r)(a_i - s) + 2r$ $(a_i - a)$. Setting this equal to zero and rearranging tells us that the optimal action for all agents i is

$$a_i = (1 - r)s + ra. \tag{4.7}$$

Integrating actions over all individuals gives us the average action: $a \equiv \int_i a_i = (1 - r)s + ra$. Collecting the a terms on the left and right sides delivers $a = s$. Plugging this average action into (4.7) reveals that the optimal action is $a_i = s$.

Note that there is a unique solution in the model. Unlike the model in section 4.2, we do not need heterogeneous information to make the equilibrium unique. For $r > 0$, there is a complementarity. But that complementarity is not strong enough to generate multiple equilibria.

Solution with heterogeneous, imperfect information. Suppose that, in addition to the knowledge of the distribution from which nature draws s, all agents have private information with precision τ_w and public information with precision τ_z. Given this information, Bayes' law (2.3) dictates that the agent's belief about the state is

$$E_i[s] = \frac{\tau_y y + \tau_w w_i + \tau_z z}{\tau_y + \tau_w + \tau_z}. \tag{4.8}$$

Let's define $\alpha_s = \tau_y/(\tau_y + \tau_w + \tau_z)$, $\alpha_w = \tau_w/(\tau_y + \tau_w + \tau_z)$, and $\alpha_z = \tau_z/(\tau_y + \tau_w + \tau_z)$. Note that $\alpha_s + \alpha_w + \alpha_z = 1$.

Each agent's optimal action minimizes (4.5). Following the same steps as in the full-information case, the first-order condition is

$$a_i = (1 - r)E_i[s] + rE_i[a]. \tag{4.9}$$

Morris and Shin (2002) show that there is a unique optimal action in this type of model. Hellwig and Veldkamp (2009) extend that argument for the case with information choice. For the purpose of this book, I will omit any discussion of uniqueness and just guess and verify the solution. Guess that

$$a_i = y + \gamma_w(w_i - y) + \gamma_z(z - y). \tag{4.10}$$

Since the mean of the private signals w_i is the true state s, our guess implies that the average action is

$$a = y + \gamma_w(s - y) + \gamma_z(z - y). \tag{4.11}$$

Therefore, agent i's expectation of the average action is

$$E_i[a] = y + \gamma_w(E_i[s] - y) + \gamma_z(z - y). \tag{4.12}$$

Substituting the expected state (4.8) into the expected average action (4.12) and then substituting both (4.8) and (4.12) into the first-order condition (4.9) yields

$$a_i = (1 - r + r\gamma_w)(\alpha_s y + \alpha_w w_i + \alpha_z z) + r((1 - \gamma_w)y + \gamma_z(z - y)). \tag{4.13}$$

Matching coefficients verifies the conjecture that the action is a linear function of each of the signals and that the linear weights are $\gamma_w = (1 - r + r\gamma_w)\alpha_w$ and $\gamma_z = (1 - r + r\gamma_w)\alpha_z + r\gamma_z$. Collecting the γ_w and γ_z terms and substituting γ_w into the expression for γ_z delivers

$$\gamma_w = \frac{\alpha_w(1 - r)}{1 - \alpha_w r} \tag{4.14}$$

and

$$\gamma_z = \frac{\alpha_z}{1 - \alpha_w r}. \tag{4.15}$$

The last step is to check if the guess (equation [4.10]) was correct by seeing if the coefficients on y add up to $1 - \gamma_w - \gamma_z$. I leave this as an exercise.

An important feature of this solution is that the weight agents put on the public signal when forming their action (γ_z) is increasing in the value of coordination r. Agents who want to do what others do make their actions more sensitive to information that others know. Whenever there is strategic complementarity in actions ($r > 0$), $\gamma_z > \alpha_z$, meaning that agents' actions react more to changes in public information than their beliefs do. Conversely, when there is strategic substitutability in actions, agents weight private signals more in their actions than in their beliefs.

Information and covariance. An important feature of this solution is that when an agent has a more precise signal about a shock, his optimal action puts a higher weight on it. For example, if the public signal z is very noisy, γ_z is smaller and actions will not be very sensitive to z. Reacting less to z means that the covariance between the average action a and z will be lower. This, in turn, lowers the covariance between a and the true state s. To see this, substitute γ_w and γ_z from (4.14) and (4.15) into the formula for the average action (4.11). Then, substitute in $z = s + \epsilon_z$ to get $a - y = (\alpha_w(1 - r) + \alpha_z)/(1 - \alpha_w r)(s - y) + \alpha_z/(1 - \alpha_w r)\epsilon_z$. Note that y is a known constant and that ϵ_z is independent of s and y. Thus, $cov(a, s) = ((\alpha_w(1 - r) + \alpha_z)/(1 - \alpha_w r))\tau_y^{-1}$. For $r < 1$, this covariance is increasing in the precision of both private and public signals (τ_w and τ_z). The result that information precision governs the covariance of average actions and the state will be an important idea in many of the results that follow.

4.4 STRATEGIC MOTIVES IN INFORMATION ACQUISITION

Hellwig and Veldkamp (2009) examine how one agent's choice to acquire information before playing a strategic game depends on others' information acquisition. In their model, signals can be purely private, purely public, or correlated and agents can observe heterogeneous exogenous signals prior to choosing their information. This section considers a simplified model with common priors where agents choose signals that are either purely private or common. The results provide intuition that will illuminate many of the results in the models that follow.

The model. The model is identical to the one in section 4.3, except that now agents can choose to acquire additional information. Specifically, they choose how much to pay $C(\tau_w, \tau_z)$ (increasing, convex, twice differentiable) to acquire a private signal $w_i \sim N\left(s, \tau_w^{-1}\right)$ and/or a common signal $z \sim \mathcal{N}\left(s, \tau_z^{-1}\right)$. The interpretation of the private signal choice is straightforward. For example, the agent might choose how much independent research to do about the state s. The common signal requires some explanation because common information is only truly common if all agents know it, which means that they must choose to observe it. Suppose that every agent gets an identical newspaper delivered to their door. Each agent begins at the start of page 1 and decides how far to read. Each additional word provides additional information, so the choice of the number of words is a choice of signal precision. Of course, the number of words is an integer. So, imagine a limiting version of this environment where words become less informative and less costly to read at the same rate. This limit economy approximates the continuous choice of signal precision examined below.

We will solve for a symmetric equilibrium: a precision τ_w^* or τ_z^* that is common to all agents.

Solving the model. The solution strategy is to work backward. Hold fixed the information agents have and solve the action game, as in the previous section. Compute agents' expected utility in that game. It will be a function of their information. Now move backward to the first period. Use this expected utility as the payoff function in the first-stage information choice game. Finally, solve for the information choices. Substitute those choices back into the solutions for the second-stage game. This is a complete solution to the game.

Solving the second-stage action game is more complicated now that one agent can potentially have different information precision than the rest of the agents. Let τ_w^*, τ_z^* be the information choice of all other agents and τ_w, τ_z be agent i's information choice. Likewise, let z^* be the public signal others see. Since the one agent has zero mass, the other agents are playing a game where the average agent has the same precision information as they do. Their optimal actions are given by the weights γ_w^* and γ_z^* on private and public information, as given in equations (4.14) and (4.15). These weights imply that the average action is $a = (1 - \gamma_w^* - \gamma_z^*)y + \gamma_w^* s + \gamma_z^* z^*$.

The agent choosing his information precision takes the form of the average action as given and chooses his own optimal action, given information precision τ_w and τ_z. Call the weights that solve this problem $\tilde{\gamma}_w$ and $\tilde{\gamma}_z$, so that $a_i = (1 - \tilde{\gamma}_w - \tilde{\gamma}_z)y + \tilde{\gamma}_w w_i + \tilde{\gamma}_z z$.

The next step is to compute expected utility, piece by piece. Substitute a_i from (4.10) into the first term of the objective (4.5). That first term becomes

$$E[(a_i - s)^2] = E[((1 - \tilde{\gamma}_w - \tilde{\gamma}_z)y + \tilde{\gamma}_w w_i + \tilde{\gamma}_z z - s)^2]. \qquad (4.16)$$

Next, rearrange the right-hand side of this equation in order to make use of a helpful shortcut. Distributing the $-s$ term yields $E[(1 - \tilde{\gamma}_w - \tilde{\gamma}_z)(y - s) + \tilde{\gamma}_w(w_i - s) + \tilde{\gamma}_z(z - s))^2]$. Since y, w, and z are independently drawn from distributions with mean s, the terms $(y - s)$, $(w_i - s)$, and $(z - s)$ have zero mean and zero covariance with each other. Thus, the expectation of all the cross-terms of the form $(y - s)(z - s)$ are zero. Therefore, (4.16) becomes

$$E[(a_i-s)^2] = (1-\tilde{\gamma}_w-\tilde{\gamma}_z)^2 E_i[(y-s)^2]+\tilde{\gamma}_w^2 E_i[(w_i-s)^2]+\tilde{\gamma}_z^2 E_i[(z-s)^2]. \quad (4.17)$$

Furthermore, the expected square of a variable minus its mean is the definition of a variance. Therefore,

$$E[(a_i - s)^2] = (1 - \tilde{\gamma}_w - \tilde{\gamma}_z)^2 \tau_y^{-1} + \tilde{\gamma}_w^2 \tau_w^{-1} + \tilde{\gamma}_z^2 \tau_z^{-1}. \qquad (4.18)$$

The second term in utility is the distance of one's action from the average action $E[(a_i - a)^2]$. The form of this term depends on whether the agent observes more public signals than others do.

Case 1: $\tau_z \leq \tau_z^*$. In this case, others observe more public signals than what i knows. From agent i's point of view, this creates noise in the average action. This noise is conditionally uncorrelated with any information i knows.

The difference between i's action and the average action is

$$(a_i - a) = \tilde{\gamma}_w(w_i - y) - \gamma_w^*(s - y) + \tilde{\gamma}_z(z - y) - \gamma_z^*(z^* - y).$$

Splitting the $(w_i - y)$ and $(z - y)$ terms into a difference of independent random variables, $(w_i - s) - (y - s)$ and $(z - s) - (y - s)$, and taking the expectation of the square yields

$$E[(a_i-a)^2] = \tilde{\gamma}_w^2 \tau_w^{-1} + (-\tilde{\gamma}_w + \gamma_w^* - \tilde{\gamma}_z + \gamma_z^*)^2 \tau_y^{-1} + E[(\tilde{\gamma}_z(z-s) - \gamma_z^*(z^*-s))^2].$$

The last term inside the expectation and the square can be split into $(\tilde{\gamma}_z - \gamma_z^*)(z - s)$ $- \gamma_z^*(z^* - z)$: $(z - s)$ is noise in i's signal; $(z^* - z)$ is the difference in two mean-s signals. Of course, z^* and z are correlated because both are signals about s. But the additional signals that others observe and i does not have signal noise that is uncorrelated with the noise in z. Therefore, $(z - s)$ and $(z^* - z)$ are independent random variables. Thus,

$$E[(a_i - a)^2] = \tilde{\gamma}_w^2 \tau_w^{-1} + (-\tilde{\gamma}_w + \gamma_w^* - \tilde{\gamma}_z + \gamma_z^*)^2 \tau_y^{-1} + (\tilde{\gamma}_z - \gamma_z^*)^2 \tau_z^{-1}$$
$$+ (\gamma_z^*)^2 (\tau_z^* - \tau_z)^{-1}. \tag{4.19}$$

Case 2: $\tau_z \geq \tau_z^*$. In this case, the additional public information that i learns, in excess of what others know, is effectively private information. Thus $z - z^*$ is treated like private information in agents' actions and in expected utility. Since there is now more effective private information, the agents' weights on private and public information change. Let $\dot{\gamma}_w$ be the optimal weight on $w_i + z - z^*$, which is a private signal with precision $(\tau_w + \tau_z - \tau_z^*)$. Likewise, let $\dot{\gamma}_z$ be i's optimal weight on the information that is common knowledge, z^*. Expected utility then takes the same form as before except that the variance of the effective private signal is $(\tau_w + \tau_z - \tau_z^*)^{-1}$ instead of τ_w^{-1}, the variance of the public signal is $(\tau_z^*)^{-1}$, and there is no last term that came from the additional public information in others' actions.

$$E[(a_i - a)^2] = \dot{\gamma}_w^2 (\tau_w + \tau_z - \tau_z^*)^{-1} + (-\dot{\gamma}_w + \gamma_w^* - \dot{\gamma}_z + \gamma_z^*)^2 \tau_y^{-1}$$
$$+ (\dot{\gamma}_z - \gamma_z^*)^2 (\tau_z^*)^{-1}. \tag{4.20}$$

The sum of (4.18) and either (4.20) or (4.19) is the negative expected utility an agent with the information set we postulated expects to get. This solution has an interesting and useful feature: expected utility does not depend on signal realizations. It only depends on the precision of each signal and the equilibrium weights on each signal in the action game. The equilibrium weights also depend only on signal precision and the parameters of the game. Therefore, there is no uncertainty about what anyone's signal utility is. Even with heterogeneous prior beliefs (meaning that the means, not the variances, of our priors differed), there would be no uncertainty about anyone's expected utility from additional information. This feature of the problem will be important when we talk about equilibrium uniqueness later on.

The main result: strategic motives in information acquisition. The main result is that the strategic motives in information choice mirror the strategic motives in actions. If actions are strategic complements ($r > 0$), then information acquisition is also complementary. Conversely, if actions are strategic substitutes, then information is a strategic substitute as well.

The marginal value of private information is

$$B(\tau_w) = -\frac{\partial}{\partial \tau_w} EL(\tau_w, \tau_z; \tau_w^*, \tau_z^*).$$

The marginal value of public information is

$$B(\tau_z) = -\frac{\partial}{\partial \tau_z} EL(\tau_w, \tau_z; \tau_w^*, \tau_z^*).$$

Proposition

$$r > 0 \iff \frac{\partial}{\partial \tau_w^*} B(\tau_w), \quad \frac{\partial}{\partial \tau_z^*} B(\tau_z) > 0$$

$$r = 0 \iff \frac{\partial}{\partial \tau_w^*} B(\tau_w), \quad \frac{\partial}{\partial \tau_z^*} B(\tau_z) = 0$$

$$r < 0 \iff \frac{\partial}{\partial \tau_w^*} B(\tau_w), \quad \frac{\partial}{\partial \tau_z^*} B(\tau_z) < 0$$

Proof. See Hellwig and Veldkamp 2009. $\qquad\qquad\square$

To see why this result holds mathematically, examine the expected loss function, (4.18) plus either (4.19) or (4.20). Since the state is exogenous, others' choices do not affect $E[(a_i - s)^2]$; they only affect the distance of one's action from the average action. Therefore, we can focus only on the second term in utility.

Suppose i learns the same amount of public information but more private information. Then, $z = z^*$, $\gamma_w > \gamma_w^*$, and $\gamma_z < \gamma_z^*$:

$$(a_i - a) = \gamma_w w_i - \gamma_w^* s + (\gamma_z - \gamma_z^*)z + (\gamma_w^* - \gamma_w + \gamma_z^* - \gamma_z)y$$

$$E[(a_i - a)^2] = (\gamma_z - \gamma_z^*)^2 \tau_z^{-1} + (-\gamma_w + \gamma_w^* - \gamma_z + \gamma_z^*)^2 \tau_y^{-1}.$$

If $r > 0$, this term enters positively in the expected loss (negatively in expected utility). To minimize this term, γ_w and γ_z should be as close as possible to γ_w^* and γ_z^*. That is information complementarity. If $r < 0$, utility is higher when this term is larger. Thus, making γ_w and γ_z very different from γ_w^* and γ_z^* raises expected utility. That is information substitutability. The same argument holds for differences in public information. To prove this formally, sign the cross-partial derivatives $\partial^2 EL / \partial \tau_w \partial \tau_w^*$ and $\partial^2 EL / \partial \tau_z \partial \tau_z^*$.

Intuitively, what is going on is that information changes the covariance between the average action and the state. That is what makes information more or less valuable. When actions exhibit complementarity ($r > 0$) and other agents have precise information (high $\tau_w + \tau_z$), $\text{cov}(a, s)$ is high. When the average action and the state covary, the agent faces more payoff uncertainty because if he chooses an action that turns out to be far away from s, it will also be far away from a and he will be penalized twice. This added utility risk raises the value of accurate information. Conversely, when actions are substitutes ($r < 0$) and other agents have precise information (high $\tau_w + \tau_z$), $\text{cov}(a, s)$ is again high, meaning that if the agent chooses an action that turns out to be far away from s, it will also be far away from a. But in this case, that covariance reduces payoff uncertainty because taking an action that is far away from a confers a utility benefit. The offsetting benefit hedges the risk of taking an action that is far away from a. Less risk lowers the value of information.

4.5 EXAMPLE: INFORMATION CHOICE AND REAL INVESTMENT

The following simple example of a strategic game with information choice illustrates the mechanism behind the main result in the preceding section. The utility function in this example takes a different form from that in the previous section, but the same logic applies to both models.

A measure-1 continuum of firms is indexed by i. Each firm maximizes expected profits. A firm's output is $[(1 - r) s + r K] k_i$, where k_i is the firm's investment, s is technology, $K = \int k_i di$ is aggregate investment, and $r < 1$ determines whether aggregate investment increases ($r > 0$) or decreases ($r < 0$) each individual firm's marginal product of capital. If investment cost is $C(k_i) = \frac{1}{2}k_i^2$, then realized profits are

$$\pi_i = [(1 - r) s + r K] k_i - \frac{1}{2} k_i^2. \tag{4.21}$$

First, nature draws s from a prior distribution $G(\cdot)$. We let $y = \int s \, dG(s)$ denote the prior mean and $\sigma^2 = \int (s - y)^2 \, dG(s)$ the prior variance of s. Second, each firm decides whether to pay a cost $C > 0$ to observe s without noise; if no cost is paid, no information is acquired, and the firm's prior and posterior about s are the same. Finally, each firm decides on its investment level k_i. A Nash equilibrium of this game is a set of choices by each firm: whether to become informed or not, an investment level k_U for a firm who remains uninformed, and an investment function $k_I(s)$ for firms who observe s. The analysis focuses on symmetric pure-strategy equilibria, in which either all firms become informed or all remain uninformed.

Results. To solve the model, work backward. Compute optimal investment decisions, taking information as given, and then compare the expected profit of informed and uninformed agents. The first-order condition for optimal investment is $k_i = (1 - r) E_i(s) + r E_i(K)$. Substituting this optimal decision into (4.21) yields expected equilibrium profits

$$E_i(\pi_i) = \frac{1}{2} [(1 - r) E_i(s) + r E_i(K)]^2. \tag{4.22}$$

We now compute expected payoffs of informed and uninformed firms in two cases.

1. All firms remain uninformed. If all firms are uninformed, their optimal investment is the prior expected level of technology: $k_i = y$ and $K = y$. Ex ante expected profits are

$$E\pi_{U,U} = \frac{1}{2} y^2.$$

If a firm deviates and chooses to become informed while all other firms remain uninformed, it invests

$$k_i = (1 - r) s + r y.$$

It realizes a profit

$$\pi_i = \frac{1}{2} [(1 - r) s + r y]^2.$$

Its expected profit (before information costs) is

$$E\pi_{I,U} = \frac{1}{2} y^2 + \frac{1}{2} (1 - r)^2 \sigma^2.$$

Thus the benefit of acquiring information, when all others are uninformed, is $E\pi_{I,U} - E\pi_{U,U} = \frac{1}{2}(1-r)^2\sigma^2$.

2. All firms become informed. If all firms are informed, their optimal investment decisions solve $k_i = K = s$. Realized profits are

$$\pi_{I,I} = \frac{1}{2}s^2.$$

Ex ante expected profits are

$$E\pi_{I,I} = \frac{1}{2}y^2 + \frac{1}{2}\sigma^2.$$

If a firm deviates and chooses to remain uninformed, while all other firms acquire information, it will invest $k_i = y$. Its prior expected profits are

$$E\pi_{U,I} = \frac{1}{2}y^2.$$

When all other agents are informed, a firm that remains uninformed loses $E\pi_{I,I} - E\pi_{U,I} = \frac{1}{2}\sigma^2$ utils.

The following payoff matrix summarizes these results.

Expected Profit	Others Are Informed	Others Are Uninformed
Become Informed	$\frac{1}{2}y^2 + \frac{1}{2}\sigma^2$	$\frac{1}{2}y^2 + \frac{1}{2}(1-r)^2\sigma^2$
Remain Uninformed	$\frac{1}{2}y^2$	$\frac{1}{2}y^2$

Since this profit is computed before subtracting the information cost, being informed is always better than being uninformed. But the utility difference is $\sigma^2/2$ if others are informed and $(1-r)^2\sigma^2/2$ if they are not. If $r > 0$, then $\sigma^2/2 > (1-r)^2\sigma^2/2$, meaning that information others learn is more valuable. Thus when investment is complementary, information is complementary. If $r < 0$, then $\sigma^2/2 < (1-r)^2\sigma^2/2$, meaning that information others learn is less valuable. When investment is a substitute, information is as well.

This information externality arises because aggregate learning choices affect the covariance of s and K and thereby the variance of the marginal product of investment. When all other firms remain uninformed, there is uncertainty only about exogenous fluctuations in productivity. When all other firms become informed, their investment level depends on technology. When investment is a complement ($r > 0$), this dependence amplifies the effect of technology changes on each firm's marginal product. More volatility makes information more beneficial. When investment is a strategic substitute ($r < 0$), aggregate investment fluctuations that covary with technology dampen the fluctuations in each firm's marginal product. When other firms are informed and their investment covaries more with technology, uncertainty about marginal productivity falls and information becomes less beneficial.

The effect of information demand on the covariance of aggregate investment K and the state s is responsible for the information complementarity. It is also important in its own right because it determines the statistical properties of macroeconomic aggregates. In an equilibrium where many investors are informed, investment and output vary more and investment and technology covary more. When multiple equilibria exist, switches between equilibria will trigger regime changes in the variances and covariances of the aggregate economic variables. Even when the equilibrium is unique, gradual changes in the amount of information observed by firms can shift variances and covariances over time.

4.6 PUBLIC INFORMATION ACQUISITION AND MULTIPLE EQUILIBRIA

Choosing how much information to learn, when the same information is available to others who choose to learn, is a problem that is conducive to multiple equilibria. In settings with coordination motives in actions, agents get strictly more marginal utility from public information than from private information. In section 4.4, we derived expected utility as a function of an individual's public and private information precision. A result that follows from that model is that agents value a marginal improvement in information when that information is known by others more than they value information that others do not know. The reason is that public information better facilitates coordination.

As an individual learns more and more public information, he eventually knows all the information that others know. At that point, any additional information is effectively private. It may be contained in the newspaper that lands on every agent's doorstep. But if those agents do not invest the resources to read that information, it remains private to the one agent who reads it. Since the value of private information is less than public information, the marginal value of reading in the newspaper drops discretely when the agent reaches the limits of public knowledge. Figure 4.1 illustrates the drop in the marginal value of public information in two cases, one where others acquire 0.35 units of public information and another case where others acquire 0.5 units of public information. Since places where the cost and benefit curves run parallel are equilibria, the first two panels show how multiple equilibria can arise. The kink makes it possible to draw a line that is tangent to the benefit curve with the same slope as the cost curve (marginal benefit and marginal cost are equal). In the bottom two panels, there is no kink in the benefit curve. Benefit and cost are parallel only for a unique level of information precision. As a consequence, choices over private information result in unique equilibria.

What this tells us is that if every agent reads five stories in the newspaper, then reading five stories can be optimal. If every agent reads six stories, then six stories can also be an optimal amount of information to acquire. This is true even if agents are given heterogeneous private signals x_i for free. The Morris and Shin (1998) trick of adding heterogeneous information to eliminate multiple equilibria does not work here because information choices depend on variances and covariances, not the levels of beliefs.

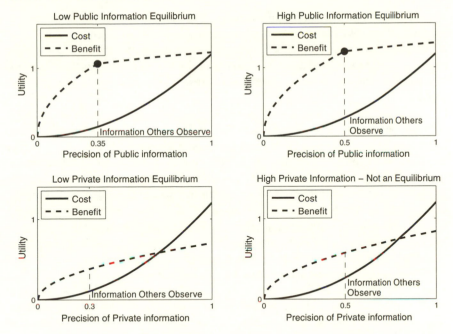

Figure 4.1 Public information equilibria can be multiple, while private information equilibrium is unique. Public information, in excess of what others observe, is private.
That creates a kink (large dot) in the benefit curve. When others observe more
information, the kink shifts and a new equilibrium is sustained. When others
observe more private information, the benefit curve rotates up. But this rotation
is not sufficiently large to sustain multiple equilibria. The high level of private
information is not an equilibrium because the benefit and cost lines are not parallel there, indicating the marginal benefit and marginal cost are not equal. The
optimal information demand rises by less than the increase in others' private
information demand. Thus, the new, higher level of information demand is not a
best response and not an equilibrium.

This result is significant because it offers some practical advice: applied theorists
are in the business of writing down models to explain observed phenomena. If
the model we write down has multiple equilibria, testing such a model will be
difficult, though not impossible. Public information choice models with action
complementarities run a high risk of generating multiple equilibria.

Myatt and Wallace (2009) show how to construct a model with a type of public
signal that preserves the equilibrium uniqueness. The objective is the quadratic
loss beauty contest objective in (4.5). Agents' priors about the state s are diffuse
$(s \sim N(0, \infty))$. There are n signals, indexed by $j \in \{1, \ldots, n\}$, of the form

$$z_{ij} = s + \eta_j + e_{ij} \tag{4.23}$$

where the noise $\eta_j \sim N(0, \tau_{\eta,j}^{-1})$ is independent across signals j, and the individual-
specific noise $e_{ij} \sim N(0, \tau_{ej}^{-1}/\chi_{ij})$ is independent across signals and individuals.
They call $\tau_{\eta j}$ the signal j's *accuracy*, τ_{ej} the signal's *clarity*, and what the agents
are allowed to choose, χ_{ij}, *attention*.

In the language of the newspaper analogy given previously, agents in this economy all get the same newspaper. That newspaper conveys some common noise to all its readers. But each reader is inattentive and interprets the newspaper differently. As readers pay more attention to the newspaper, they can discern its true meaning and can achieve a common interpretation of the public signal that it contains.

Agents choose actions a_i and attention $\{\chi_{ij}\}_{j=1}^n$ to maximize (4.5) subject to a limit on total attention, $f(\chi_1, \ldots, \chi_n)$. The authors focus on equilibria with symmetric strategies. If we guess that actions are linear in signals, then $a_i = \sum_j \gamma_{ij} z_{ij}$. Looking for a symmetric equilibrium implies that no agent wants to deviate from some weights $\gamma_{ij} = \gamma_j \ \forall i$. Integrating yields the average action $\bar{a} = \int a_i di = \sum_j \gamma_j (s + \eta_j)$. Substituting $\bar{a}$ back into the first-order condition and computing the expectations would deliver the equilibrium weights γ_j. But this approach is messy because forming expectations about $s + \eta_j$ requires using every signal. Instead, the authors determine expected utility for arbitrary action weights γ and then choose the optimal weights directly to maximize agents' utility.

If agent j chooses weights γ_{ij}, then his unconditional expected distance of his action from the state is $E[(a_i - s)^2] = \sum_j \gamma_{ij}^2 (\tau_{\eta j}^{-1} + \tau_{ej}^{-1}/\chi_{ij})$. The distance of j's action from the average action has two components: one that is the loss from having different signal realizations and the other that is realized if j chooses different weights γ from the other agents. Since the signal errors are independent across signals, we can rewrite $E[(a_i - \bar{a})^2] = \sum_j E[(\gamma_{ij} z_{ij} - \gamma_j (s + \eta_j))^2]$. Taking the expectation and constructing the weighted sum of the two expected loss terms delivers

$$EL = r\left[\sum_j \frac{\gamma_{ij}^2}{\tau_{ej}\chi_{ij}} + (\gamma_{ij} - \gamma_j)^2 \tau_\eta^{-1} \right] + (1-r)\left[\sum_j \gamma_{ij}^2 (\tau_{\eta j}^{-1} + \tau_{ej}^{-1}/\chi_{ij}) \right].$$

(4.24)

The optimal action is described by the weights γ_{ij} that minimize this expression, subject to the constraint that $\sum_j \gamma_{ij} = 1$. If $\phi_j^{-1} \equiv r\tau_{\eta j}^{-1} + \tau_{ej}^{-1}/\chi_{ij}$, then the symmetric equilibrium is $\gamma_j = \phi_j/(\sum_{k=1}^n \phi_k)$.

In Hellwig and Veldkamp's work (2009), if an agent deviated from the symmetric equilibrium and learned more public information, the additional information was effectively private. Thus, it had a discretely different marginal value. In work by Myatt and Wallace (2009), agents who learn more public information are continuously reducing the noise in their signal about what others know. There is none of the discreteness of the public information choice problem. Just as in the private information choice problem, the continuity ensures a unique fixed point.

4.7 BROADER THEMES AND RELATED LITERATURE

The theme that the strategic motives in information choice mirror the strategic motives in actions will reemerge in different forms throughout the book. It plays an important role in information acquisition price-setting models such as those by Maćkowiak and Wiederholt (2009b) and Reis (2006) and will come back in models of investment choice, such as those by Grossman and Stiglitz (1980) and Van Nieuwerburgh and Veldkamp (2010).

This result should give you some powerful intuition about what the information choice equilibrium might look like in a broad range of strategic games. If the game is one with complementarities, like, for example, increasing returns to aggregate investment, technology spillovers, Bertrand (price) competition, or a simple preference for behaving like others, then information choice will likely be complementary as well. What does this imply? For starters, people will want to learn the same information. As we will see later on, this may lead them to behave similarly. There is also the possibility that multiple equilibria arise. If everyone else learns about variable x, you will want to as well. But if everyone is learning about variable y, that becomes the optimal thing to learn about. Even with a unique equilibrium, there could be small changes in state variables that cause sudden switches in the equilibrium. Such theories can generate excess volatility.

If the game is one of substitutes, what does this imply? In many market environments, when many agents all want to buy good a, a becomes expensive and buying it delivers less net utility to other agents. Markets with Cournot competition (firms choose quantities to produce), returns to specialization or spatial location models are also situations where agents want to behave differently from other agents. In these environments, agents will want to learn information that others do not. This may involve mixed strategies over what to learn. Seemingly identical agents may learn different pieces of information and be led to take different actions. This mechanism can deliver endogenous heterogeneity that resembles a form of market segmentation.

The global games literature. The literature on coordination games with a continuum of agents and heterogeneous information is often referred to as the "global games" literature. What follows are works, both theoretical and with a wide variety of applications, in this literature. For theoretical works on equilibrium multiplicity or uniqueness, see Hellwig 2002 or Angeletos and Werning 2006. For applications of these ideas to price adjustment and business cycles, see Woodford 2002, Hellwig 2005, Lorenzoni 2009, or Ziera 1999. Ozdenoren and Yuan (2007) use complementarity between financial and real investment to generate excess volatility in asset prices and use heterogeneous information to make their equilibrium unique. For applications to financial crises, see Morris and Shin 1998, Goldstein and Pauzner 2005, Angeletos, Hellwig, and Pavan 2007, or Hellwig, Mukherji, and Tsyvinski 2005. See Stromberg 2001 or Edmond 2005 for models of political economy. These are only a few examples of recent work in this literature. Finally, although not in the global games tradition, Vives 1984 and 1988 also look at the strategic motives in information acquisition.

4.8 EXERCISES

1. Show that the coefficients on y in equation (4.13) add up to $1 - \gamma_z - \gamma_w$. *Hint*: Don't forget to use the fact that $\alpha_s + \alpha_w + \alpha_z = 1$. Interpret this fact. What does it tell us about the relationship between signals and actions?

2. In the model of section 4.4, show that when actions are complements $r > 0$, it is not optimal for one agent to deviate from a symmetric equilibrium by acquiring more or less public information than other agents do.

3. The bulk of Morris and Shin's 1998 work is about why the equilibrium with heterogeneous information is unique. Give a short summary (one paragraph) of how they go about proving this claim.

4. In Morris and Shin 1998, how does uncertainty about other speculators' signals affect the probability of a successful attack? Derive a comparative static and then discuss your result intuitively.

5. Using Morris and Shin 1998, show that if successful speculation is profitable, even in the best state ($f(1) < e^* - t$), and k is the signal of the speculator who is indifferent between speculating or not, then $min(\theta^*, k + \varepsilon) = \theta^*$.

6. Suppose an agent has a choice over the precision of a correlated signal that takes the form $v = w + z$, where w and z are signals about s with equal precision and where w is private and z is public in the sense of section 4.4. Utility is given by equation (4.5). and actions are strategic substitutes ($r < 0$). What level of signal precision constitutes an equilibrium?

PART II

Information Choice with Complementarity in Actions

Chapter Five

Disclosing Public Information

While most of the models in this book feature agents who are choosing how much information to learn, this chapter examines the choice of how much information to disclose to others. Typically, the agent deciding whether or not to disclose is a central bank or a government statistical agency that seeking to maximize social welfare. They are choosing whether or not to reveal a piece of information (or how much to reveal) to all market participants.

We usually think of more information as welfare improving because it facilitates efficient market outcomes. But a recent literature has questioned this conventional wisdom. This chapter examines four reasons why revealing information might be socially costly. The fact that the information revealed will be made public is important because public signals convey information not just about an unknown state but also about what other agents know. Thus, disclosing public information can facilitate coordination. One potential problem is that it can cause too much coordination, relative to a social optimum, in settings where there are coordination externalities. Another drawback is that public information releases can deter agents from acquiring or transmitting private information. A third issue is that more information can cause beliefs and, therefore, market prices to be more volatile. Finally, when price-setters have complete information about monetary policy, that policy may cease to have any effect on real economic activity. This is often referred to as monetary neutrality. In such cases, disclosing information can rob the central bank of its ability to stabilize economic fluctuations. This chapter explores these ideas and uses them to frame an active debate in the monetary policy literature: Should a central banker reveal to the public everything that he or she knows about the state of the economy?

5.1 PAYOFF EXTERNALITIES AND THE SOCIAL VALUE OF INFORMATION

5.1.1 Coordination and Overreaction to Public Information

Recall the exogenous-information quadratic loss "beauty contest" model from the previous chapter (section 4.3). The optimal action was

$$a_i = y + \frac{\alpha_w(1-r)}{1-\alpha_w r}(w_i - y) + \frac{\alpha_z}{1-\alpha_w r}(z - y). \tag{5.1}$$

Notice how an increase in the value of the private signal w_i affects the optimal action differently from an increase in the value of the public signal z. In particular, if $r > 0$, and the relative precisions of private information and public information are equal ($\alpha_w = \alpha_z$), then an increase in the public signal affects the action more. The effect of an increase in the private signal is scaled down by $(1 - r)$. The greater the complementarity, the less agents care about private, relative to public, information. Also, because $\alpha_z/(1 - \alpha_w r)$ rises in r, stronger complementarity makes agents' actions more sensitive to public information.

A public signal carries two types of information: it tells the agents something about the state s, and it tells them something about what others' beliefs are, which affects the average action a. In contrast, a private signal tells the agent something about the state but nothing about what others know. So when agents want to coordinate their actions with others' actions ($r > 0$), the public signal is more useful for that purpose, so they weight it more. If agents want to take actions that are different from what others do ($r < 0$), then giving more weight to private information achieves that goal.

5.1.2 Morris and Shin's Social Cost of Public Information

The overreaction to public information, relative to private information, can make additional public information welfare reducing. This is the main point of Morris and Shin's 2002 work. To make this point, we need to change the utility function from the previous chapter by adding one term:

$$U_i = -(1 - r)(a_i - s)^2 - r(a_i - \bar{a})^2 + r \int_0^1 (a_j - \bar{a})^2 dj. \qquad (5.2)$$

The last term, the newly added one, depends only on the actions that other players take. Since each agent has zero mass, he does not affect the value of this integral. Thus, the last term is irrelevant to the agents' decision problem. The optimal action a_i is the same as it was in section 4.3. The role of this last term is to introduce a payoff externality that affects social welfare.

Social welfare is defined as the integral over all individuals' welfare: $W \equiv \int_0^1 U_i di$. When we evaluate this integral, the second and third terms of utility cancel each other out:

$$W = -(1 - r) \int_0^1 (a_i - s)^2 di. \qquad (5.3)$$

This tells us that social welfare is only improved when agents' actions are closer to the state s. Thus, coordination offers private benefits but no social benefits. To the extent that agents' desire to coordinate trades off with their desire to take actions close to s, coordination is socially costly. This insight (that coordination is socially costly) is key to understanding Morris and Shin's result. Because public information facilitates coordination, it will turn out to be social welfare reducing as well.

Substituting the optimal actions from (5.1) into the welfare function (5.3) and taking the integral over agents' private signals yields

$$W = -\frac{1 - r}{(1 - \alpha_w r)^2} \left\{ (1 - \alpha_w - \alpha_z)^2 (y - s)^2 \right.$$
$$\left. + \alpha_w^2 (1 - r)^2 \int_0^1 (w_i - s)^2 di + \alpha_z^2 (z - s)^2 \right\}.$$

Next, take expectations over $(y - s)^2$ and $(z - s)^2$, using the fact that the error in priors $(y - s)$ and the signal noises $(z - s)$ and $(w_i - s)$ are mutually independent

$$E[W] = -\frac{1 - r}{(1 - \alpha_w r)^2} \left\{ (1 - \alpha_w - \alpha_z)^2 \tau_y^{-1} + \alpha_w^2 (1 - r)^2 \int_0^1 (w_i - s)^2 di + \alpha_z^2 \tau_z^{-1} \right\}.$$

Substitute $\tau_w^{-1} = \int_0^1 (w_i - s)^2 di$. The proof of this equality is left as an exercise. Replacing the relative precisions α with the absolute precisions τ, we get

$$E[W] = -(1 - r) \left(\frac{1}{\tau_y + (1 - r)\tau_w + \tau_z} \right)^2 \left\{ \tau_y^2 \tau_y^{-1} + \tau_w^2 (1 - r)^2 \tau_w^{-1} + \tau_z^2 \tau_z^{-1} \right\}.$$

$$E[W] = (1 - r) \left[-\frac{\tau_y + (1 - r)^2 \tau_w + \tau_z}{(\tau_y + (1 - r)\tau_w + \tau_z)^2} \right].$$

Finally, take a partial derivative of expected welfare, with respect to the precision of public information:

$$\frac{\partial E[W]}{\partial \tau_z} = -(1 - r) \left[\frac{-\tau_y - (1 - 2r)(1 - r)\tau_w - \tau_z}{(\tau_y + (1 - r)\tau_w + \tau_z)^3} \right]. \tag{5.4}$$

When $0 < r < 1$, this expression is positive if and only if

$$\frac{\partial E[W]}{\partial \tau_z} > 0 \iff \frac{\tau_y + \tau_z}{\tau_w} > (2r - 1)(1 - r). \tag{5.5}$$

This tells us that if public information (which includes both the common prior and the public signal because both are common knowledge) is sufficiently precise, then adding more public information is welfare improving. Furthermore, when coordination motives are not very strong ($r < 0.5$), then public information is always welfare improving. But in cases where agents have a strong desire to coordinate and the existing public information is noisy, adding to the precision of public information can cause agents to put too much weight on it. They coordinate, at the expense of choosing actions that are further away from the true state, on average. Because social welfare is linked to the distance of actions from the true state, these are situations where public information is socially costly.

5.1.3 Can Private Information Also Be Socially Costly?

If there is a positive rather than a negative coordination externality, then the same arguments in the previous section can be applied to private information. Consider the utility function

$$U_i = -(1 - r)(a_i - s)^2 - r \int_0^1 (a_j - \bar{a})^2 dj \tag{5.6}$$

where $0 < r < 1$. The interpretation is that each agent has an incentive only to make his action as close as possible to the unknown state s, but he benefits when all agents' actions are more coordinated. This creates a positive coordination externality.

Suppose that each agent observes a private signal x_i and a public signal y about the state s, with precisions τ_x and τ_y. Since the optimal action will be $a_i^* = E_i[s] = (\tau_x x_i + \tau_y y)/(\tau_x + \tau_y)$, welfare will be a weighted sum of the conditional variance of each agent's beliefs about s and the dispersion of those beliefs:

$$\int_0^1 U_i di = -(1-r)\frac{1}{\tau_x + \tau_y} - r\frac{\tau_x}{(\tau_x + \tau_y)^2}. \tag{5.7}$$

Notice that this expression is strictly increasing in the precision of public information τ_y. Public information is unambiguously welfare increasing here because it helps agents choose actions closer to s and to coordinate better.

Differentiating reveals that $\partial(\int U_i di)/\partial \tau_x < 0$ if $\tau_x < (2r - 1)\tau_y$. This means that when private information is noisy, relative to public information, then giving agents more private information is welfare reducing. When agents get more precise private information, they base their actions more on this private information and end up taking actions that are very different from each other. This dispersion in actions is what reduces welfare.

5.1.4 A More General Approach

Angeletos and Pavan (2007) unify these findings. They classify economies into four types. First are economies in which the equilibrium is efficient under both complete and incomplete information. In these economies, information is always welfare improving. Second are economies where actions are efficient under complete information, but actions are too coordinated under incomplete information. (This was the case in the work by Morris and Shin 2002.) In these types of settings, public information can reduce welfare. Third are economies where actions are efficient under complete information, but actions are insufficiently coordinated under incomplete information. This is the case that the utility function (5.6) represents. In these settings, private information can reduce welfare. Fourth are economies where actions are inefficient, even with complete information, because there is some other non-information-related distortion in the economy. Because bringing the economy closer to its full-information counterpart does not necessarily increase welfare, either more private or public information could be welfare reducing.

Rather than considering different types of utility and social welfare functions, Cornand and Heinemann (2008) and Myatt and Wallace (2008) generalize the types of signals that agents can observe. Cornand and Heinemann consider revealing the public signal to only a subset of agents. They find that it is socially optimal to provide public information at its maximum precision but that when coordination externalities are present, it may be optimal not to give that information to all agents. Myatt and Wallace consider signals that are imperfectly correlated. Each signal has some private and public component that cannot be disentangled. They interpret this type of signal as an announcement with "limited clarity." The main result is that perfectly private or public signals are never optimal. Instead, limited clarity is what achieves the optimal degree of coordination.

5.1.5 The Central Bank Transparency Debate

The Morris and Shin result that information disclosure could be bad raised many concerns for central bankers. There had been many recent struggles for central banks to open up their decision-making process to greater scrutiny. Proponents of transparency argued that openness would coordinate public expectations on the bank's goals, making price stability easier to attain. The result that public information might be socially costly caused some to rethink their positions and many others to write in defense of transparency.

The debate over the merits of central bank transparency is a rapidly growing literature that I could not attempt to cover comprehensively. One strand of this literature includes works that are closely related to the Morris-Shin framework. Svensson (2006) takes the Morris-Shin model and calibrates some of its parameters to match facts about price-setting in the United States. He argues that existing public information is sufficiently precise that increasing its precision would be welfare enhancing. Hellwig (2005) takes a standard micro-founded price-setting model and disputes the idea that coordination is not socially beneficial. He shows that when price-setting is coordinated, relative prices of goods are aligned to efficiently allocate the goods. If coordination is socially beneficial, more public information that facilitates such coordination is as well. In a different application, Angeletos and Pavan (2004) show that investment coordination can be welfare improving, making public information about productivity socially beneficial. The remaining sections of this chapter summarize other major strands of this literature.

5.2 PUBLIC INFORMATION CROWDS OUT PRIVATE INFORMATION

Another reason that public information could be socially costly is that it inhibits the transmission of private information. Whereas the previous two sections built externalities into agents' payoffs, this argument relies on information externalities. It stipulates that how information is used to form actions affects other agents' ability to learn from those actions. Amador and Weill (2011) show that increasing the precision of public information causes agents to weight it more heavily, and private information less heavily, in their actions. Because actions are observed with some noise, a smaller private information component makes actions less informative about what private information others know. Because information diffuses only when actions reveal private information that the observer did not already know, more public information eventually makes agents less informed. In short, public information crowds out private information.

5.2.1 Amador and Weill 2009

The following is a 2-period model that illustrates the effect that Amador and Weill (2009) build into an infinite-horizon, continuous-time model. Consider a continuum of agents indexed by i with payoffs that depend on the agent's action in periods 1 and 2, a_{1i} and a_{2i}, and an unknown state x:

$$U = -(a_{1i} - x)^2 - (a_{2i} - x)^2. \qquad (5.8)$$

Prior beliefs are diffuse. Before taking their first action, each agent observes a private signal z_{1i} and a public signal Z_1 of x, with precisions π_1 and Π_1, respectively:

$$z_{1i} = x + w_{1i} \quad w_{1i} \sim i.i.d. N(0, \pi_1^{-1}) \tag{5.9}$$

$$Z_1 = x + W_1 \quad W_1 \sim N(0, \Pi_1^{-1}). \tag{5.10}$$

After taking their first action, but before taking their second action, each agent observes a private and a public signal about the average first action $A \equiv \int a_{1i} di$:

$$z_{2i} = A + w_{2i} \quad w_{2i} \sim i.i.d. N(0, p^{-1}) \tag{5.11}$$

$$Z_2 = A + W_2 \quad W_2 \sim N(0, P^{-1}) \tag{5.12}$$

Thus, the agents' problem is to choose a_{1i}, given their time-1 information set $\{z_{1i}, Z_1\}$ and to choose a_{2i}, given their time-2 information set $\{z_{1i}, Z_1, z_{2i}, Z_2\}$ to maximize (5.8).

Equilibrium outcomes. The crowding-out effect is when an increase in the precision of the exogenous public signal (Π_1) decreases the precision of the period-2 public and private signals Π_2 and π_2. Begin with the first-order condition with respect to a_{1i}, which yields optimal period-1 actions:

$$a_{1i}^* = E[x|z_{1i}, Z_1] = \frac{\pi_1 z_{1i} + \Pi_1 Z_1}{\pi_1 + \Pi_1}. \tag{5.13}$$

To figure out what π_2 and Π_2 are, we need to know what the information content of the average action A is. Integrating a_i over all individuals and using the fact that $\int z_{1i} di = x$ yields

$$A = \frac{\pi_1 x + \Pi_1 Z_1}{\pi_1 + \Pi_1}. \tag{5.14}$$

Notice that the average action A becomes less sensitive to changes in the true state x as public information becomes more precise ($\partial A / \partial x$ falls as Π_1 rises).

Substituting the A into (5.11) tells us that the endogenous private signal is $z_{2i} = (\pi_1 x + \Pi_1 Z_1)/(\pi_1 + \Pi_1) + w_{2i}$. This signal is informative about x, but its mean is not x. Since the agent knows Z_1 at the time when he observes z_{2i}, he subtracts that from the signal and divides by $\pi_1/(\pi_1 + \Pi_1)$ to get an unbiased signal of x:

$$\tilde{z}_{2i} \equiv z_{2i} + \frac{\Pi_1}{\pi_1}(z_{2i} - Z_1) = x + \frac{\pi_1 + \Pi_1}{\pi_1} w_{2i}. \tag{5.15}$$

The variance of this signal is $Var[x|z_{2i}, Z_1] = Var[w_{2i}]((\pi_1 + \Pi_1)/\pi_1)^2 = p^{-1}(\pi_1 + \Pi_1)^2/\pi_1^2$. Thus, the signal precision is

$$\pi_2 = \frac{p\pi_1^2}{(\pi_1 + \Pi_1)^2}. \tag{5.16}$$

Making the same substitution into (5.12) tells us that the unbiased public signal is $\tilde{Z}_2 \equiv Z_2 + (\Pi_1/\pi_1)(Z_2 - Z_1)$. Its precision is

$$\Pi_2 = \frac{P\pi_1^2}{(\pi_1 + \Pi_1)^2}. \tag{5.17}$$

The key result is that Π_2 and π_2 are decreasing in Π_1. In other words, more precise initial public information lowers the precision of subsequent signals. This is the crowding-out effect. The reason this happens is that agents who have more precise public information put less weight on their private information when choosing their period-1 action. This makes the average period-1 action less informative. To see why, consider an extreme case where period-1 actions were a function only of the public signal Z_1. Then observing A would only reveal Z_1. But the agents already know Z_1, so A or any noisy signal of A would reveal no new information. When actions are not so extreme and they convey private information, the informativeness of the noisy signals of A will depend on how much weight agents put on that private information. A larger weight (higher $\frac{\pi_1}{\pi_1 + \Pi_1}$) increases the signal-to-noise ratios of z_{2i} and Z_2. Changes in x become easier to observe when those changes are larger, relative to the size of the noise coming from w_{2i} and W_2. Thus, when agents put more weight on their private information in their period-1 actions, the period-2 signals convey more information.

This crowding-out effect would be present even if the only endogenous signal was the public one, Z_2. Why have a private signal z_{2i} as well? The presence of this signal amplifies the crowding-out effect in future periods. To see why this is the case, consider the optimal period-2 action:

$$a_{2i}^* = E[x|z_{1i}, Z_1, z_{2i}, Z_2] = \frac{\pi_1 z_{1i} + \Pi_1 Z_1 + \pi_2 \tilde{z}_{2i} + \Pi_2 \tilde{Z}_2}{\pi_1 + \Pi_1 + \pi_2 + \Pi_2}. \qquad (5.18)$$

When agents observe the endogenous signals in period-3, both Z_1 and Z_2 will be known to them. The period-2 average action will reveal new information to the extent that agents put weight on their exogenous private signal z_{1i} and their endogenous private signal z_{2i}. As in period-1, more precise exogenous public information lowers the weight put on z_{1i}. But now it also lowers the weight put on z_{2i}. So, more public information obscures both exogenous and endogenous private information. In an infinite-horizon model, Amador and Weill can show the amplified crowding-out effect is sufficiently strong that more initial public information eventually leads agents to have less total information. The conclusion is ironic: giving agents more public information can cause them to be less well-informed.

Amador and Weill (2011) embed this mechanism in a cash-in-advance model where households observe the prices of goods but cannot disentangle productivity from money supply shocks. When the central bank provides more precise public information about the money supply (or about productivity), households' production and purchasing decisions depend less on their private information and more on public information. This can make prices less informative.

5.2.2 Complementary Public and Private Information

While the idea that public information crowds out private information is intuitively appealing, it is possible to generate the reverse conclusion. Here is an example of a setting where disclosing public information facilitates the transmission of private information. It is loosely based on work by Gosselin, Lotz, and Wyplosz (2008).

A central bank chooses two actions, a_1 and a_2, to maximize a quadratic social welfare function. It is meant to represent the idea that in a new-Keynesian model, the optimal period-1 interest rate a_1 depends on the expected future interest rate $\bar{E}[a_2]$ and expected inflation $\bar{E}[s]$. Since the economy returns to steady state in period 3, the optimal period-2 interest rate depends only on inflation s. The quadratic form is purely for tractability.

$$U = U_1 + U_2 \quad \text{where } U_1 = -(a_1 - \bar{E}[a_2] - \bar{E}[s])^2 \text{ and } U_2 = -(a_2 - s)^2, \quad (5.19)$$

where $\bar{E}$ represents the average expectation of a continuum of agents, indexed by i. These agents do not choose actions but only form their expectations.

Agents and the central bank form expectations using Bayes' law. No one knows s exactly, but everyone observes noisy signals. Agents are endowed with signals $x_i = s + \eta_i$ where $\eta_i \sim i.i.d.N(0, \sigma^2)$. This implies that the average expectation is perfectly accurate: $\bar{E}[s] = s$. The central bank's signal is $x_{CB} = s + \eta_{CB}$ where $\eta_{CB} \sim N(0, \sigma^2)$ and η_{CB} and η_i are independent.

The agents also have common prior beliefs about the central bank's signal error. They observe $y = \eta_{CB} + \eta_y$ where $\eta_y \sim N(0, \sigma_y^2)$. Combining y with the knowledge that η_{CB} is mean-0 results in a posterior belief $E[x_{CB}|x_i, y] = x_i + y\sigma_y^{-2}/(\sigma_y^{-2} + \sigma^{-2})$.

In addition to this prior information, there is one endogenous signal. After the bank chooses a_1, agents form their expectations, but before the bank chooses a_2, everyone observes the period-1 component of the payoff U_1.

Outcome with disclosure. Suppose the central bank publicly announces its signal before the agents form their expectations. The first-order condition for the central bank's period-2 action yields

$$a_2 = E_{CB}[s]. \quad (5.20)$$

Conjecture that the bank learns s perfectly from observing the period-1 payoff. Then $a_2 = s$. In that case, the agents' expectations about the period-2 action and the period-2 shock are the same: $\bar{E}[a_2] = \bar{E}[s] = s$. Therefore, $U_1 = -(a_1 - 2s)^2$. Since the bank knows what action a_1 it took, it can invert U_1 to perfectly learn what s is. Thus, the conjecture is verified.

Since the bank knows s, it can set $a_2 = s$ and ensure that $U_2 = 0$. Expected utility is

$$E[U] = -(a_1 - \bar{E}[a_2] - \bar{E}[s])^2. \quad (5.21)$$

The first-order condition for a_1 yields $a_1 = E_{CB}^1[\bar{E}[a_2] + \bar{E}[s]] = 2x_{CB}$, because x_{CB} is the central bank's expectation of s, conditional on its period-1 information set and because $a_2 = s$. Thus,

$$E[U] = -(2x_{CB} - 2s)^2 = -4\sigma^2. \quad (5.22)$$

This argument does not prove that the conjectured solution is unique. But Gosselin, Lotz, and Wyplosz (2008) do prove uniqueness. The logic is that agents have no reason to use their signal y to forecast the bank's information x_{CB} if the bank tells them directly what x_{CB} is. By preventing agents from using y, the bank ensures that there is only one unknown variable in U_1. As long as the bank can invert U_1 to learn s, it will learn the true state.

Outcome with opacity. If the central bank does not reveal its signal x_{CB}, then agents will use their signal y to forecast it. The bank's optimal actions take the same form as before: $a_2 = E[s|x_{CB}, U_1]$ and $a_1 = E[\bar{E}[a_2] + \bar{E}[s]|x_{CB}]$.

We conjecture that the central bank's expectation $E[s|x_{CB}, U_1]$ is a linear combination of the true state s, the agents' signal y, and the central bank's own signal x_{CB}:

$$a_2 = \alpha_1 s + \alpha_2 x_{CB} + (1 - \alpha_1 - \alpha_2)y. \qquad (5.23)$$

Then, agent i's expectation of a_2 is $E[a_2|x_i, y] = \alpha_1 x_i + \alpha_2(x_i + y\sigma_y^{-2}/(\sigma_y^{-2} + \sigma^{-2})) + (1 - \alpha_1 - \alpha_2)y$. Therefore, the average expectation of the central bank's action is $\bar{E}[a_2] = \alpha_1 s + \alpha_2(s + y\sigma_y^{-2}/(\sigma_y^{-2} + \sigma^{-2})) + (1 - \alpha_1 - \alpha_2)y$. As before, the average expectation of the state is unbiased $\bar{E}[s] = s$.

The central bank chooses its first action. Substituting $\bar{E}[a_2]$ into the first-order condition and using the fact that y is the sum of two mean-zero variables,

$$a_1 = (1 + \alpha_1 + \alpha_2)x_{CB}. \qquad (5.24)$$

The central bank's period-1 utility is

$$U_1 = -\left(\frac{\alpha_2 \sigma_y^{-2}}{\sigma_y^{-2} + \sigma^{-2}} \eta_{CB} + \left(1 - \alpha_1 - \frac{\alpha_2 \sigma^{-2}}{\sigma_y^{-2} + \sigma^{-2}}\right) \eta_y \right)^2. \qquad (5.25)$$

This utility realization is informative. Therefore, the central bank transforms it into $-U_1^{1/2}(\sigma_y^{-2} + \sigma^{-2})/(\alpha_2 \sigma_y^{-2})$, which is an unbiased signal about η_{CB}. But that signal has noise that comes from the presence of the random variable η_y. Because this signal depends on both η_{CB} and η_y, the central bank cannot invert it to back out its expectation error $\eta_{CB} = x_{CB} - s$. This shows why with opacity, the central bank loses its ability to know the true state s. The verification of the conjectured solution in (5.23) and the derivation of α_1 and α_2 are left as an exercise.

The interpretation of this result is that when a central bank publicly releases its information, that eliminates the need for price-setters to second-guess what the bank knows. As a result, price-setters base prices only on their information about fundamentals, not on their information about central bank beliefs. This makes prices more informative to the central bank, which can use that information to set better policy. In essence, releasing public information turns Fed-watchers into inflation-watchers.

5.2.3 Private Information Makes Public Disclosures More Informative

Duffie, Giroux, and Manso (2010b) show that private and public information can be complementary in another way as well. In their setting, a continuum of agents are endowed with signals about a random variable X, where the signal noise is independent across agents. Let the precision of these initial signals be σ_s^{-2}. Agents are chosen at random to publicly disclose their posterior beliefs.

When such public announcements are the only source of new information, agents learn slowly. The only new information revealed by each announcement is what private signal the announcer was endowed with. Any other information contained in the announcer's posterior belief must have come from some previous public announcement, which is not new information to the other agents. When signals are normally distributed, each announcement increases the precision of agents' beliefs by σ_s^{-2}.

Now suppose that instead of public announcements, there are private meetings. Each agent meets another randomly chosen agent at a Poisson rate λ. At each meeting, the agents reveal their posterior beliefs to each other. Duffie, Giroux, and Manso (2010b) show that the distribution of posterior beliefs converges to X at the rate λ.

When there are both private meetings and public announcements, then the information content of the public announcements is enhanced. When an agent has exchanged information with other agents first and then is chosen to announce his posterior beliefs, he reveals both what he knew initially and what he learned from others. Since what he has learned from meetings with others was not publicly announced, it is also new information to almost all other agents. Thus, the precision of the new information in the public signal is greater than σ_s^{-2}. This is another sense in which private information exchange and public announcements can be complementary.

The set of tools used in this chapter and those developed by Duffie, Giroux, and Manso (2010a) and Duffie, Malamud, and Manso (2009) are useful for studying many problems where information diffuses gradually through a population of agents who meet randomly. This environment is similar to that discussed by Amador and Weill (2011). The main difference is that the agents in Duffie, Malamud, and Manso's work (2009) reveal their posterior beliefs to each other and can always extract all the new information that the other knows. The Amador and Weill (2011) agents observe each other's actions, which gives them a noisy signal about what new information the other agent knows. The signal-to-noise ratio of another agent's action depends on how much public information that agent knows. So, public information can make actions less informative in Amador and Weill's work (2011), while that type of effect is not possible in Duffie, Malamud, and Manso's work (2009).

5.3 MORE INFORMATION INCREASES PRICE VOLATILITY

The simplest form of this argument is that if asset values are stationary, more precise information makes expected asset values more volatile. To see why this is true, consider an agent who has an information set $\mathcal{I}$ and forms an expectation about an asset value v:

$$v = E[v|\mathcal{I}] \pm e. \tag{5.26}$$

If the agent's beliefs are unbiased, then $E[e] = 0$ and there is zero correlation between e and $E[v|\mathcal{I}]$. Taking the variance of both sides of this equation tells us that $Var(v) = Var(E[v|\mathcal{I}]) + Var(e)$. Getting more precise information means that the variance of the expectation error $Var(e)$ is smaller. Since the unconditional variance of asset payoffs is exogenous, for the equality to hold, it must be that more precise information raises $Var(E[v|\mathcal{I}])$.

Thus, if asset prices are determined by a representative investor's expected value of an asset, then giving that investor more precise information (be it public or private) will increase the variance of the asset price. This effect is amplified if investors have heterogeneous information and want their valuation of the asset to correspond closely to the valuations of other investors. Then, in addition to this simple effect of information on belief volatility, there is also the Morris-Shin effect, described in section 5.1.1: more information will also facilitate coordination. Using the same argument as above, we can show that more precise information about the average valuation makes beliefs about the average valuation more volatile as well. If each individual wants his or her value to align with the average value, this effect will amplify the volatility in estimates of the asset's value and therefore in the asset's price.

5.4 PUBLIC INFORMATION MAKES MONEY NEUTRAL

One of the earliest arguments made against central bank transparency was that it would render monetary policy impotent (Cukierman and Meltzer 1986). In many settings with common knowledge, the money supply only affects the units that prices are denominated in. When prices adjust to absorb money supply shocks, real economic quantities remain unchanged (Lucas 1972). In order for monetary policy to have some role in stabilizing the economy, there must be some friction that breaks this neutrality result. A large literature in monetary economics assumes that the friction is an information asymmetry: price-setters do not know what money supply the central bank chooses. This information asymmetry is what allows a central bank's actions to dampen fluctuations in economic activity. Since risk-averse agents prefer less economic volatility and information asymmetry is what allows the bank to lower volatility, eliminating that asymmetry by disclosing public information can be socially costly.

Following this insight, researchers such as Faust and Svensson (2002) noted that transparency is not an all-or-nothing choice. More nuanced questions arose about whether the central bank should hide its money supply choices or make those common knowledge, or instead hide its inflation target. That discussion takes us away from the theme of information choice toward a detailed discussion of monetary policy. (see Geraats 2002 and Carpenter 2004 for surveys of this literature). The following chapter will explore the workings of asymmetric information models that make money non-neutral.

5.5 BROADER THEMES AND PATHS FOR FUTURE RESEARCH

These theories provide much insight about important differences between public and private information. But they ultimately do not resolve the following question: Is full disclosure the best policy for a government or central bank? They provide a number of competing arguments pro and con. What is lacking is a way of evaluating these competing claims. This theoretical literature raises interesting questions for more applied work. For example, what are the testable implications of these theories? How can we measure private and public information? Do we count newspaper articles, lines of text from Federal Open Market Committee (FOMC) meetings, look at bond risk premia, options prices, or bid-ask spreads? How is monetary policy information being spread? Through centralized channels, as shown by Morris and Shin (2002), or through decentralized observations of others' behavior, as demonstrated by Amador and Weill (2011)? Or perhaps the mechanism of transmission does not matter if we can show that information releases make prices better predictors of future outcomes. There is an obvious opening for future research here. Someone who has knowledge of the applied models and can devise creative ways to quantify them could try to weigh these competing effects.

But the information disclosure policy of central banks is not the only application of the tools in this chapter. One application shows how public information could be harmful because it facilitates speculative currency attacks. A second considers the opposite situation, where coordinated actions are good. It shows how a leader that can induce followers to coordinate by getting them to overweight public information can maximize the value of a firm.

5.5.1 Speculative Currency Attacks

Goldstein, Ozdenoren, and Yuan (2011) have developed a model in which the central bank would like to commit not to observe public information. As discussed in section 5.1, public information is harmful because it encourages coordination, which is socially costly. But instead of public information being a signal that the bank discloses, here it is the average action of speculators (i.e., the size of the speculative attack) that is publicly observable and that the bank would like to ignore.

The model is a modified version of the Morris and Shin (1998) currency speculation model described in section 4.2. In that model, the central bank abandoned a currency peg if a sufficiently large fraction of speculative currency traders attacks the currency. The fraction depended on the state of the economy, which was known to the bank but not to the speculators. In this model, the central bank does not know the state of the economy and does not know what speculators know about the state of the economy. Therefore, it learns from speculators' actions.

This is a one-shot game. First, both the central bank and the speculators receive exogenous, heterogeneous information regarding the random state of the fundamental: the central bank receives a private signal only, while each speculator gets a private and a common signal about the fundamental. Second, the speculators decide whether to attack the currency or not. The central bank observes the attack and then decides whether to maintain the existing exchange rate system or to abandon it.

A coordination motive is built into the original Morris and Shin problem because speculation is only profitable if a sufficiently large attack induces the government to abandon the currency peg. A new additional coordination motive comes from the fact that the central bank learns from speculators' actions. Upon observing a large currency attack, the bank infers that the speculators must have observed signals indicating weak economic fundamentals. This makes the bank more prone to abandon the currency peg, which makes attacking the currency more profitable. Thus, learning by the central bank creates a situation where large speculative attacks change the beliefs of the bank in such a way as to make attacking more profitable. The authors call this informational complementarity. If the bank could commit to ignore the information contained in the size of the speculative attack, it could eliminate this additional complementarity. Of course, this would not be a credible commitment. After the speculators have chosen their actions, the bank would then choose to use all the information available to it. Thus, this is another mechanism that can make the availability of public information socially costly.

5.5.2 A Coordination-Based Theory of Leadership

Reversing the sign of the Morris-Shin externality (2002) can make private information, rather than public information, socially costly. According to Bolton, Brunnermeier, and Veldkamp (2008), agents fail to fully internalize the social benefits of coordination. As a result, there is a role for a leader who induces agents to over-weight public information, relative to private information, to achieve better coordination.

A continuum of agents, indexed by i, has utility

$$\Pi_i = -(a_i - a_L)^2 - \int_0^1 (a_j - \bar{a})^2 dj - (a_L - \theta)^2 \quad \text{for } i, j \in [0, 1] \cup \{L\}. \quad (5.27)$$

The first term is decreasing in the distance between the agent's action a_i and the action of a leader a_L. The second term is the externality: agent i suffers when all agents take actions that are further away from the average action $\bar{a}$. Since each agent has zero mass, their own action has zero marginal effect on this term. Thus, agents benefit when all take similar actions, but none has any direct incentive to do so. The third term says that the agent prefers when the leader takes an action that is close to an unknown optimal action θ.

Each follower's optimal action minimizes the first term in the utility function. They ignore the second term because, having zero mass, their actions do not affect it. They ignore the third term because only the leader's action affects it. To minimize the first term, they set $a_i = E_i[a_L]$. In contrast, the leader's action minimizes the third term. The leader ignores the first term because it is always zero ($i = L$). Likewise, the second term is also invariant to the choice of a_L. To minimize the third term, the leader chooses $a_L = E_L[\theta]$.

The leader and each agent get a private signal about θ, upon which they form their prior beliefs. The leader then makes his signal s_1 public. (This is always optimal because it facilitates coordination.) This disclosure is interpreted as announcing a direction for the organization. The agents combine the leader's signal with their own, using Bayes' law, and choose their actions a_i. Finally, the leader gets an additional signal s_2, updates his beliefs, and chooses a_L. The coordination problem arises because of this second signal. It makes a_L unknown to the agents at the time when they choose their own actions a_i. Thus, they use their private information to forecast s_2 and thus a_L. Since agents' private signals differ, $a_i = E_i[a_L]$ differs, which causes actions to be imperfectly coordinated.

In this setting, a good leader is one who can induce agents to place more weight on his publicly announced signal s_1 and less weight on their own private signals. The leader achieves this if he can credibly commit to put less weight on his own private signal s_2 in his action. A "resolute" leader is one who believes that his first signal is more precise than it truly is and, therefore, weights it more heavily than the second signal. Such a leader can achieve a more efficient degree of coordination.

5.6 EXERCISES

1. In the model of section 5.1, prove that $E[\int_0^1 (w_i - s)^2 di] = \tau_w^{-1}$.

2. In the model of section 5.1, if nature draws the state s from a distribution with lower variance and this distribution is common knowledge, is this good or bad for social welfare? Under what conditions?

3. What if we reversed the sign on coordination externality, the last term in equation (5.2). If welfare is still the integral over all agents' individual utilities, what would this model say about the social value of public information? Consider the case where $r > 0$ and the case where $r < 0$.

4. Suppose the individuals' utility is

$$U_i = -(1 - r)(a_i - s)^2 - r(a_i - \bar{a})^2 + (1 - r) \int_0^1 (a_j - s)^2 dj$$

where $r > 0$.

(a) Is the amount of coordination less than, more than, or equal to the socially efficient level?

(b) If welfare is still the integral over all agents' individual utilities, can public information be welfare reducing?

(c) Can private information be welfare reducing?

5. In the model with complementarity between private and public information (section 5.2.2), prove that the conjectured solution (equation [5.23]) is a valid solution. Solve for α_1 and α_2 as a function of the model's variance parameters.

Chapter Six

Informational Inertia and Price-Setting

Much of the work on imperfect information and information choice in macroeconomics has been done in the context of price-setting models. One of the most fundamental questions macroeconomics faces is why monetary policy appears to have real effects on the economy. In frictionless models, prices are typically proportional to the money supply, so that money simply determines the units of account but not real output. The question put differently is: Why is the covariance of prices with the money supply so much lower than what standard models predict? Since information choice governs the covariance between choice variables (prices) and states (the money supply), it is a tool well-suited to address this problem.

The chapter proceeds by describing a sequence of models. Each builds on the ideas of the one before. A central question in monetary economics is how the supply of money affects real output. Lucas (1972) sets the stage for this literature by arguing that the key is imperfect information about aggregate variables such as the price level and the money supply. A problem with the Lucas model is that it does not explain why output has a *delayed* reaction to changes in the money supply. Woodford (2002) argues that a combination of heterogeneous information and coordination motives in price-setting can create inertia in prices. Since money supply and price levels are published frequently, imperfect, heterogeneous information presumably arises because accessing or processing this public information is costly. Reis (2006) investigates the predictions of a model with fixed costs of updating beliefs. But firms that do not update their beliefs frequently should not react promptly to any shocks. Yet, they appear to react aggressively to firm-specific shocks, just not to monetary shocks. According to Maćkowiak and Wiederholt (2009b), firms optimally choose to learn more about firm-specific than monetary shocks because the firm-specific shocks generate more volatility in their optimal price. Finally, Woodford (2008) incorporates both the fixed-cost friction of Reis (2006) and the rational inattention friction of Maćkowiak and Wiederholt (2009b) into one framework in order to assess their relative importance.

While the specific messages about price-setting and monetary policy are mostly of interest to people who work in this area, the models in this chapter could describe many dynamic problems where actions and information choices depend on what others choose. As such, the chapter explores two broad questions that extend beyond the application to monetary economics. *Question #1: Why do some shocks seem to matter while others do not?* Prices of goods, or equity, production, and investment decisions, all respond differently, depending on the type of shock. Rational inattention offers one potential explanation for why that might be.

Question #2: Why do actions exhibit inertia? Investors are slow to rebalance their portfolios. Consumers are slow to adjust their consumption in response to income shocks. Some industries lag the business cycle more than others. One explanation could be that the incentives to process aggregate information may differ according to the type of information or according to the agent and the nature of the shocks they face.

6.1 LUCAS-PHELPS MODEL

The original Lucas (1972) model is richer than the one presented here. It has over-lapping generations, a more general utility function, two islands, and uncertainty about both the supply of money that old agents have and the number of young agents working on each island. This original model is difficult to work with. The simplified model presented below misses some of the micro-foundations but will give a clear picture of the kind of informational problem agents face.

There is a continuum of goods in the economy, each produced by a single repre-sentative producer i. Each producer can transform labor L_i, one-for-one, into good i output Y_i:

$$Y_i = L_i. \tag{6.1}$$

Utility is defined over the consumption of a composite good C and labor:

$$U_i = C_i - \frac{1}{\gamma} L_i^\gamma, \tag{6.2}$$

where $\gamma > 1$. The composite good C_i is constructed so as to deliver an aggregate demand for good i that depends on aggregate income Y, good i's price P_i, relative to the price of the consumption aggregate, and z_i, a random, mean-zero shock to the preference for good i:

$$Y_i^d = Y \left(\frac{P_i}{P} \right)^{-\eta} \exp(z_i). \tag{6.3}$$

Aggregate income is defined such that $\ln(Y) \equiv \int_i \ln(Y_i) di$. Aggregate demand for goods depends on the real money supply M and the aggregate price level P:

$$Y = M/P, \tag{6.4}$$

where the price level is defined such that $\ln(P) = \int_i \ln(P_i) di$.[1] Finally, an individ-ual's budget constraint is

$$P C_i = P_i Y_i. \tag{6.5}$$

Equilibrium. An equilibrium is a set of utility-maximizing labor L_i and consump-tion C_i choices that respect the budget constraint and prices that equate demand and supply. Substituting the budget constraint (6.5) and the production function (6.1)

---

[1] Specifying demand directly like this is obviously a shortcut. See Lorenzoni 2009 for a micro-founded model that delivers this form of aggregate demand.

into the individual's utility (6.2) delivers $E[U_i] = E[P_i L_i / P] - (1/\gamma)L_i^\gamma$. The first-order condition in L_i reveals that the optimal choice of labor is

$$L_i = E\left[\frac{P_i}{P}\right]^{1/(\gamma-1)}. \tag{6.6}$$

Equilibrium prices with full information. With full information, we can drop the expectation operator in (6.6). To simplify the analysis, transform the problem into logarithms. Let lowercase variables denote logs. For example $l_i \equiv \ln(L_i)$.

The log of supply (6.6) is $1/(\gamma - 1)(p_i - p)$. The log of demand (6.3) is $y - \eta$ $(p_i - p) + z_i$. Equating these two expressions and rearranging delivers the equilibrium price:

$$p_i = p + \frac{\gamma - 1}{1 + \eta(\gamma - 1)}(y + z_i). \tag{6.7}$$

Since the log aggregate price is defined to be an average of the log individual prices,

$$p = \int p_i \, di = p + \frac{\gamma - 1}{1 + \eta(\gamma - 1)}(y + 0). \tag{6.8}$$

Subtracting p on both sides leaves log output $y = 0$, meaning that aggregate output Y is always $e^0 = 1$. Using the aggregate demand equation (6.4), it also tells us that $M = P$. In short, money is neutral. A large supply of money only affects prices, not output.

Equilibrium prices with incomplete information. The key assumption that causes money to have real effects is that agents do not know the aggregate price level. When choosing how much to produce or work, individuals can see the price of their good p_i, but the aggregate price level p, the money supply m, and the good-specific demand shock z_i are all unobserved. They believe these shocks to be normally distributed: $m \sim N(E[m], V_m)$ and $z_i \sim N(0, V_z)$. If p is a linear function of m and z_i, then p will have an unconditional (not conditional on observing p_i) normal distribution: $p \sim N(E[p], V_p)$ for some values $E[p]$ and V_p. After production takes place, the aggregate price level and money supply are revealed so that consumers' demand can depend on p and m.

Along with the limited-information assumption, many versions of this model make a simplifying assumption: certainty equivalence. When choosing their optimal labor supply, agents form an expectation $E_i[p_i - p] \equiv E[p_i - p|p_i]$ and then treat that expectation as if it were the truth. Since the log optimal labor supply (log of equation [6.6]) with full information is $1/(\gamma - 1)(p_i - p)$, the certainty equivalent of optimal labor is

$$l_i = \frac{1}{\gamma - 1}E_i[p_i - p]. \tag{6.9}$$

The interpretation is that agents work harder when they believe that the relative price of their good $(p_i - p)$ is high. Money has real effects because when money is abundant, most agents observe a high price for their good. But each agent cannot tell whether their price is high because their good's relative price is high or because the aggregate price level is high. So, they place some probability on each cause. If their expected relative price rises, they work harder, which increases output.

The equilibrium price is determined by equating supply (6.9) with demand. Demand is the same as in the full-information model (the log of equation [6.3]). Using (6.4) to substitute out y,

$$\frac{1}{\gamma - 1}(p_i - E_i[p]) = m - p - \eta(p_i - p) + z_i. \tag{6.10}$$

Note that this is a linear relationship between p and p_i, with normally distributed noise $m + z_i$. Since Bayes' law for normal variables is also a linear relationship, $E_i[p]$ will be linear as well. Thus, p_i must be equal to a linear function of p, plus noise. In other words, there are some coefficients a and b such that $p_i = a + bp + \epsilon_i$ where $\epsilon_i \sim N(0, V_e)$. Since we know that p is always the average log price, $p = \int p_i di = a + bp + 0$. This can only hold for every aggregate price if $a = 0$ and $b = 1$. Thus,

$$p_i = p + \epsilon_i \quad \epsilon_i \sim N(0, V_e).$$

This is useful because it tells us that the price of an individual good is an unbiased signal about the aggregate price level.

Next, use Bayes' law to combine this information in the individual good price with the aggregate price to get a conditional expectation $E_i[p]$. As explained in chapter 2, the conditional expectation (the posterior belief) is a weighted sum of the prior and signal, where the weights are the relative precisions of each. Thus,

$$E_i[p] = \frac{V_e}{V_p + V_e}E[p] + \frac{V_p}{V_p + V_e}p_i. \tag{6.11}$$

The next step is to substitute for $E_i[p]$ in the labor supply equation (6.9). Define $\alpha \equiv V_e/(V_p + V_e) \cdot 1/(\gamma - 1)$ and collect terms to get

$$l_i = \alpha\,(p_i - E[p]). \tag{6.12}$$

Averaging over i delivers aggregate production ($\int_i l_i di = y$) and using the aggregate demand relationship $y = m - p$ yields

$$m - p = \alpha\,(p - E[p]). \tag{6.13}$$

Taking the unconditional expectation of both sides of (6.13) tells us that $E[m] - E[p] = 0$. Thus, $E[p] = E[m]$. The unconditional expected price level is the expected money supply. This parallels the result in the full-information model. When m and p were known, we had $m = p$.

Substituting in $E[m]$ for $E[p]$ in (6.13) and rearranging, we can express the aggregate price level as a function of the expected and actual money supply:

$$p = \frac{\alpha}{1 + \alpha}E[m] + \frac{1}{1 + \alpha}m. \tag{6.14}$$

This captures the idea that inflation can be driven by changes in monetary policy m or changes in expectations $E[m]$.

Output depends on the difference between actual and expected money supply. Using the aggregate demand relationship $y = m - p$ again reveals that

$$y = \frac{\alpha}{1 + \alpha}(m - E[m]). \qquad (6.15)$$

The term $m - E[m]$ captures money surprises: the difference between realized and expected money supplies. The main result of the Lucas-Phelps model is that money supply surprises cause output to rise. This is important because it creates a role for monetary policy to have real effects on economic activity.

6.2 A RECIPE FOR INERTIA

The Lucas island model's results are important because they describe how monetary policy can be used to manage the real economy. They embody an expectations-augmented Phillips' curve—the idea that when inflation (or money growth) is higher than expected, the economy's output will be above trend. The problem with Lucas's explanation is that once producers produce and turn into consumers, they observe all posted prices. If the aggregate price level from period t is known in period $t + 1$, then the real effects of monetary policy should be only one-period-lived. Yet, in the data, monetary policy has its greatest effect on output six quarters after the monetary shock, and after ten quarters, this effect is still one-third the size of the peak effect (Woodford 2002).

Of course, one could argue about the length of periods in the Lucas model. But with all the information released daily through financial market prices and published quarterly by government bureaus, it is difficult to defend the idea that aggregate price information is not available more than two years after the fact.

Woodford (2002) argues that public information about the aggregate price level is readily available. The friction is that firms cannot process all the information they observe. They can observe it freely, but figuring out what it means and how to use it to set their good's price requires some mental energy, called capacity, which is in limited supply. This limited ability to process information is modeled as an exogenous noisy signal that each firm gets about the state of the economy, whose signal noise is independent of other firms' signals. That noisy signal informs firms about the current and past periods' states so that beliefs converge slowly to the truth.

Woodford makes a second important change to the Lucas model: he introduces a complementarity into the payoff structure. It gives firms an incentive to coordinate price-setting. In order to coordinate effectively, they want to forecast other firms' beliefs. Learning about what others know is a much slower process than learning the value of an exogenous state variable. This is because higher-order beliefs are much more uncertain than first-order beliefs (see section 4.1). This slow updating helps monetary policy shocks have long-lived effects. We investigate a simplified version of that model where log GDP is a random walk.

There is a continuum of firms, indexed by i. Each firm optimally chooses its price p_{it} to maximize its expected profit. Woodford (2002) shows that a standard profit maximization objective can be approximated by the following second-order utility function:

$$U = E_{it}\left[\bar{u} - r(p_{it} - p_t)^2 - (1 - r)(p_{it} - q_t)^2\right], \tag{6.16}$$

where $p_t \equiv \int p_{it} di$ and q_t are the (log) time-t aggregate price level and nominal GDP and E_{it} denotes firm i's expectations, based on its time-t information set. The parameter r measures the degree of complementarity in price-setting. The higher r is, the more aggregate prices matter relative to fundamental shocks and the stronger the complementarity in price-setting is.

The log of nominal GDP is a random walk with a known drift g and an unknown innovation u_t:

$$q_t = g + q_{t-1} + u_t \quad u_t \sim N(0, \sigma_u^2). \tag{6.17}$$

Finally, the information each firm receives each period is a noisy signal of current nominal GDP:

$$z_{it} = q_t + v_{it}, \tag{6.18}$$

where v_{it} is i.i.d.$N(0, \sigma_v^2)$ across individuals and over time. More capacity to process information corresponds to a lower σ_v.

Characterizing the model's solution. The first-order condition for an optimum reveals that $p_{it} = r E_{it}[p_t] + (1 - r)E_{it}[q_t]$. If we average over all firms, we get the aggregate price level as a function of the average beliefs $\bar{E}_t[p_t]$ and $\bar{E}_t[q_t]$,

$$p_t = r\bar{E}_t[p_t] + (1 - r)\bar{E}_t[q_t]. \tag{6.19}$$

This model describes a form of a coordination game with heterogeneous expectations. Just as in section 4.1, the aggregate action (p_t in this case) can be described as an infinite sum of higher-order expectations. To see this, recursively substitute for p_t on the right side of the equality to get $p_t = \sum_{k=1}^{\infty}(1 - r)r^{(k-1)}q_t^{(k)}$, where the superscript (k) represents the kth-order average expectation. For example, $q_t^{(1)} = \bar{E}_t[q_t]$ is the average belief about q_t, while $q_t^{(2)} = \bar{E}_t[q_t^{(1)}]$ is the average belief about the average belief of q_t, and so forth. Working with this infinite sum is intractable. Morris and Shin (2002) avoid this problem by conjecturing and then verifying a symmetric strategy for firms. Woodford (2002) instead conjectures that q_t and p_t are sufficient state variables and that they have a linear law of motion.

Define $x_t \equiv [q_t \ p_t]'$ to be the 2×1 vector of state variables. Then the conjectured law of motion is

$$x_{t+1} = c + Mx_t + mu_{t+1}, \tag{6.20}$$

where the unknown coefficients are c (2×1), M (2×2), and m (2×1) and where u_{t+1} is the innovation to GDP in (6.17).

Note that (6.18) and (6.20) comprise the observation and state equations of a Kalman filter. Using equation (2.8), we can express agent i's expected value of state x at time t as

$$E_{it}[x_t] = c + M E_{i(t-1)}[x_{t-1}] + k_t(z_{it} - E_{it}[q_t]), \tag{6.21}$$

where k_t is the Kalman gain. Integrating this expectation over agents and using the fact that the signals z_{it} have mean q_t gives the average expectation

$$\bar{E}_t[x_t] = c + M\bar{E}_{t-1}[x_{t-1}] + k_t(q_t - \bar{E}_t[q_t]).$$ (6.22)

Note that the Kalman gain is identical across agents because we have assumed that all have the same prior and signal variances.

The next step is to solve for the unknown coefficients in the vector c and the matrix M. $c(1) = g$, $M(1, 1) = 1$, and $M(1, 2) = 0$. Recall that x_t has two rows, one for GDP and one for aggregate price. Therefore, equation (6.22) has two rows, which we can write out separately. The assumption that GDP is a random walk (6.17) tells us what the coefficients in the first row of (6.22) are: The first row becomes $\bar{E}_t[q_t] = g + \bar{E}_{t-1}[q_{t-1}] + k_t(1)(q_t - \bar{E}_t[q_t])$. The second row is $\bar{E}_t[p_t] = c(2) + M(2, 1)\bar{E}_{t-1}[q_{t-1}] + M(2, 2)\bar{E}_{t-1}[p_{t-1}] + k_t(2)(q_t - \bar{E}_t[q_t])$. To determine the unknown coefficients, substitute these two expressions in for $\bar{E}_t[q_t]$ and $\bar{E}_t[p_t]$ in (6.19) to get

$$p_t = r\left[c_2 + M(2, 1)\bar{E}_{t-1}[q_{t-1}] + M(2, 2)\bar{E}_{t-1}[p_{t-1}]\right] + (1 - r)$$
$$\times \left[g + \bar{E}_{t-1}[q_{t-1}]\right] + ((1 - r)k_t(1) + rk_t(2))\left[q_t - \bar{E}_t[q_t]\right].$$ (6.23)

The constant terms on the right side must be equal to c_2. The coefficients on q_t are $M(2, 1) = (1 - r)k_t(1) + rk_t(2)$. Finally, the remaining terms must equal $M(2, 2)p_{t-1}$. Substituting for $M(2, 1)$ in $M(2, 2)$ and rearranging yields $M(2, 2) = 1 - (1-r)k_t(1) - rk_t(2)$. The fact that there exist coefficients that solve this system of equations verifies the conjectures.

The final step is to solve for the Kalman gain k_t. To do this, use the Kalman filter formulas (2.9) and (2.10), substituting in the above solution for M. This produces a set of two equations in two unknowns, k_t and the posterior variance Σ_t. The solution takes the form $M(2, 1) = 1/2[-\gamma + (\gamma^2 + 4\gamma)^{1/2}]$, where $\gamma \equiv (1 - r)\sigma_u^2/\sigma_v^2$. Recall that $M(2, 1)$ is the sensitivity of the average price to GDP. A key result is that this sensitivity is decreasing in the degree of pricing complementarity r. That means that more complementarity in prices reduces the sensitivity of prices to innovations in GDP ($M(2, 1)$ falls) and increases the extent to which prices depend on the previous period's prices ($M(2, 2)$ rises). In other words, the recipe for inertia is a mix of complementarity in actions and heterogeneous information.

6.3 INATTENTIVENESS IN PRICE-SETTING

"Inattentiveness" is a term used to describe models where firms can occasionally observe the entire history of events. It is as if the price-setter knows nothing about demand or monetary innovations until he, one day, receives a newspaper and fully updates his knowledge of the past and present states of the world. According to Mankiw and Reis (2002), information arrives randomly. Arrival times are a Poisson process. Gabaix and Laibson (2002) and Reis (2006) introduce information choice. Information updates are costly and firms choose when to incur that cost.

Dynamic models with information choice are notoriously hard to solve. Inattentiveness simplifies these problems by making past learning choices irrelevant each time a firm decides to learn. Using a learning technology where acquiring information means learning all past shock realizations perfectly is a way of truncating the state space. Inattentiveness also offers a succinct way of describing agents' information. Each information set is summarized by the last date at which the agent acquired information.

The following model, a version of Reis's 2006 work, builds on the quadratic-loss model from the previous chapter.[2] As before, coordination motives in actions (here, price-setting) imply coordination motives in information acquisition. This generates additional inertia, beyond that shown by Woodford (2002). The additional effect is that as firms move away from perfect information, the value of any single firm becoming informed diminishes. As firms acquire information less frequently, prices become more sticky.

The model. Time is discrete and infinite. There is a measure-1 continuum of firms, indexed by i. Each firm's objective is to minimize their loss function:

$$E\left\{\sum_{t=0}^{\infty}\beta^t\left[\left(p_t^i - p_t^*\right)^2 + D_t^i C\right]\right\}, \tag{6.24}$$

where p_t^i denotes firm i's (log-)price in period t; $D_t^i \in \{0, 1\}$ is its decision to acquire information (update); p_t^* is an unknown, stochastic target price that a firm with full information would set; $\beta \in (0, 1)$ is the firm's discount rate; and $C > 0$ is the cost of information acquisition.

As in new-Keynesian models of monopolistic competition, the target price is

$$p_t^* = (1 - r)m_t + rp_t, \tag{6.25}$$

where m_t is the log of nominal demand in period t; $m_t - p_t$ is the log of real demand; $p_t = \int_0^1 p_t^i di$ is the average log price; and $r > 0$ measures strategic complementarity or real rigidity in price-setting. For simplicity, we assume that demand follows a random walk, with innovations $\varepsilon_t \sim i.i.d.N(0, \sigma^2)$:

$$m_t = m_{t-1} + \varepsilon_t. \tag{6.26}$$

Information choices. If firm i last updated in period $\hat{\tau}$, it enters period t with an information set that contains the demand realizations from every period up to and including $\hat{\tau}$: $I_{\hat{\tau}} = \{m_\tau\}_{\tau=0}^{\hat{\tau}}$. If this firm updates in the current period ($D_t^i = 1$), its information set contains all demand realizations up to the current date: $I_t = \{m_\tau\}_{\tau=0}^{t}$. If the firm does not update at date t ($D_t^i = 0$), its information set is $I_{\hat{\tau}}$; it does not observe any new information about the state, including endogenous variables like the aggregate price level. The idea is that firms can always see prices, but using them to infer demand or to recompute their own optimal price incurs a cost.

---

[2] The quadratic objective function comes from a second-order approximation to a micro-founded model. Ball and Romer (1990) derive this price-setting model from first principles. A technical appendix to Hellwig and Veldkamp 2009 shows that their foundations produce the same objective in a setting with costly information.

The following notation describes aggregate information choices. At date t, let $\lambda_{t,\hat{\tau}}$ denote the measure of firms who last updated in period $\hat{\tau} \leq t$, and $\Lambda_{t,\hat{\tau}} \equiv \sum_{\tau=\hat{\tau}}^{t} \lambda_{t,\tau}$ be the measure of firms who have last updated between dates $\hat{\tau}$ and t. Let $D_{t,\hat{\tau}} \in [0, 1]$ denote updating choices: the probability that a firm who last updated in period $\hat{\tau}$ will update in period t. $\{\lambda_{t,\hat{\tau}}\}$ is defined recursively as $\lambda_{t,\hat{\tau}} = (1 - D_{t,\hat{\tau}})\lambda_{t-1,\hat{\tau}}$ for $\hat{\tau} < t$; the measure of firms who have up-to-date information is $\lambda_{t,t} = \sum_{\tau=0}^{t-1} D_{t,\tau}\lambda_{t-1,\tau}$.

Equilibrium. An equilibrium is a sequence of information choices by every firm i, $\{D_t^i\}$, and prices, $\{p_{i,t}\}$, that are measurable with respect to i's information set and maximize (6.24), taking as given the choices of all other firms.

Prices and indirect utility. The first-order condition of (6.24) with respect to price dictates that firm i that last updated at date $\hat{\tau}$ sets a price equal to its expected target price at time t: $p_t^i = E\left(p_t^*|I_{\hat{\tau}}\right) = (1 - r)E\left(m_t|I_{\hat{\tau}}\right) + rE\left(p_t|I_{\hat{\tau}}\right)$. Since demand is a random walk, $E\left(m_t|I_{\hat{\tau}}\right) = m_{\hat{\tau}}$. We can then guess and verify that price is also a random walk, $E\left(p_t|I_{\hat{\tau}}\right) = p_{\hat{\tau}}$. If so, the average of all firms' prices is a weighted sum of the expected target price of firms who have last updated their information in period $\hat{\tau}$, $p_t = \sum_{\tau=0}^{t} \lambda_{t,\tau} E\left(p_t^*|I_{\tau}\right) = \sum_{\tau=0}^{t} \lambda_{t,\tau}\left((1 - r)m_{\tau} + rp_{\tau}\right)$. Recursively substituting in for p_{τ} reveals that the average price is a weighted sum of all past demand innovations:

$$p_t = \sum_{\tau=0}^{t} \frac{\Lambda_{t,\tau}(1 - r)}{1 - r\Lambda_{t,\tau}} \varepsilon_{\tau}. \tag{6.27}$$

The proof of this result is left as an exercise.

Substituting this result into (6.25) tells us that the target price process is $p_t^* = \sum_{\tau=0}^{t} \frac{1-r}{1-r\Lambda_{t,\tau}}\varepsilon_{\tau}$. Firms who last updated at date $\hat{\tau}$ set a price $E\left(p_t^*|I_{\hat{\tau}}\right) = \sum_{\tau=0}^{\hat{\tau}} \frac{1-r}{1-r\Lambda_{t,\tau}}\varepsilon_{\tau}$. Their expected one-period loss depends on all the demand innovations since the last update:

$$L_{t,\hat{\tau}} = E\left[E\left(p_t^*|I_{\hat{\tau}}\right) - p_t^*|I_{\hat{\tau}}\right]^2 = \sum_{\tau=\hat{\tau}+1}^{t} \left(\frac{1-r}{1-r\Lambda_{t,\tau}}\right)^2 \sigma^2. \tag{6.28}$$

The longer it has been since a firm has updated its information, the higher its incentives to update in the current period. Consequently, an equilibrium is characterized by threshold dates such that firms who last updated at date $\hat{\tau} < \tau_t^*$ update at date t, while those who last updated at $\hat{\tau} > \tau_t^*$ find not updating strictly optimal.

Complementarity in information choice. When prices are complements ($r > 0$), there is complementarity in information acquisition (updating). When prices are strategic substitutes ($r < 0$), the converse is true. This general principle in static models (section 4.4) reappears in dynamic price-setting. Information complementarity is important because it generates delays in price adjustment, which price-setting models are designed to explain.

To see where updating complementarity arises, consider firms' per-period loss from not updating (6.28). For any $\tau = \hat{\tau} + 1, ..., t$, $\partial L_{t,\hat{\tau}}/\partial \Lambda_{t,t-\tau} > 0$, if and only if $r > 0$. The more firms are aware of a shock that has occurred since the firm last updated, the higher the per-period loss of not being aware of this shock, if prices are complementary. This is the complementarity in updating decisions: the more recently other firms have updated, the higher the cost to a firm of not updating in the current period.

The complementarity in updating delays price adjustment. To illustrate this, we next consider one equilibrium of this updating game. This particular equilibrium has been the focus of previous work (Reis 2006). In this equilibrium, updating decisions are *staggered*, meaning that all firms update after a fixed number of periods T, and each period a fraction $1/T$ of the firms updates. This means that if $\tau < t - T$, then $\lambda_{t,\tau} = 0$ and $\Lambda_{t,\tau} = 1$, but if $t - T < \tau \leq t$, then $\lambda_{t,\tau} = 1/T$ and $\Lambda_{t,\tau} = (t - \tau + 1)/T$. Therefore, a firm who last updated at date $\hat{\tau}$ has 1-period loss at date t:

$$
L_{t,\hat{\tau}} = \begin{cases} \sigma^2 \sum_{v=1}^{t-\hat{\tau}} \left(\frac{1-r}{1-rv/T} \right)^2 & \text{if } \hat{\tau} > t - T \\ L_{t,\hat{\tau}+1} + \sigma^2 & \text{if } \hat{\tau} \leq t - T. \end{cases} \tag{6.29}
$$

Complementarity ($r > 0$) generates delays in price adjustment through two channels. First, because many other firms have prices based on old information, firms that do update temper their reactions to recent information. This is the effect Woodford (2002) identified and it shows up here in equation (6.27). Second, complementarity reduces the frequency of information acquisition. This effect shows up as $L_{t,\hat{\tau}}$ decreasing in r in equation (6.29). When pricing complementarity causes firms to temper their reactions to new information, the loss incurred from having old information is smaller. As other firms delay updating, this loss falls even more. Firms that update information less frequently have more inertia in their prices.

More generally, complementarity and covariance are mutually reinforcing. With more incomplete information, the covariance of average prices and demand falls. As that covariance falls, demand innovations contain less information about changes in average price. If demand innovations are less useful for coordinating price-setting, the incentive for a firm to update its information about demand diminishes. If firms update less, the covariance of prices and demand falls even further. This feedback is a key feature of the incomplete-information price-setting models that allows them to match the degree of price inertia in the data.

6.4 RATIONAL INATTENTION MODELS OF PRICE-SETTING

The next model, a version of one created by Maćkowiak and Wiederholt (2009b), has similar objectives to the inattentiveness model from the last section. However, it uses a different learning technology. Instead of choosing when to learn and update completely about all past shock realizations, firms continuously observe noisy information flows about two random variables, an aggregate and a firm-specific variable. The learning choice is how much attention to allocate to each shock. First we will explore a partial equilibrium model and then discuss how the authors embed the mechanism in a general equilibrium model.

The model. In each period t, a firm i chooses its price to maximize its expected profit π,

$$\max_{P_{it}} E[\pi(P_{it}, \bar{P}_t, Y_t, Z_{it})|s_i^t]. \tag{6.30}$$

Profit depends on the firm's own price P_{it}, the average of other firms' prices $\bar{P}_t$, an aggregate state (aggregate output) Y_t, and a firm-specific shock (productivity) Z_{it}. The expectation of profits is conditioned on the firm's information set, which is the sequence of all signals they have observed up to time t, s_i^t.

The authors solve for the steady state of the model. Then, they reexpress the objective in terms of log-deviations from that steady state. For example, $x = \ln X_t - \ln X^{steady\ state}$ and the profit function is now $\hat{\pi} = \pi(P^{ss}e^{p_{it}}, P^{ss}e^{\bar{p}_t}, Y^{ss}e^{y_t}, Z^{ss}e^{z_{it}})$. Next, they do a second-order Taylor approximation of the objective around the steady state. They show that the optimal price that comes out of the first-order condition is

$$p_{it} = E\left[\bar{p}_t - \frac{\pi_{PY}}{\pi_{PP}}y_t - \frac{\pi_{PZ}}{\pi_{PP}}z_{it}|s_i^t\right], \tag{6.31}$$

where $\pi_{ij} \equiv \partial^2\pi/\partial i\,\partial j$ and $\pi_{PP} < 0$. Notice that the coefficient on the average price in the price-setting rule is positive. This is a coordination motive in price-setting.

The authors rewrite this optimal price by breaking it into two pieces. The first term, $\Delta_t \equiv \bar{p}_t - \frac{\pi_{PY}}{\pi_{PP}}y_t$, is the profit-maximizing response to aggregate conditions. The second term is the optimal response to idiosyncratic conditions:

$$p_{it} = E\left[\Delta_t - \frac{\pi_{PZ}}{\pi_{PP}}z_{it}|s_i^t\right]. \tag{6.32}$$

Finally, the expected loss from not setting the full-information optimal price p_{it}^* takes a quadratic form (because of the second-order Taylor approximation):

$$EL = \frac{|\pi_{PP}|}{2}E\left[(p_{it} - p_{it}^*)^2\right]. \tag{6.33}$$

Firms minimize this expected loss. The aggregate and firm-specific shocks are assumed to be white noise processes, with mean zero and variances σ_Δ^2 and σ_z^2.

Information choice. Firms get signals each period about the aggregate and the firm-specific shock. The aggregate and firm-specific signals are not correlated with each other, nor are the signal errors correlated across firms:

$$s_{1it} = \Delta_t + \epsilon_{it} \tag{6.34}$$

$$s_{2it} = z_{it} + \psi_{it}, \tag{6.35}$$

where $\epsilon_{it} \sim N(0, \sigma_\epsilon^2)$ and $\psi_{it} \sim N(0, \sigma_\psi^2)$. The assumption that signal noise is independent across agents implies that all signals are *private information*. As in section 4.6, this ensures a unique equilibrium.

What firms are choosing is the precision of the two signals. This choice is bounded by a constraint on the mutual information of signals and the two random shocks. Recall that the entropy (mutual information) constraint limits the determinant of the posterior variance-covariance matrix of the shocks, relative to their prior variance-covariance matrix (section 3.2). Since the z and Δ shocks are independent, their variance-covariance matrix is diagonal and its determinant is the product of the variances. Therefore, the entropy (capacity) constraint can be expressed as

$$\frac{\hat{\sigma}_\Delta^{-2}\hat{\sigma}_z^{-2}}{\sigma_\Delta^{-2}\sigma_z^{-2}} \le e^{2K}. \tag{6.36}$$

There is an additional constraint that the signal variances cannot be negative. This implies that the posterior variances are always weakly lower than the prior variances.

Each choice of signal precision will map one-for-one into a choice of posterior belief precision about the two shocks: $\hat{\sigma}_\Delta^{-2} = \sigma_\Delta^{-2} + \sigma_\epsilon^{-2}$ and $\hat{\sigma}_z^{-2} = \sigma_z^{-2} + \sigma_\psi^{-2}$. Thus, the information choice problem can be expressed as a choice of posterior variances: Choose $\hat{\sigma}_\Delta^2$ and $\hat{\sigma}_z^2$ to minimize (6.33) subject to (6.36), $\hat{\sigma}_\Delta^2 \le \sigma_\Delta^2$, and $\hat{\sigma}_z^2 \le \sigma_z^2$.

Optimal attention allocation. Substituting the optimal price (6.31) into the objective (6.33), and using the fact that $E[(\Delta_t - E[\Delta_t|s_{1it}, s_{2it}])^2] = \hat{\sigma}_\Delta^2$ and $E[(z_{it} - E[z_{it}|s_{1it}, s_{2it}])^2] = \hat{\sigma}_z^2$, yields

$$EL = \frac{|\pi_{PP}|}{2}\left(\hat{\sigma}_\Delta^2 + \left(\frac{\pi_{PZ}}{\pi_{PP}}\right)^2\hat{\sigma}_z^2\right). \tag{6.37}$$

Since the expected loss is increasing in both conditional variances, the capacity constraint will always bind. Use the capacity constraint (6.36) to substitute out $\hat{\sigma}_z^{-2}$. The first-order condition of the resulting single-variable optimization is

$$\frac{|\pi_{PP}|}{2}\left(1 - \left(\frac{\pi_{PZ}}{\pi_{PP}}\right)^2\frac{e^{-2K}\sigma_\Delta^2\sigma_z^2}{\hat{\sigma}_\Delta^4}\right) = 0. \tag{6.38}$$

Under the optimal allocation of attention, the ratio of posterior to prior precision of beliefs about the aggregate shock is

$$\frac{\hat{\sigma}_\Delta^{-2}}{\sigma_\Delta^{-2}} = \left|\frac{\pi_{PP}}{\pi_{PZ}}\right|e^K\frac{\sigma_\Delta}{\sigma_z}. \tag{6.39}$$

This, of course, is only the solution if it is not less than 1 and not greater than e^{2K}. If the ratio were less than 1, the posterior variance would be higher than the prior variance. This means that the firm forgets; it knows less about Δ after observing its signal than it did before. We do not allow firms to choose to forget information in this way. If the ratio were greater than e^{2K}, then the firm would be acquiring more information than its capacity allows. If the ratio is between 1 and e^{2K}, then the corresponding conditional variance of the firm-specific shock is $e^{-2K}\sigma_\Delta^2\sigma_z^2/\hat{\sigma}_\Delta^2$.

Interpreting the solution. When the ratio $\hat{\sigma}_\Delta^{-2}/\sigma_\Delta^{-2}$ is 1, its minimum, then no attention is being paid to aggregate (Δ) shocks. Greater values mean more attention to aggregates.

The optimal attention allocation depends on both properties of the profit function and the unconditional variances of the aggregate and firm-specific shocks. The more sensitive profits are to the interaction between prices and firm-specific shocks, the higher π_{PZ}. That makes devoting more attention to aggregate shocks less valuable, which raises the optimal posterior variance on aggregate shocks $\hat{\sigma}_{\Delta}^2$. Conversely, it makes devoting more attention to firm-specific shocks more valuable and lowers $\hat{\sigma}_z^2$. That is not surprising, but it helps explain what determines the attention allocation. When aggregate shocks have higher unconditional volatility, it is also optimal to devote more attention to them. Thus, firms want to devote more attention to the shock that their price is more sensitive to and the shock that is more volatile.

The question of how much inertia in price-setting this model generates is ultimately an empirical one. Thus the authors calibrate the stochastic processes to measures of the volatility of nominal aggregate demand shocks and the volatility of firm-level shocks as measured by the average size of a firm's price change. They calibrate the preference parameters to match price sensitivities used in the monetary literature. They find that firms optimally allocate 94 percent of their attention to firm-specific conditions. The primary reason that little attention is paid to aggregate shocks is that firm-specific shocks are about ten times more volatile.

Because price-setters devote so little attention to aggregate shocks, prices do not covary highly with these shocks. As a result, monetary policy has very little contemporaneous effect on prices. It gradually moves prices as new information is processed at a slow rate.

The more general lesson is that in environments with multiple random shocks to optimal actions, firms will tend to devote more attention to the most volatile shocks. That can make actions appear unresponsive to the more subtle changes in their environments.

Attention allocation in a production economy. The reason monetary economists want to understand what makes prices unresponsive to aggregate monetary shocks is because it is precisely that unresponsiveness that causes monetary policy to have real effects on output and consumption. To gauge those effects, Maćkowiak and Wiederholt (2009a) extend the framework described above from a partial equilibrium with exogenous aggregate output to general equilibrium. Households choose consumption and wages and firms choose labor inputs and set prices. Each observes only noisy signals about aggregate technology shocks, and monetary policy (interest rate) shocks, and firm-specific productivity shocks. Firms pay least attention to monetary shocks, pay more attention to productivity shocks, and pay the most attention to micro-level shocks. As before, this result follows from the calibrated relative volatilities of each type of shock. The firm-specific and individual-specific shocks are the most volatile, followed by aggregate productivity and lastly monetary policy.

Modeling rational inattention in an equilibrium model raises lots of questions. For example, if output is unknown, then the agent cannot choose both consumption and savings. They can choose one and the other must be a residual. Another issue is how information revealed by equilibrium prices is incorporated into the information constraint. Here, instead of writing the information flow constraint in

terms of the prior and posterior variances of each shock, Maćkowiak and
Wiederholt constrain the amount of information that actions contain about the
optimal, full-information action. For example, suppose a firm chooses price p
and labor input l. Given full information about the state of the economy, the firm
would choose p^*, l^*. Then this constraint would bound the mutual information
$\mathcal{I}(\{p, l\}, \{p^*, l^*\})$. This constraint represents the same physical learning process
as the constraint on signal precisions. If actions are conditioned on any kind of
signal that contains information about the true state, mutual information $\mathcal{I}$ rises.
Thus, the constraint incorporates the effect of all information from both exogenous signals and endogenous sources such as market prices. Because learning from
market prices requires capacity, this model does not need to introduce shocks that
make market prices noisy to keep information heterogenous. The information flow
restriction ensures that all firms extract noisy heterogeneous information, even from
public signals like prices.

The key result is that changes in monetary policy produce delayed, hump-shaped
consumption and output responses, just as they do in the data. While Mackowiak
and Wiederholt solve pieces of this model analytically, the main results are numerical in nature. (For more details, see Maćkowiak and Wiederholt 2009a).

6.5 ARE PRICES STATE DEPENDENT OR TIME DEPENDENT?

One way of seeing the contribution of information choice models in monetary economics is that they advance the debate about whether prices adjust in response to
changes in economic conditions (state dependence) or whether they adjust at regu-
lar intervals (time dependence). An example of a state-dependent price adjustment
model is one with a fixed adjustment cost or "menu cost" to update prices. In such
a model, whether the firm decides to update its price depends on its state variables,
specifically, the distance between its current price and its optimal price. An example of a time-dependent price adjustment model is one where firms update prices
every T periods. This is often referred to as Calvo (1983) pricing.

The problem with state-dependent pricing is that it generates little rigidity in
aggregate prices. Golosov and Lucas (2007) show that even though very few firms
adjust prices each period, the aggregate price adjusts quickly to changes in the state
because it is the firms whose prices have the furthest to adjust that do the adjusting.
This *selection effect* is mitigated in time-dependent models because the firms do
not choose to adjust prices when adjustment is most valuable. They adjust prices
when their time comes.

However, many oppose Calvo pricing because it lacks microeconomic foundations. Why would a firm wait the required number of periods to adjust its price
if some event just happened that makes non-adjustment very costly? Models with
inattentiveness, like the one by Reis (2006), attempt to provide micro-foundations
for a Calvo-like model. Reis's answer to the criticism of the Calvo model is that
when an event that warrants a big price adjustment takes place, firms may not react
because they are not paying attention. They are not paying attention to market
events because attention is costly.

Models with rational inattention, like those by Woodford (2002) and Maćkowiak and Wiederholt (2009b), have a constant flow of information that firms can react to. Thus, they are more like state-dependent models than time-dependent models. But imperfect information reduces the dependence of prices on the state. These models generate non-trivial price rigidity because the imperfect information works to mitigate the selection effect. If firms do not know how far their prices are from the optimal price, then some firms that should adjust do not adjust and some of the price adjusters make only small adjustments. (See also Moscarini 2004 on this point.)

Recent work on information frictions in monetary economics attempts to integrate both state and time dependence in one framework. In Woodford's work (2008), firms face a fixed cost of acquiring perfect information and updating their prices, just like the models of inattentiveness. Whereas inattentive firms get no information about the state in between price updates, these firms get new noisy signals every period, just like the firms with rational inattention. The state-dependent and time-dependent models are two limiting cases of Woodford's model. When the signal observed each period is perfectly precise, the model becomes a simple menu-cost model with a fixed cost of price adjustment. That is state dependence. When the signal contains no information, then the firm's decision about whether to update its price depends only on the number of periods since it last updated. That is time dependence. Calibrating such a model could give us an idea of which assumption is closer to the truth.

A hybrid model of rational inattention and inattentiveness. Woodford (2008) constructs a model where a firm chooses how much information to acquire rather than how to allocate its attention. As seen in Reis's work (2006), the firm can pay a fixed cost at discrete dates to observe perfect information about the current and past states of the economy. But in between these updates, it can observe a flow of noisy information about the state, as seen in work by Maćkowiak and Wiederholt (2009b). This is meant to capture the idea that it is costly both to adjust prices and to monitor the economy to know when to adjust.

Woodford writes the problem in terms of the *price gap* x, the discrepancy between a firm's chosen price and the price that would be optimal under full information. The firm's prior belief is that $x \sim f(x)$. At each date, the firm observes a signal s about x. The mutual information of s and x is denoted $I(s, x)$. The firm can choose the precision of the signal s. A more precise signal will have higher mutual information I, which has a constant marginal cost θ. This is the *rational inattention* part of the model.

The firm uses its signal s to update its beliefs about x using Bayes' law. Then it makes a choice about whether or not to adjust prices. The adjustment choice variable is $\delta(s)$, which is 1 if prices adjust and 0 otherwise. If the firm adjusts its price, it gets perfect information about the current (and past) values of x. This is the *inattentiveness* part of the model.

The objective of the firm depends on the benefit from updating, net of the updating cost $L(x)$. This benefit is the firm's value if it pays the updating cost, updates, and sets the price gap to zero, minus its value with price gap x. Thus, the firm chooses a quantity $I(s, x)$ and the function $\delta(s)$ to maximize its objective:

$$E[\delta(s)L(x)] - \theta I(s, x). \tag{6.40}$$

The first term is a product because the firm only gets benefit $L(x)$ if it updates and sets $\delta(s) = 1$.

Woodford proves that the optimal policy involves acquiring a signal that takes on only two values ($s \in \{0, 1\}$) and using an updating function that prescribes a review whenever the signal is 1 ($\delta(s) = s$). Given these features, the question for the firm is, how precise a signal do they want? The precision of the signal is described by a function $\Lambda(x)$ that gives the probability that $s = 1$, given that the true state is x. Woodford calls this a *hazard function* because it is the probability that a firm will decide to fully update its information and reset its price to the optimal full-information price.

To solve for the optimal hazard function, we need to express the mutual information I in terms of $\Lambda(x)$. To express mutual information, we first need to know the probability of state x conditional on signal s. This conditional (posterior) probability is given by Bayes' law:

$$f(x|s = 0) = \frac{f(x)(1 - \Lambda(x))}{1 - \bar{\Lambda}}, \quad f(x|s = 1) = \frac{f(x)\Lambda(x)}{\bar{\Lambda}}, \tag{6.41}$$

where $\bar{\Lambda}$ is the prior probability of observing $s = 1$: $\bar{\Lambda} \equiv \int \Lambda(x) f(x) dx$.

Recall from section 3.2 that the entropy of a variable $x \sim f(x)$ is $H(x) = -E[\ln f(x)]$ and conditional entropy is $H(x|y) = -E[\ln f(x|y)]$. Therefore, the entropy of x, conditional on the signal s, is $H(x|s) = -\bar{\Lambda}E[\ln f(x|s = 1)] - (1 - \bar{\Lambda})E[\ln f(x|s = 0)]$. Finally, mutual information is entropy minus conditional entropy (equation [3.1]). Replacing the expectation $E[\ln f(x)]$ with the integral $\int \ln(f(x)) f(x) dx$ and doing the same substitution for the conditional entropy term yields

$$I(s, x) = -\int \ln(f(x)) f(x) dx + \bar{\Lambda} \int \frac{f(x)\Lambda(x)}{\bar{\Lambda}} \ln\left(\frac{f(x)\Lambda(x)}{\bar{\Lambda}}\right) f(x) dx$$

$$+ (1 - \bar{\Lambda}) \int \frac{f(x)(1 - \Lambda(x))}{1 - \bar{\Lambda}} \ln\left(\frac{f(x)(1 - \Lambda(x))}{1 - \bar{\Lambda}}\right) f(x) dx. \tag{6.42}$$

We can write the log of a product as a sum of logs and thereby extract all the $\ln(f(x))$ terms. They all cancel each other out. Collecting the remaining terms under one integral reveals that mutual information is

$$I(s, x) = \int \left[\Lambda(x) \ln\left(\frac{\Lambda(x)}{\bar{\Lambda}}\right) + (1 - \Lambda(x)) \ln\left(\frac{1 - \Lambda(x)}{1 - \bar{\Lambda}}\right)\right] f(x) dx.$$

Next, break up both log ratio terms into the difference of logs. Also, write the integral over four additive terms as the sum of four integrals. Note that $-\ln(\bar{\Lambda})$ and $-\ln(1 - \bar{\Lambda})$ do not vary in x and can therefore be extracted from the integral, leaving $-\ln(\bar{\Lambda}) \int \Lambda(x) f(x) dx = -\ln(\bar{\Lambda})\bar{\Lambda}$ and $-\ln(1 - \bar{\Lambda}) \int (1 - \Lambda(x))$

$f(x)dx = -\ln(1 - \bar{\Lambda})(1 - \bar{\Lambda})$ as two of the four terms. Thus,

$$I(s, x) = \int \Lambda(x) \ln(\Lambda(x)) f(x) dx$$
$$+ \int (1 - \Lambda(x)) \ln(1 - \Lambda(x)) f(x) dx - \bar{\Lambda} \ln(\bar{\Lambda}) - (1 - \bar{\Lambda}) \ln(1 - \bar{\Lambda}).$$

Combine the first two terms in one integral and examine the term inside that integral. Using the definition of entropy again, note that this term is the entropy of the signal s, conditional on the hazard function $\Lambda(x)$: $E[log(p(s = 0|\Lambda(x))) + log(p(s = 1|\Lambda(x)))] = -H(s|\Lambda(x))$. Likewise, the last two terms are the entropy of s, conditional on the prior probability $\bar{\Lambda}$. That conditional entropy is $H(s|\bar{\Lambda})$.

Substituting mutual information into the firm's objective function (6.40) and using the fact that $\Lambda(x)$ is the probability $Prob[\delta(s) = 1|x]$ delivers the firm's maximization problem:

$$\max_{\Lambda(x)} \int \Lambda(x)L(x) - \theta H(s|\Lambda(x)) f(x) dx + \theta H(s|\bar{\Lambda}). \qquad (6.43)$$

Woodford establishes that a first-order approach characterizes the unique global solution to this problem. In each state x that has positive measure ($f(x) > 0$), the first derivative of the objective with respect to Λ must be zero:

$$\left(L(x) - \theta \frac{\partial H(s|\Lambda(x))}{\partial \Lambda(x)} \right) f(x) + \theta \frac{\partial H(s|\bar{\Lambda})}{\partial \bar{\Lambda}} \frac{\partial \bar{\Lambda}}{\partial \Lambda(x)} = 0 \quad \forall x \text{ such that } f(x) > 0.$$
$$(6.44)$$

Simple differentiation reveals that $\partial H(s|\Lambda(x))/\partial \Lambda(x) = \ln(\Lambda(x)/(1 - \Lambda(x)))$ and $\partial \bar{\Lambda}/\partial \Lambda(x) = f(x)$. Since we are looking at states where $f(x) > 0$, we can cancel the $f(x)$ terms and express the optimal hazard function as

$$\ln \left(\frac{\Lambda(x)}{1 - \Lambda(x)} \right) = \ln \left(\frac{\bar{\Lambda}}{1 - \bar{\Lambda}} \right) + \frac{L(x)}{\theta}. \qquad (6.45)$$

This condition is what pins down the optimal degree of rational inattention. One of the features of this model is that there is little incentive to allocate much attention to x because adjusting the price allows the firm to get periodic updates with perfect information.

Woodford goes on to describe how in a dynamic model, prior beliefs $f(x)$ arise endogenously from past signals. He also links the payoff function $L(x)$ to economic fundamentals in an equilibrium model of monopolistically competitive firms.

A calibrated version of this model delivers a realistic degree of price inertia to changes in monetary policy. For small shocks, these results are similar to what the time-dependent model predicts. The reason is that some firms whose prices are far away from the optimal prices (a large $|x|$) do not know this. Because of the information frictions, such firms have prices that are "sticky," meaning that they fail to react to changes in the monetary environment.

6.6 BROADER THEMES AND PATHS FOR FUTURE RESEARCH

The mechanisms explored in this chapter, particularly the interaction between coordination motives and heterogeneous information, can be used to explain many situations where aggregate actions exhibit inertia.

Consumption inertia and excess sensitivity. Two empirical puzzles about consumer behavior cannot be explained by a standard, rational expectations, permanent income hypothesis (PIH) model. The first puzzle is excess consumption smoothness: aggregate consumption growth is much smoother than short-run aggregate income growth in the U.S. data and smoother than what the PIH predicts. The second puzzle is excess sensitivity: when the shock is anticipated, aggregate consumption is actually more sensitive than the PIH predicts.

Luo (2008) shows that a model with rational inattention can explain these facts. Agents have quadratic utility and face permanent (random walk) and transitory (moving average) shocks to their income. They do not observe income but can acquire noisy signals about it.

The main result is that a smaller information-processing capacity dampens the response of consumption to the permanent and transitory income shocks in the short run but amplifies the response in the long run. The short-run response is dampened because, as we have seen many times now, imperfect information makes actions less correlated with the unobserved state variable. The long-run response is amplified because agents who have high income but do not increase their consumption accumulate wealth that allows them to have even higher consumption in future periods.

Insensitivity of asset prices to some shocks. Just like goods prices, equity prices can be slow to incorporate some kinds of news and quick to incorporate others. Hong, Stein, and Yu (2007) give the example of Amazon's stock price. It initially reacted mostly to information about the number of clicks on its Web site and not to earnings announcements, even though earnings announcements seemed more relevant to future dividends. In the savings-consumption context, tax cuts seem to affect consumption behavior differently than equivalent tax rebates. In the world of corporate debt markets, investors react more to a ratings downgrade than to an upgrade. These types of phenomena could potentially be explained by a model of attention allocation. Maćkowiak and Wiederholt (2009b) show us that more volatile variables are more valuable to pay attention to. This same effect could take the form of a dynamic reallocation effect: in times when a variable has higher expected volatility, firms track it closely and react quickly to it. When a variable is expected to be relatively constant, changes in its value may not affect firms' behavior because they choose to allocate their attention to something else.

Similarly, there are events where private information does not effect aggregate actions but public information does. For example, some news stories do not affect the price of a stock the first time they are printed but do when they are later reprinted in a higher-circulation publication (Huberman and Regev 2001). An effect that Reis (2006) highlights is that when firms want to coordinate, the incentive to acquire information that is closer to common knowledge is stronger than the incentive to acquire information that most others will choose not to observe.

Overreaction to recent news in asset markets. In section 6.2 we saw how the combination of coordination motives and heterogeneous information was a potent force for inertia. The idea was that if you wanted to take an action (e.g., set a price) that is close to the actions others choose, you want to react more to public information than to private information. When firms get updated information only infrequently, older information is more public. Newer information is known by only the firms that have updated their information sets since the new event took place. Thus, firms put more weight on old, more public information, which makes their actions slow to evolve.

But what if the strategic motives in actions are characterized by substitutability rather than complementarity? Chapter 7 will show that investment decisions are characterized by such substitutability. If firms want to take actions that differ from what others do, they want to weight private information more and public information less. When firms get updated information only infrequently, newer information is more private. Thus, weighting newer information more is optimal. Such logic might explain why there is excess volatility in asset markets.

Ratings agencies. The tools in this chapter could also be used to ask normative questions. For example, a ratings firm has a large number of assets to follow and has limited information-processing resources available to re-rate assets. Which assets should they collect more information on to potentially re-rate? If ratings agencies follow this optimal procedure for re-rating, can firms take actions that manipulate this process? Can they make investments that minimize their chances of being re-rated when their performance is poor and maximize it when performance is strong? A framework like the one presented here where firms re-set ratings, instead of prices, could be useful for answering such questions.

Monitoring and moral hazard. Another application of rational inattention and inattentiveness models is to rethink questions about optimal monitoring that arise in applied micro and corporate finance. For example, if a manager has to monitor many different operations, how does he allocate his attention among them? How does the manager's compensation scheme affect his allocation choice?

Central bank transparency revisited. The main question raised in the previous chapter is whether a central bank or other public authority should reveal information publicly. Morris and Shin (2002) argue that if coordination produces private benefits, but not public benefits, then too much coordination, which is facilitated with public information, can be welfare reducing. According to Amador and Weill (2011), when agents know lots of public information, their actions reveal little private information and others learn little that is new from observing them.

This chapter introduced information choice not by the government but by the firms who set the prices. The possibility that the government's information disclosure might interact with firms' information choice could create another rationale for withholding public information. The argument is that public information can deter information acquisition. If agents with public information acquire less private information, aggregate information could suffer and social welfare with it.

6.7 EXERCISES

1. Prove the result in equation (6.27). Conjecture that the price p_t is a linear combination of past money supply innovations $\epsilon_{t-\tau}$. Then use equations (6.25) and (6.26) to verify the conjecture and solve for the undetermined coefficients.

2. Suppose that all the firms updated their information periods ago but no firm has updated it since. Is it an equilibrium? Express the current price as a function of demand innovations.

3. If more firms planned more recently, how does this affect one firm's loss from not planning? *Hint*: express your answer as a partial derivative.

4. Prove that if $r > 0$ and if all firms choose to update in even periods, then any given firm strictly prefers to update in even periods rather than in odd periods.

5. Verify the expression for the optimal price (equation [6.31]) in Maćkowiak and Wiederholt 2009b.

6. Assume now that the firms process information subject to a linear information-processing constraint using Maćkowiak and Wiederholt 2009b. What is the solution to this version of the model? Explain it carefully.

PART III
Information Choice with Substitutability in Actions

Chapter Seven

Information Choice and Investment Choice

What features of an asset make its payoffs valuable to learn about? Some of the very first equilibrium models of information acquisition with many agents were written about asset markets. These canonical models provide a useful framework for modeling information choice not just in financial markets but also in production economies.

While previous chapters focused on settings where actions were primarily characterized by coordination motives, here we begin to examine settings of strategic substitutability. This is perhaps the more common case in economics because it arises naturally from the role that prices play in allocating goods: agents typically prefer to buy goods (or assets) that others do not want to buy because the goods others demand will be more expensive. As in the model of section 4.4, this causes information acquisition to be a strategic substitute as well.

Investment choice differs from the previous models in another respect as well. The choice of which price to set or which action to take did not generate any economies of scale in information acquisition. With investment, choosing to invest more in an asset makes learning about that asset's payoff more valuable. However, to keep this chapter focused on strategic substitutability, we will postpone the discussion of returns to scale until the next chapter.

The first section explores the one-asset general equilibrium model of Grossman and Stiglitz (1980). In that model, investors choose whether or not to acquire a signal about the risky asset. Substitutability takes the following form: the value of acquiring the signal diminishes as more investors acquire it. The second section builds the framework of an equilibrium model with multiple risky assets. Investors have heterogeneous information, but they are not able to choose their information. The third section introduces information choice in that framework. Substitutability reemerges. Because investors prefer to buy low-demand assets that have lower prices, they also prefer to learn about assets that others know less about. As a consequence, ex ante identical investors may choose to learn about different assets and therefore hold different portfolios. These portfolios differ from the diversified portfolios prescribed by standard portfolio theory. Thus, introducing information choice in an investment choice model can alter basic prescriptions of portfolio theory. The fourth section examines the various forms that entropy-based information constraints might take in an equilibrium model.

7.1 A ONE-ASSET MODEL WITH INFORMATION CHOICE

Grossman and Stiglitz (1980) build a rational expectations equlibrium model of information acquisition in an endowment economy with one risky asset. The information choice is discrete. Investors acquire a signal or not. The key result is that the value of the signal declines as more investors choose to observe it. Much subsequent work has built on this framework.

Model. This is a static model, which we can break down into three periods. In period 1, each investor i chooses whether to purchase a signal ($L_i = 1$) or not ($L_i = 0$). In period 2, investors observe signals and equilibrium prices and choose how much to invest in a riskless asset m_i and a risky asset q_i. In period 3, the payoffs of both assets and the investors' utility are realized.

There is a continuum of ex ante identical investors, indexed by i, with expected utility

$$U_i = -E_i[e^{-\rho(W_i - cL_i)}], \tag{7.1}$$

where W is wealth at the end of the period and cL represents a monetary cost of acquiring information. There are two assets. One offers a riskless return r. The other pays a risky amount $f = \theta + e$. The first component of the risky payout is the part that agents can learn about. It is $\theta \sim N(\bar{\theta}, \sigma_\theta^2)$. θ can be observed at a cost c. The second component is not learnable: $e \sim N(0, \sigma_e^2)$. The two components are independent of each other.

The price of the riskless asset is one (a numeraire). The price of the risky asset is p, an endogenous amount that will be determined in equilibrium.

Each agent is endowed with m_i^0 units of the riskless asset and q_i^0 units of risky asset. The aggregate endowment of the risky asset is $\bar{x} + x = \int q_i^0 di$. The second component of this endowment is random: $x \sim N(0, \sigma_x^2)$. The random asset supply assumption serves two related purposes: it prevents prices from perfectly revealing the true payoff of the asset, and it prevents agents from refusing to trade (see Milgrom and Stokey 1982). This assumption has been interpreted in many different ways including the presence of irrational noise traders, random endowment shocks, or shocks to traders, needs for liquid assets.[1] Thus, each agent's budget constraint is

$$m_i + pq_i = m_i^0 + pq_i^0, \tag{7.2}$$

where m_i and q_i are the number of shares of the riskless and risky assets the agent chooses to hold. End-of-period wealth is the sum of the payoffs from the risk-free and risky assets, $W_i = rm_i + fq_i$. Using the budget constraint to substitute in for m_i, wealth is $W_i = r(m_i^0 + pq_i^0) + (f - pr)q_i$.

A noisy rational expectations equilibrium. The concept of equilibrium that Grossman and Stiglitz use is the following: agents choose whether to purchase information ($L_i \in \{0, 1\}$) to maximize expected utility (7.1), given prior information. Agents choose their portfolio investments (m_i and q_i) to maximize their expected

---

[1] See Biais, Bossaerts, and Spatt 2010 for a model with endowment shocks and Uhlig 1990 for a model of a production economy with noise in equilibrium prices.

utility, given any information they purchased and given the information contained in the realized equilibrium asset price.

The reason this equilibrium concept can feel counterintuitive is that the realized price of the risky assets will depend on agents' asset demand. How can they know that price and use it when they form their demands? One justification for this equilibrium concept is the idea of tatonnement; demands and prices adjust iteratively until they converge. Another mechanism that would achieve this equilibrium is a menu auction. Suppose a continuum of agents submit a menu of prices, and quantities that they would be willing to purchase at each price, that is, they submit a demand function $q_i(p)$. Then an auctioneer sold each share at the market-clearing price. The price and allocation that would result are the same as the noisy rational expectations equilibrium.

Solving the model. We begin by solving the period-2 investment choice problem and then working backward to determine the value of observing the signal in period 1. Substitute in for W. Then take the expectation of the utility function. That expectation is conditional on investor i's signal (if he purchased a signal) and the risky asset price:

$$U_i = -E_i[\exp(-\rho q_i(f - pr))]\exp(-\rho r(m_i^0 + pq_i^0))\exp(\rho c L_i).$$

In period 2, the terms $\exp(-\rho r(m_i^0 + pq_i^0))$ and $\exp(\rho c L_i)$ are positive constants because the information choice L_i has already been made. They will not affect the maximization problem, except that the choice of information will affect the information set that the expectation E_i is conditioned on. The remaining term $\exp(-\rho q_i(f - pr))$ is a log-normal variable because the price times the risk-free rate pr is known and f is normally distributed. If agent i believes that f has mean $E_i[f]$ and variance $V_i[f]$, then the conditional mean of the log-normal term in utility is

$$-E_i[\exp(-\rho q_i(f - pr))] = -\exp\left(-\rho q_i(E_i[f] - pr) + \frac{\rho^2}{2}q_i^2 V_i[f]\right). \quad (7.3)$$

These calculations highlight some helpful features of exponential (also called constant absolute risk aversion [CARA]) preferences. First, these preferences work well for information-based models because taking the expectation of an exponential function of a normal random variable is analytically tractable. Second, initial wealth does not matter. Rich and poor people regard equal gambles the same way. Both want to hold the same amount of risky assets. This eliminates a potential source of heterogeneity that would be complicated to keep track of. While there are many objections to this form of utility and to the idea of normally distributed payoffs that are unbounded, solving models with most other sets of assumptions is analytically intractable and computationally challenging.[2]

---

[2] See Muendler 2005 for a model with alternative distributional assumptions on payoff shocks. See Van Nieuwerburgh and Veldkamp 2010 for a model of information choice with constant relative risk aversion (CRRA) preferences and log-normally distributed payoffs.

Step 1: Solve for portfolios and prices. Start with the portfolio problem—the last problem to be solved and then work backward. Suppose investor i believes $f \sim N(E_i[f], V_i[f])$, conditional on everything he knows at the investment date.

The first-order condition for q_i is $-\rho(E_i[f] - pr) + \rho^2 V_i[f]q_i = 0$. Rearranging this condition yields the optimal portfolio,

$$q_i = \frac{1}{\rho} V_i[f]^{-1}(E_i[f] - pr). \tag{7.4}$$

The budget constraint is then satisfied with purchases of the riskless asset m_i. Note that this solution does not rule out negative holdings (short sales) of either the risky or the riskless asset.

At this point, we can drop the i subscript and consider just two types of investors, informed (I) and uninformed (U). Informed investors are those that have paid to observe θ. They still do not know exactly what the asset payoff is because they do not know e. Uninformed investors do not know θ or e. Both sets of investors will observe the asset price p.

The first-order condition (7.4) holds for both informed and uninformed investors. The difference between the two is their conditional expectations and variances of f. Substitute the correct posterior mean and variance to get the asset demands of informed investors q^I:

$$q^I = \frac{1}{\rho} \sigma_e^{-2}(\theta - pr). \tag{7.5}$$

For uninformed investors, the asset demand q^U is more complicated because uninformed investors learn something about θ from observing the asset price p. At the same time, asset prices are influenced by uninformed investors' demand for the asset. This is a fixed-point problem. We need to solve for p and q^U jointly.

Step 2: Determine risky asset price. The price of the risky asset is determined by the market clearing condition:

$$\lambda q^I + (1 - \lambda)q^U = \bar{x} + x.$$

We employ a "guess and verify" solution method. The hypothesis is that the price is a linear function of θ and of x: $p = A + B\theta + Cx$ for some coefficients A, B, and C. Using this price function, we can figure out what this price implies for risky asset demands, substitute those demand functions into the market clearing conditions, and match coefficients to verify the hypothesis.

For the uninformed investors, use the Bayesian updating formula for normal variable (equations [2.3] and [2.4]) to combine the prior belief that $\theta \sim N(\bar{\theta}, \sigma_\theta^2)$ and the signal from the price $(p - A)/B \sim N(\theta, (C/B)^2 \sigma_x^2)$. The posterior variance is

$$\sigma_{\theta|p}^2 \equiv Var[\theta|p] = (\sigma_\theta^{-2} + ((C/B)^2 \sigma_x^2)^{-1})^{-1}.$$

The posterior mean is

$$\hat{\mu} \equiv E[\theta|p] = \sigma_{\theta|p}^2 \left(\sigma_\theta^{-2}\bar{\theta} + \frac{1}{(C/B)^2 \sigma_x^2} \frac{p - A}{B} \right).$$

Since θ and e are independent, the conditional variance of f is the sum of the conditional variances $\sigma_{\theta|p}^2 + \sigma_e^2$. Substituting in the conditional mean and variance of f for $E_i[f]$ and $V_i[f]$ in (7.4) delivers the optimal portfolio for an uninformed investor:

$$q^U = \frac{\hat{\mu} - pr}{\rho(\sigma_{\theta|p}^2 + \sigma_e^2)}. \tag{7.6}$$

The last step is to add the two demand expressions—(7.5) and (7.6)—together, weighting them by λ and $(1 - \lambda)$ and setting them equal to $\bar{x} + x$. The resulting expression is linear in x and θ. Each shows up in only one place and is additive with p. Everything else is just constant coefficients. This confirms the guess of a linear price rule. The coefficients A, B, and C can be solved for by matching coefficients.

On average, informed agents demand more. Uninformed and informed investors have equal conditional expectations of the payoffs, in expectation, $E\left[\hat{\mu}\right] = \theta$, but the conditional variance for informed agents is lower: $\sigma_e^2 < \sigma_{\theta|p}^2 + \sigma_e^2$. Lower conditional variance means higher demand for assets with positive expected returns. In other words, investors prefer to take larger positions in less risky assets. This becomes important because it means that, on average, higher information demand will increase asset demand and raise the equilibrium price of the asset.

Step 3: Determine the value of information. Now that we know how much of the risky asset each type of investor holds, we can compare the expected utility of the informed and uninformed investors. This tells us how valuable information is. To take expected utility, proceed in *three* steps, using the law of iterated expectations. First, condition on signals and the asset price. Then condition only on the asset price. Finally, take the unconditional expectation, which depends only on prior information, $E[e^{-\rho W}] = E[E[E[e^{-\rho W}|E[f], p]|p]]$.

To simplify the expressions, we will ignore the constants in the investors' utility function. Let $U^U = E[e^{-\rho q(f-pr)}]$ for the uninformed investor and let U^I be the same piece of expected utility for the informed investor.

Expected utility for uninformed investor. The uninformed investor forms a posterior belief about f that is conditioned only on prior information and the asset price p. Thus, taking an expectation conditional on $E[f]$ and p is the same as conditioning on p alone.

The uncertainty about the payoff conditional on p is $V[f|p] = \sigma_e^2 + \sigma_{\theta|p}^2$. Let $\hat{\mu} \equiv E[f|p]$. Recall that the mean of a log-normal variable is the exponential of the mean, plus one-half the variance. Applying this rule delivers expected uninformed investors' utility U^U:

$$E[U^U|p] = -\exp\left(\frac{-(\hat{\mu} - pr)^2}{\sigma_e^2 + \sigma_{\theta|p}^2} + \frac{1}{2}\left(\frac{\hat{\mu} - pr}{\sigma_e^2 + \sigma_{\theta|p}^2}\right)^2 (\sigma_e^2 + \sigma_{\theta|p}^2)\right).$$

Combining terms yields

$$E[U^U|p] = -\exp\left(-\frac{1}{2}\frac{(\hat{\mu} - pr)^2}{\sigma_e^2 + \sigma_{\theta|p}^2}\right).$$

There is a second expectation over p that we have not taken. It turns out that we will not need to.

Expected utility for informed investor. Let U^I denote informed investors' utility before subtracting their information cost. Applying the same rule for the mean of a log-normal yields

$$E[U^I|\theta, p] = E[e^{-\frac{1}{2}(\theta-pr)^2\sigma_e^{-2}}], \tag{7.7}$$

where θ replaced $\hat{\mu}$ as the informed investors' conditional mean and σ_e^2 is their conditional variance.

The next step is to take an expectation over the realization of the signal θ but not over the realized price p. This is an expectation of an exponential of a quadratic normal. Section 7.6 details the general formula for computing such expectations and shows that

$$-E[e^{-\frac{1}{2}(\theta-pr)^2\sigma_e^{-2}}] = -\sqrt{\frac{\sigma_e^2}{\sigma_e^2+\sigma_{\theta|p}^2}}\exp[-\frac{1}{2}\frac{(\hat{\mu}-pr)^2}{\sigma_e^2+\sigma_{\theta|p}^2}].$$

Note that the second term is the expected utility of an uninformed agent $E[U^U|p]$ (times (-1)).

Therefore, the difference in the two utilities, and the value of information, is

$$E[U^I|p] - E[U^U|p] = \left(\sqrt{\frac{\sigma_e^2}{\sigma_e^2+\sigma_{\theta|p}^2}} - 1\right)E[U^U|p].$$

Step 4: Equilibrium demand for information. Since all investors are identical ex ante, each must be indifferent between learning or not learning. The next step is to add the cost of information and write out the indifference condition to solve for λ, the fraction of the population that is informed.

The previous expression is the value of information, before accounting for the information cost. This cost is multiplicative: the utility function (7.1) can be rewritten as $U_i = -E[e^{-\rho W_i}]e^{\rho c L_i}$. Since $L_i = 1$ for the informed investor and is 0 for the uninformed investor, the benefit of information, net of the information cost, is

$$\left(\sqrt{\frac{\sigma_e^2}{\sigma_e^2+\sigma_{\theta|p}^2}}e^{\rho c} - 1\right)E[U^U|p].$$

In equilibrium, this net benefit must be zero because that makes investors ex ante indifferent between being informed or uninformed. Since $E[U^U|p] \neq 0$ for any finite level of wealth, this indifference condition implies that

$$\sqrt{\frac{\sigma_e^2+\sigma_{\theta|p}^2}{\sigma_e^2}} = e^{\rho c}. \tag{7.8}$$

Recall that this condition should allow us to solve for the fraction of investors that choose to become informed. Where does the fraction of informed agents λ enter in this equilibrium condition? It enters through $\sigma_{\theta|p}^{-2} = \sigma_\theta^{-2} + ((C^2/B^2)\sigma_x^2)^{-1}$ because the weight of asset supply shocks in the price, C, is decreasing in λ and the weight on the signal, B, is increasing in λ. Grossman and Stiglitz (1980) never solve explicitly for λ. Instead, they use these relationships to talk about properties of information demand.

What do we learn from Grossman and Stiglitz (1980)? The value of information is related to the square root of the ratio of payoff variance with the information to the payoff variance without the information. Lots of things do not matter: the level of payoffs, wealth, the risk-free rate, etcetera. Risk aversion matters only because it determines the utility cost of paying the information cost.

Another important finding is that strategic substitutability reappears: the more people acquire information, the less that information is worth. When λ increases, the weight on θ in the price (coefficient B) rises. In other words, the price has more information content: $\sigma_{\theta|p}^2$ falls. If the payoff is less variable without purchasing information, the value of information goes down. Grossman and Stiglitz call this the "fundamental conflict between the efficiency with which markets spread information and the incentives to acquire information" (1980, 105).

7.2 MULTIPLE ASSETS AND EXOGENOUS INFORMATION

Consider a Grossman-Stiglitz type of environment where instead of one risky asset, there are many risky assets. As before, the market price imperfectly aggregates information. Instead of agents who choose their information, we will consider individuals who are endowed with their information. But the information they are endowed with is heterogeneous. Everyone has their own prior beliefs with their own mean and variance. Using this setting, Admati (1985) asks questions such as, what effect does more precise private information have on the price of an asset?

There is a continuum of agents. It is a static model where agents are endowed with heterogenous signals about asset payoffs. They combine these signals with information from the equilibrium prices to form their optimal investment choices. Finally, they observe asset payoffs and get utility from their final wealth.

As before, preferences are exponential: $U_i = E_i[-e^{-\rho_i W_i}]$, where ρ_i is risk aversion of individual i and W is their final wealth. There are N risky assets with payoffs given by the $N \times 1$ vector f. Those payoffs are exogenous but unknown. There is a riskless asset with return $r > 1$. The budget constraint is the same as in the previous section but now in vector form: $W_i = (W_{0i} - q_i'p)r + q_i'f$, where W_{0i} is initial wealth, q_i is the $N \times 1$ vector of asset quantities agent i chooses to hold, and p is the $N \times 1$ vector of risky asset prices.

Individual i has exogenously given prior beliefs about asset payoffs: $f \sim i.i.d.$ $N(\mu_i, \Sigma_i)$. The supply of the risky assets is random. It is $\bar{x} + x$, where $x \sim N(0, \sigma_x^2 I)$.

As in the previous section, the equilibrium is a noisy rational expectations equilibrium.

Solving for portfolios and prices. Begin by rewriting preferences and substituting in the budget constraint. The expected part of wealth is just a constant multiplier. It can be dropped because maximizing a function times a positive constant yields the same optimal choice. The simplified objective is

$$U_i = E_i[-e^{-\rho_i q_i'(f-pr)}]. \tag{7.9}$$

Although investors do not choose to observe any information in the model, they do learn from the information contained in prices. Suppose that the price is a linear function of the true asset payoffs f and the asset supply shocks x. We can write the linear function as

$$rp = A + Bf + Cx, \tag{7.10}$$

with unknown coefficients A ($N \times 1$), and ($N \times N$) matrices B and C. (When we solve for the coefficients at the end, we will verify that this linear conjecture is in fact an equilibrium.) This implies that $B^{-1}(rp-A) = f+B^{-1}Cx$. Since the supply shock vector x is assumed to be a mean-zero, normally distributed random variable, this is an unbiased signal about the asset payoffs f. Let $s(p) \equiv B^{-1}(rp - A)$ denote this signal. The signal noise $B^{-1}Cx$ has variance-covariance matrix $\sigma_x^2 B^{-1}C(B^{-1}C)'$. Let Σ_p denote this variance.

Bayes' law tells us how to combine prior beliefs and the information in price to form posterior beliefs. Investor i will have posterior beliefs that $f \sim N(\hat{\mu}_i, \widehat{\Sigma}_i)$ where

$$\widehat{\Sigma}_i = (\Sigma_i^{-1} + \Sigma_p^{-1})^{-1} \tag{7.11}$$

and

$$\hat{\mu}_i = \widehat{\Sigma}_i(\Sigma_i^{-1}\mu_i + \Sigma_p^{-1}s(p)). \tag{7.12}$$

This raises the question, what information do prices contain? What are the unknown coefficients A, B, C that underlie $s(p)$ and Σ_p? It turns out that this depends on investors' asset demands. But asset demands depend on beliefs, which are partly determined by the information contained in prices. In other words, this is a fixed-point problem. To solve this problem, we take $s(p)$ and Σ_p as given, solve the investment demand problem, determine equilibrium prices, and then match coefficients to solve for $s(p)$ and Σ_p.

Taking the first-order condition of (7.9) with respect to q_i delivers investor i's optimal portfolio. Given posterior beliefs $f \sim N(\hat{\mu}_i, \widehat{\Sigma}_i)$, that portfolio is

$$q_i = \frac{1}{\rho_i}\widehat{\Sigma}_i^{-1}(\hat{\mu}_i - pr). \tag{7.13}$$

To solve for the asset price, impose the market clearing condition. It says that demand for the asset must equal supply: $\int q_i di = x + \bar{x}$. Substituting (7.13) for the asset demand and then (7.12) for $\hat{\mu}_i$ delivers

$$\int \frac{1}{\rho_i}\widehat{\Sigma}_i^{-1}\left(\widehat{\Sigma}_i(\Sigma_i^{-1}\mu_i + \Sigma_p^{-1}s(p)) - pr\right)di = x + \bar{x}.$$

Next, we define two pieces of notation. The first is the average of agents' initial precision, weighted by their risk tolerance, $\Psi \equiv \int \frac{1}{\rho_i}\Sigma_i^{-1}di$. The second is the harmonic mean of risk aversion, $\bar{\rho} \equiv (\int \rho_i^{-1}di)^{-1}$. Using the fact that heterogeneity in means μ_i is uncorrelated with heterogeneity in variances Σ_i and risk aversions ρ_i, we can rewrite the market clearing condition as

$$\Psi \int \mu_i di + \frac{1}{\bar{\rho}} \Sigma_p^{-1} s(p) - \int \frac{1}{\rho_i} \widehat{\Sigma}_i^{-1} di \; pr = x + \bar{x}.$$

Since all investors' beliefs are distributed i.i.d. around the true payoffs f, and since (7.11) implies that $\widehat{\Sigma}_i^{-1} = \Sigma_i^{-1} + \Sigma_p^{-1}$, the market clearing equation becomes

$$\Psi f + \frac{1}{\bar{\rho}} (\Sigma_p^{-1} s(p) - \Sigma_p^{-1} rp) - \Psi rp = x + \bar{x}. \tag{7.14}$$

The last step is to substitute in $s(p)$ and Σ_p, solve for the price p, and use the method of undetermined coefficients to solve for A, B, and C. Recall that $s(p) = B^{-1}(rp - A)$ and $\Sigma_p = \sigma_x^2 B^{-1} C (B^{-1} C)'$. Substituting these two expressions into (7.14), solving for rp, and matching coefficients yields the following solution:

$$A = -\bar{\rho}(\bar{\rho}\Psi + \Sigma_p^{-1})^{-1} \bar{x}$$
$$B = I \tag{7.15}$$
$$C = -\Psi^{-1}.$$

A is the unconditional expected return. It is risk aversion times the posterior belief of a synthetic "average" agent, whose information set is the mean of all agents' signals and whose precision is the mean of all agents' precisions. If risk aversion is the same for all agents, then $A = -\rho \widehat{\Sigma}_a^{-1} \bar{x}$, where $\widehat{\Sigma}_a^{-1} \equiv \int \widehat{\Sigma}_i^{-1} di$.

C is the sensitivity of the price to asset supply shocks. The more uncertain the synthetic "average" agent is initially (high $\widehat{\Sigma}_a$), the more an increase in supply decreases an asset's price.

Interpreting the results. What assets command high prices (and therefore lower returns)? Assets about which agents have less uncertainty (Σ_a is low) command high prices because less risky assets are more valuable to risk-averse investors. Assets that are less abundant (small $\bar{x}$) have higher prices because scarcity raises the asset's price. In contrast, assets that are more abundant need to have lower prices to induce the average investor to hold more of that asset so that the market can clear. Assets with small asset supply shocks (low σ_x^2) have higher prices because their prices are more revealing. This makes the average investor better informed about their true value. Better information about the payoff makes the asset less risky to investors, who therefore value it more.

What assets do investors want to hold? Recall that $q_i = \frac{1}{\rho_i} \widehat{\Sigma}_i^{-1} (\hat{\mu}_i - pr)$. They want to hold assets that they are optimistic about (high $\hat{\mu}_i$), assets they know lots about (high $\widehat{\Sigma}_i^{-1}$), and assets that command high returns (low pr).

A note about uniqueness. We have not ruled out other possible non-linear equilibrium price functions. To my knowledge, no one has shown that this solution is unique. What to do about it? Nothing, just keep it in mind. Of course, if you are looking for a tough problem to crack and you have the tools to do it, proving whether this solution is unique or not is a useful problem to solve.

Compute expected utility. To analyze information choices in the next section, we will need to know the expected utility that results from each information set. Begin by computing expected utility conditional on prices. After observing prices, f is the only random variable: $f \sim N(\hat{\mu}_i, \widehat{\Sigma}_i)$. Use the formula for the expectation of a log-normal variable to obtain

$$E[U|p, \hat{\mu}_i] = E[-e^{-\rho_i q_i'(f-pr)}|\hat{\mu}_i, p] = -\exp\left[-\rho_i q_i'(\hat{\mu}_i - pr) + \frac{\rho^2}{2}q_i'\widehat{\Sigma}_i q_i\right].$$

(7.16)

Substituting in for q_i and rearranging delivers

$$E[U|p, \hat{\mu}_i] = -\exp\left[-\frac{1}{2}(\hat{\mu}_i - pr)'\widehat{\Sigma}_i^{-1}(\hat{\mu}_i - pr)\right].$$

(7.17)

Since the exponential operator is a monotonically increasing function, this is equivalent to maximizing $\frac{1}{2}(\hat{\mu}_i - pr)'\widehat{\Sigma}_i^{-1}(\hat{\mu}_i - pr)$.

7.3 MULTIPLE ASSETS WITH INFORMATION CHOICE

Starting with the model from the previous section, the next step is to add an information choice that precedes the investment choice. While the Grossman and Stiglitz (1980) model in section 7.1 could predict what fraction of investors would choose to purchase a given signal, this model features a choice between signals.[3] Investors can acquire a fixed amount of information (they have a fixed capacity) and they choose which assets to learn about (how to allocate their capacity). We have worked out what expected utility an investor would have in that setting with any posterior beliefs $\hat{\mu}_i$ and $\widehat{\Sigma}_i$. The next step is to use this expected utility as an objective function in an information choice problem.

In this model, there are three pieces of information that the investor takes into consideration when he forms his portfolio. Each investor has his prior belief $f \sim (\mu_i, \Sigma_i)$. As shown in Admati's work (1985), prices also contain information, so that $E[f|p] = f + e_p$ where $e_p \sim N(0, \Sigma_p)$. Finally, the agent chooses a vector of signals about the payoffs of each asset to observe $\eta = f + e_\eta$, where $e_\eta \sim N(0, \Sigma_\eta)$. Investor i's posterior mean and variance $\hat{\mu}_i$ and $\widehat{\Sigma}_i$ incorporate all three pieces of information. As before, we assume that asset payoffs and signal noise are independent, so that Σ and Σ_η are diagonal.

Model setup. When an investor chooses his signal distribution, he does not know what his signal realization will be. Therefore, his posterior belief $\hat{\mu}_i$ is also uncertain. To compute unconditional expected utility, we need to take an expectation over $\hat{\mu}_i$ in (7.17). This is an expectation of an exponential of squared normal variables. Section 7.6 details the formula for computing such expectations and shows

---

[3] This section builds an equilibrium model, similar to Van Nieuwerburgh and Veldkamp 2009, but with preferences like those explored in Van Nieuwerburgh and Veldkamp 2010, and a different information constraint than either work.

that the expected value is

$$E[U] = - \left(|\Sigma|/|\widehat{\Sigma}|\right)^{-1/2} \exp\left(-\frac{1}{2} E[\hat{\mu}_i - pr]' \Sigma^{-1} E[\hat{\mu}_i - pr]\right). \quad (7.18)$$

The expectation operator E is unconditional. It is based only on the information in the investor's prior beliefs. This is all he knows at time 1, when he chooses what signals to acquire. The signal choice does not affect these unconditional expectations. Signal choices do not systematically affect $\hat{\mu}$ because investors do not expect signals to make them more or less positive about asset payoffs: $E_i[\hat{\mu}] = \mu_i$. Signal choices do not affect prices because the investor is one in a continuum of investors. Therefore, the investor chooses signals to maximize the first term, $-\left(|\Sigma|/|\widehat{\Sigma}|\right)^{-1/2}$.

There are two constraints governing how the investor can choose his signals. First is the *capacity constraint*. As in section 3.2, this constraint takes the form of a bound on the mutual information of priors and priors plus signals:

$$|\Sigma^{-1} + \Sigma_\eta^{-1}| \le e^{2K}|\Sigma^{-1}|. \quad (7.19)$$

Whereas before $\Sigma^{-1} + \Sigma_\eta^{-1}$ was the precision of posterior beliefs, that is no longer true because posterior beliefs also contain information inferred from prices.

Second is the *no-forgetting constraint*:

$$\Sigma_\eta \quad \text{positive semi-definite.} \quad (7.20)$$

Without this constraint, the investor could choose to forget what he knows about one variable in order to obtain a more precise signal about another.

Simplifying assumption: independent assets, independent signals. Suppose that Σ is diagonal and Σ_η is diagonal, then their inverses are diagonal and the sum and product of these inverses are diagonal as well. Therefore, $\widehat{\Sigma}$ will also be diagonal. To solve the model with correlated assets, simply use the variance decomposition tools from section 3.8. See section 7.7 for more details.

7.3.1 Gains to Specialization

To solve for the optimal learning strategy, the first step is to show that the objective is convex. This convexity represents the increasing returns that create gains to specialization.

In a multivariate optimization problem like this one, a second derivative of the objective function does not determine whether the problem is convex or not. To be convex in each choice variable, the problem must have a positive bordered Hessian.[4] This Hessian is a pain to compute. The simplest way to establish convexity is to write the problem so that utility is additively separable in the choice variables and the constraint is a simple sum constraint. If a problem has these features and has a utility function with a positive second derivative in each of its choice variables, it is a convex problem and therefore has a corner solution.

---

[4] For a discussion of bordered Hessians and the second-order necessary and sufficient conditions for an interior optimum, see Chiang 1984, p 381.

To put the problem in this form, take the log of the objective and the log of both sides of the constraint. Let $\Sigma(j)$ denote the jth diagonal entry of any matrix Σ. Then do a change of variable. Let $x_j = \ln(\Sigma^{-1}(j) + \Sigma_\eta^{-1}(j))$, so that $\Sigma_\eta^{-1}(j) = \exp(x_j) - \Sigma^{-1}(j)$. The problem becomes

$$\max_{\{x_j\}_{j=1}^N} \sum_{j=1}^N \ln(\Sigma_p^{-1}(j) + \exp(x_j)) \quad s.t. \sum_{j=1}^N x_j < 2K - \ln(|\Sigma|) \quad \text{and}$$

$$x_j \geq \ln(\Sigma^{-1}(j)) \; \forall j.$$

The second derivative of the objective in x_j is $\left(\Sigma_p^{-1}(j)\exp(x_j)\right)/(\Sigma_p^{-1}(j) + \exp(x_j))^2$, which is always positive, for every asset j.

This establishes that investors will use all their capacity to learn about one asset. If they learn exclusively about asset j, the precision of that signal can be determined by setting $\Sigma_\eta^{-1}(j') = 0$ for all $j' \neq j$ in (7.19). The resulting signal precision is $\Sigma_\eta^{-1}(j) = \Sigma^{-1}(j)(e^{2K} - 1)$.

7.3.2 Identical Investors Hold Different Portfolios

The next step in solving the model is to determine which asset each investor learns about. Suppose an investor learns about asset j; his expected utility would be proportional to

$$U_1 \propto \prod_{j'=1}^N (\Sigma^{-1}(j') + \Sigma_p^{-1}(j')) \frac{\Sigma^{-1}(j)e^{2K} + \Sigma_p^{-1}(j)}{\Sigma^{-1}(j) + \Sigma_p^{-1}(j)}.$$

Since the product term is common to all assets, the greatest expected utility comes from learning about the asset with the highest *learning index*, defined as

$$\mathcal{L}_j = (\Sigma^{-1}(j)e^{2K} + \Sigma_p^{-1}(j))/(\Sigma^{-1}(j) + \Sigma_p^{-1}(j)). \tag{7.21}$$

The learning index has two important features. First, it is decreasing in $\Sigma_p^{-1}(j)$. Combining (7.15) and the solution for Σ_p reveals that $\Sigma_p^{-1} = \sigma_x^{-2}\widehat{\Sigma}_a^{-1}\widehat{\Sigma}_a^{-1}$. Since $\widehat{\Sigma}_a^{-1}$ is the average of agents' information precision, the precision of the information contained in prices is increasing in the precision of the average investors' posterior beliefs. Thus, when many investors learn about asset j, $\widehat{\Sigma}_a(j)$ and $\Sigma_p^{-1}(j)$ rise, and the learning index $\mathcal{L}_j$ falls. *This is strategic substitutability in information choice.*

Second, the learning index is increasing in $\Sigma^{-1}(j)$. Thus, investors prefer to learn about assets they initially know more about. If investors initially have heterogeneous beliefs with different values of $\Sigma^{-1}(j)$, then the investors who have more precise initial information about asset j would be more likely to learn about it. This effect forms the basis of a theory of home bias shown in work by Van Nieuwerburgh and Veldkamp (2009).

Equilibrium information allocation. At the time when they choose what information to acquire, all investors are identical. Therefore, if they learn about different assets, they must be indifferent between each asset that anyone is learning about. Otherwise, someone could improve his utility by changing his information choice.

Therefore, we can describe the equilibrium information allocation as an identical mixed strategy that each investor adopts. Each strategy involves devoting all capacity to one asset j: $\Sigma_\eta^{-1}(j) = \Sigma^{-1}(j)(e^{2K} - 1)$, with a probability $\pi(j)$. This strategy pins down an average level of signal precision $(\Sigma_\eta^a)^{-1}$, which, in turn, determines Σ_p and a set of learning indices $\mathcal{L}$. Optimality requires that if $\pi(j), \pi(k) > 0$, then $\mathcal{L}_j = \mathcal{L}_k$.

Portfolio allocation. What does this result mean for portfolio allocation? Conditional on each investor's information, the investor's portfolio is the one prescribed by Admati's model (7.13). This portfolio can be decomposed into the diversified benchmark portfolio that an investor with no capacity would hold, $q^{div} = \frac{1}{\rho}\Sigma^{-1}(\mu - pr)$, and the number of extra shares of asset j that will be held due to learning, q^{learn}. q^{learn} is random because it depends on the realization of the investor's signal. In expectation, it is

$$E[q^{learn}] = \frac{e^{2K} - 1}{\rho \Sigma_j}(\mu_j - p_j r), \tag{7.22}$$

where j is the asset the investor optimally learns about. Thus, when ex ante identical investors learn about different assets (j differs), they hold different portfolios.

This is a useful result because standard investment theory is challenged by the low degree of diversification in observed portfolios. An equilibrium model where investors all hold the same assets must be one where all investors hold the market portfolio. Otherwise, the asset market cannot clear. Thus, the under-diversification puzzle stated differently is about why seemingly similar investors hold such different portfolios from one another. A joint learning-investment model can rationalize these differences.

7.4 INTERPRETING INFORMATION CONSTRAINTS
IN EQUILIBRIUM

In an equilibrium model, prices are an additional source of information. This raises the question of how such information should be incorporated in the information constraints. Minor differences in model interpretation can drastically change the results. In this section, we consider alternative forms of the information constraints and the optimal learning strategies and portfolios that they deliver.

The model in the previous section excluded the information in prices from both the no-forgetting constraint and the capacity constraint. The no-forgetting constraint requires the signal variance-covariance matrix Σ_η to be positive semidefinite. The capacity constraint (7.19) bounds the distance between priors and priors plus private signals. The interpretation is that investors do not use up any capacity learning from prices. They still learn from prices ($\hat{\mu}$ and $\widehat{\Sigma}$ still include price information). But the feasible signal set for any investor does not depend on how much information prices contain. In other words, the set of matrices Σ_η that satisfy the capacity constraint (7.19) does not depend on Σ_p. This formulation avoids externalities that arise when one investor's ability to acquire signals depends on market prices, which in turn depend on what others have learned.

Another formulation that leaves each investor's feasible information set indepen-dent of others' information choices is one that bounds the distance between priors Σ and posteriors $\widehat{\Sigma}$. It effectively charges investors capacity in order to process the information contained in the equilibrium prices. But adopting the analogous no-forgetting constraint in the equilibrium model ($\widehat{\Sigma}^{-1}(j) \geq \Sigma^{-1}(j), \forall j$) does not prevent investors from forgetting information in prices. It only prevents them from forgetting information in their prior beliefs. Investors must observe asset prices in order to satisfy their budget constraint. But they do not necessarily use that information to infer each asset's payoff. Some might consider such an agent irrational. But it is not inconceivable that investors might see a price and yet not take the time to figure out what information that price contains. Such a constraint could be interpreted as a constraint on the ability to draw logical inferences from observed information.

An alternative no-forgetting constraint prohibits investors from forgetting or ignoring information from their priors or from prices: $\widehat{\Sigma}^{-1}(j) \geq \Sigma^{-1}(j) + \Sigma_p^{-1}(j)$, $\forall j$. In this formulation, other investors' information choices change what signals are feasible to acquire. Suppose other investors could increase their capacity K. This would make prices more informative. If the capacity constraint charges investors for information learned from prices, then more informative prices leave less residual capacity available to allocate to signals. The idea that when others have more capacity an investor is able to learn less is not intuitive.

Another alternative capacity constraint is one that treats information in prices like prior information: $|\widehat{\Sigma}^{-1}| \leq e^{2K}|\Sigma^{-1} + \Sigma_p^{-1}|$. The problem with this formula-tion is that it creates complementarity. If there are gains to specialization, then in-vestors want to learn more about assets they already have more precise information about. If many investors learn about asset j, then the price of asset j reveals lots of information to other investors about the payoff f_j. More precise information about f_j makes those other investors also want to learn about asset j. Mondria (2010) shows that this set of assumptions generates multiple equilibria. Specifically, there is always an equilibrium where prices are perfectly revealing ($\Sigma_p^{-1} = \infty$), which allows investors' posterior beliefs to be infinitely precise ($\widehat{\Sigma}^{-1} = \infty$).

An indifference result. All three of these alternative formulations deliver a sur-prising result: investors are indifferent between any allocation of capacity. Since the exponential term in (7.18) comprises only variables the investor takes as given and is positive, then maximizing this objective is equivalent to maximizing $-\left(|\Sigma|/|\widehat{\Sigma}|\right)^{-1/2}$. Since Σ is exogenous, this is equivalent to maximizing $|\widehat{\Sigma}|$. But if the capacity constraint bounds $|\widehat{\Sigma}|$, then every information allocation that exhausts capacity delivers equal expected utility. In other words, the agent prefers more capacity to less but is indifferent about how to allocate that capacity.

Result. *Given a capacity constraint of the form $|\widehat{\Sigma}| \geq K$, an investor with CARA utility $E[-\exp(-\rho W)]$ is indifferent between any allocation of his capacity.*

This result is useful because one could use it to argue that almost any portfolio is the result of some rational information choice. On the other hand, this is not an easily testable theory because its prediction is so vague. Note that the model in section 7.3 does not produce indifference because its capacity constraint (7.19) does not bound $\hat{\Sigma}$. Rather, it bounds $\Sigma^{-1} + \Sigma_\eta^{-1}$.

The reason indifference arises has more to do with the utility costs and benefits of returns to scale in information than it does with the strategic substitutability in information choice. Therefore, I postpone the discussion of indifference until the next chapter. Just be aware that many of the alternative ways of formulating the capacity constraint leave the investor indifferent about what to learn about, even in an equilibrium model.

7.5 BROADER THEMES AND PATHS FOR FUTURE RESEARCH

Much research has already built on the ideas and models in this chapter. This section begins by describing some of what has already been done and then describes possibilities for future research.

Work building on Grossman and Stiglitz 1980. Verrecchia (1982) and Hellwig (1980) extend this type of model, for example, to allow agents to choose the precision of their signal. The more recent related work is by Peress, who uses information costs to explain limited stock market participation (2004) and looks at the tradeoff between risk-sharing and information production (2010). Garcia and Vanden (2005) and Kacperczyk, Van Nieuwerburgh, and Veldkamp (2010) use information acquisition to formulate a theory about the role of mutual funds.

There are a few works that overturn the strategic substitutability in information acquisition result. For example, Barlevy and Veronesi (2000) and Breon-Drish (2011) use a non-normal distribution of shocks. This causes prices to be a very flat function of average beliefs in some regions and steeper in others. If more agents learning results in a flatter price function, then price becomes less informative. If prices reveal less information, then acquiring private information can become more valuable. Another mechanism is used by Li and Yang (2008). They consider a richer model where speculators have little prior information but can acquire additional information and well-informed entrepreneurs can choose between investing in financial assets and in real assets. In this setting, when speculators acquire more information, they drive entrepreneurs out of the financial market and make the price level less informative.

Another related literature, pioneered by Wang (1993), works out the equilibrium asset prices in a setting with long-lived assets. Agents in these models have heterogeneous information. Solving for information choice in this setting is an open area for research.

The literature on market microstructure differs from the work covered in this book because it is typically not using models where a competitive market determines equilibrium asset prices. Rather, there is a market-maker who intermediates trade (e.g., Kyle 1985) and much more focus on price dynamics. What the literature on microstructure has in common is that much of it focuses on information frictions. (For a review of related market microstructure work, see O'Hara 1995 or Brunnermeier 2001). One feature that this chapter's framework cannot handle is the presence of large investors whose trades have price impact. Using the Kyle framework (1985), Bernhardt and Taub (2005) work out a multi-asset model with large, strategic investors.

Application: home bias. In settings with strategic substitutability in actions, agents want to have different information sets. This motive can lead them to amplify small initial differences in beliefs. If each investor initially has more information about his home-country assets, and investors want to make their information sets as different as possible from those of other investors, they learn more about the assets they have an initial information advantage in. Learning more about an asset reduces the risk of that asset and makes it more desirable to hold. (Risk-adjusted returns rise.) Van Nieuwerburgh and Veldkamp (2009) build a model with this logic to explain why investors seem to over-weight their home-country assets in their equity portfolios, a phenomenon known as the home bias.

Applications in continuous time. Huang and Liu (2007) use a continuous-time, information-choice model with one risky asset and one investor to examine the interaction between information acquisition and the quantity of the risky asset held or traded. Although the authors call their learning technology "rational inattention," it is a periodic updating process, more similar to what we have called inattentiveness.

Abel, Eberly, and Panageas (2007) use a continuous-time model where there are costs to information updating and adjusting the stock of risky assets (like a brokerage fee). Borrowing tools from the literature on costly capital adjustment, they characterize the optimal portfolio adjustment rule and show that small information costs can generate substantial portfolio inertia.

Application: pricing assets. In an equilibrium model, when the average investor learns more about an asset, its risk and expected return fall. Since information acquisition systematically changes assets' expected returns, a model that does not account for information choice should have systematic pricing errors. Van Nieuwerburgh and Veldkamp (2009) argue that this theory can help explain prediction errors of the capital asset pricing model (CAPM).

In both a heterogeneous information model and a standard CAPM, an asset's expected return is proportional to its beta and to the market return. But the betas in the two models differ. The CAPM beta is the coefficient of a least-squares estimate of $R_{it} - r = \alpha + \beta^i_{CAPM}(R_{mt} - r)$; it measures the *unconditional* relationship between asset i's returns and market returns. The learning model generates a beta that is *conditional* on information the average investor knows.

According to Admati (1985), asset prices and returns are identical to an economy where a representative investor believes that payoffs are distributed $N(E_a[f], \widehat{\Sigma}_a)$; $E_a[f]$ is the average expectation and $\widehat{\Sigma}_a$ is the harmonic average covariance of our heterogeneously informed investors. Moments conditional on these average beliefs are denoted with an a subscript.

Result. *If the market payoff is defined as $f_m = \sum_{k=1}^{N}(\bar{x} + x_k)f_k$, the market return is $R_m = f_m \left(\sum_{k=1}^{N}(\bar{x} + x_k)p_k \right)^{-1}$, and the return on an asset i is $R_i = f_i/p_i$, then the equilibrium price of asset i can be expressed as $p_i = \frac{1}{r}(E_a[f_i] - \rho \, Cov_a[f_i, f_m])$. The equilibrium return is $E_a[R_i] - r = \beta_a^i(E_a[R_m] - r)$, where $\beta_a^i \equiv Cov_a[R_i, R_m]/Var_a[R_m]$.*

Assets the average investor learns more about should have lower betas, and therefore lower returns, than what the CAPM predicts. To see why, note that $\beta_{CAPM} = Corr[R_i, R_m] \; Std(R_i)/Std(R_m)$ and $\beta_a = Corr[R_i, R_m]Std_a(R_i)/Std_a(R_m)$. The correlation terms are the same because learning does not change the correlation structure; it reduces the standard deviation. If the average investor learned as much about asset i as about all other assets in the market, then the ratio of standard deviations would be the same, with or without learning. But if the average investor learned more about asset i, then $Std_a(R_i)/Std_a(R_m)$ would fall. For these assets, $\beta_a^i < \beta_{CAPM}^i$.

Future directions: the industrial organization of the financial industry. One way to interpret the theories about information acquisition in financial markets is that they model portfolio managers (intermediaries) who are deciding what to learn about. But that raises a question: Should individual investors diversify their portfolios by investing a little bit with many specialized portfolio managers? The reason why investors should concentrate their portfolios with one portfolio manager may have to do with efficient pricing of investment services. If a manager were to sell information, information resale would undermine profits. To avoid resale, intermediaries typically manage investors' portfolios. In a competitive equilibrium, fund managers offer quantity discounts to induce more investment in their fund (Admati and Pfleiderer 1990). Quantity discounts make investing in many funds costly. If competitive pricing of portfolio management services induced investors to invest with few funds, optimal under-diversification would reappear.

One place to start with this line of research is with Admati and Pfleiderer (1986). They derive the optimal price and quantity strategy for a monopolist who sells information that only he can deliver. One distinction to keep in mind is that there is a difference between selling information directly (selling a newsletter) and indirectly (selling portfolio management services). Selling information directly places no limits on how many shares of an asset an investor can trade on with that information. Newsletters cannot be sold only to those who will trade a limited amount based on the information they contain. That is not legal or enforceable. Indirect information sale is priced per unit of asset under management. Portfolio managers can limit the size of their fund and thereby limit the number of shares being traded with any given piece of proprietary information. Admati and Pfleiderer (1990) explore this distinction and its implications for information sales.

7.6 APPENDIX: COMPUTING EXPECTED UTILITY

Wealth in a portfolio choice model is a product of the asset payoff and the quantity purchased of each asset. Typically, the payoff is a normally distributed variable.

When portfolio choices depend on information observed and that information is not known in advance, the quantity invested is also a random variable, typically also normally distributed. Thus, wealth is a quadratic function of normal variables (also called a Wishart variable). To compute expected exponential (CARA) utility, we need to take an expectation of the exponential of this quadratic normal form.

The general formula for the mean of the exponential of a multivariate quadratic form of a normal variable is the following: If $z \sim N(0, \Sigma)$,

$$E[e^{z'Fz+G'z+H}] = |I - 2\Sigma F|^{-1/2} \exp\left[\frac{1}{2}G'(I - 2\Sigma F)^{-1}\Sigma G + H\right]. \quad (7.23)$$

One risky asset: the Grossman-Stiglitz case. The $\theta - pr$ term in the informed investor's expected utility is a random variable, conditional on the information in price p. Its mean is $\hat{\mu} - pr$ and its variance is $var[\theta|p] = \sigma_{\theta|p}^2$. Expected utility (7.7) is an expected exponential of a quadratic normal. To use the formula (7.23), the random variable must have zero mean. The mean-zero random variable is $\theta - \hat{\mu}$. Rewriting (7.7) as a quadratic form of $\theta - \hat{\mu}$ results in coefficients

$$F = -\frac{1}{2}\sigma_e^{-2}$$

$$G' = -(\hat{\mu} - pr)\sigma_e^{-2}$$

$$H = -\frac{1}{2}(\hat{\mu} - pr)^2\sigma_e^{-2}$$

$$\Sigma = \sigma_{\theta|p}^2.$$

Applying the formula yields:

$$E[U^I|p] = -|I - 2\sigma_{\theta|p}^2\left(-\frac{1}{2}\right)\sigma_e^{-2}|^{-1/2} \exp\left[\frac{1}{2}(\hat{\mu} - pr)^2\sigma_e^{-4}(I + \sigma_{\theta|p}^2\sigma_e^{-2})^{-1}\right.$$

$$\left. \times \sigma_{\theta|p}^2 - \frac{1}{2}(\hat{\mu} - pr)^2\sigma_e^{-2}\right].$$

Note that if we multiply numerator and denominator by σ_e^2, $(I + 2\sigma_{\theta|p}^2(\frac{1}{2})\sigma_e^{-2})^{-1} = \frac{\sigma_e^2}{\sigma_e^2 + \sigma_{\theta|p}^2}$.

$$E[U^I|p] = -\left(\frac{\sigma_e^2}{\sigma_e^2 + \sigma_{\theta|p}^2}\right)^{1/2} \exp\left[\frac{1}{2}(\hat{\mu} - pr)^2\sigma_e^{-2}\left(\sigma_e^{-2}\frac{\sigma_e^2}{\sigma_e^2 + \sigma_{\theta|p}^2}\sigma_{\theta|p}^2 - 1\right)\right]$$

Canceling $\sigma_e^2\sigma_e^{-2}$ yields

$$E[U^I|p] = -\left(\frac{\sigma_e^2}{\sigma_e^2 + \sigma_{\theta|p}^2}\right)^{1/2} \exp\left[\frac{1}{2}(\hat{\mu} - pr)^2\sigma_e^{-2}\left(\frac{\sigma_{\theta|p}^2}{\sigma_e^2 + \sigma_{\theta|p}^2} - \frac{\sigma_e^2 + \sigma_{\theta|p}^2}{\sigma_e^2 + \sigma_{\theta|p}^2}\right)\right].$$

Collecting terms in the numerator and noticing that $\sigma_{\theta|p}^2 - \sigma_{\theta|p}^2 = 0$,

$$E[U^I|p] = -\left(\frac{\sigma_e^2}{\sigma_e^2 + \sigma_{\theta|p}^2}\right)^{1/2} \exp\left[\frac{1}{2}(\hat{\mu} - pr)^2\sigma_e^{-2}\left(\frac{-\sigma_e^2}{\sigma_e^2 + \sigma_{\theta|p}^2}\right)\right].$$

Since $\sigma_e^{-2}(-\sigma_e^2) = -1$,

$$E[U^I|p] = -\left(\frac{\sigma_e^2}{\sigma_e^2 + \sigma_{\theta|p}^2}\right)^{1/2} \exp\left[-\frac{1}{2}\frac{(\hat{\mu} - pr)^2}{\sigma_e^2 + \sigma_{\theta|p}^2}\right].$$

Multiple risky assets in partial equilibrium. We start with a model where an investor takes the asset price p as given. Only asset payoffs and signals are random.

The unconditional expectation of CARA utility, after substituting in the budget constraint $W = rW_0 + q'(f - pr)$, is

$$E[U] = -E[\exp(-\rho(rW_0 + q'(f - pr)))].$$

Since r and W_0 are not choice variables and are multiplicative constants, we can drop these without changing the optimization problem. Substituting in the optimal portfolio in (7.13) and canceling out ρ in the denominator and numerator yields

$$E[U] = -E[\exp(-(\hat{\mu} - pr)'\widehat{\Sigma}^{-1}(f - pr))].$$

Using the law of iterated expectations, we take expectations in two steps. First, we compute an expectation over f, conditional on all signals. Payoffs f have a mean of $\hat{\mu}$ and a variance of $\widehat{\Sigma}$. Using the formula for the mean of a log-normal variable to compute the expectation over f yields

$$E[U] = -E\left[\exp\left(-\frac{1}{2}(\hat{\mu} - pr)\widehat{\Sigma}^{-1}(\hat{\mu} - pr)\right)\right].$$

The second expectation is taken over the unknown posterior belief $\hat{\mu}$. $\hat{\mu}$ has mean μ and variance $\Sigma - \widehat{\Sigma}$. However, this is not a log-normal variable anymore because $\hat{\mu}$ enters as a square. This is a Wishart variable. To compute its expectation, it is useful to rewrite the objective function in terms of the mean-zero variable $\hat{\mu} - \mu$:

$$E[U] = -E\left[\exp\left\{-\frac{1}{2}[(\hat{\mu} - \mu)'\widehat{\Sigma}^{-1}(\hat{\mu} - \mu) + 2(\mu - pr)'\widehat{\Sigma}^{-1}(\hat{\mu} - \mu)\right.\right.$$
$$\left.\left. + (\mu - pr)'\widehat{\Sigma}^{-1}(\mu - pr)]\right\}\right].$$

Applying the formula for the expected exponential of a Wishart (7.23) yields

$$E[U] = -|I - 2(\Sigma - \widehat{\Sigma})\left(-\frac{1}{2}\widehat{\Sigma}^{-1}\right)|^{-1/2}$$

$$\times \exp\left\{\frac{1}{2}(\mu - pr)'\widehat{\Sigma}^{-1}\left(I - 2(\Sigma - \widehat{\Sigma})\left(-\frac{1}{2}\widehat{\Sigma}^{-1}\right)\right)^{-1}\right.$$

$$\left. \times (\Sigma - \widehat{\Sigma})\widehat{\Sigma}^{-1}(\mu - pr) - \frac{1}{2}(\mu - pr)'\widehat{\Sigma}^{-1}(\mu - pr)\right\}$$

$$= -|I + (\Sigma\widehat{\Sigma}^{-1} - I)|^{-1/2}$$

$$\times \exp\left\{\frac{1}{2}(\mu - pr)'\widehat{\Sigma}^{-1}((I + (\Sigma\widehat{\Sigma}^{-1} - I))^{-1}(\Sigma\widehat{\Sigma}^{-1} - I) - I)(\mu - pr)\right\}.$$

After combining terms, expected utility simplifies to equation (7.18).

Multiple risky assets in general equilibrium. In the general equilibrium model, equilibrium asset prices are not known at time 1 and are correlated with $\hat{\mu}$ because both are related to the true asset payoffs f. Writing posterior beliefs as a function of prior beliefs and the signal $\eta = f + e$, where e is signal error, and replacing pr with $A + f + Cx$ from equation (7.15), we get $\hat{\mu} - pr = \widehat{\Sigma}(\Sigma^{-1}\mu + \Sigma_\eta^{-1}(f + e)) - A - f - Cx$. This has mean $-A$ and prior variance $(\widehat{\Sigma}\Sigma_\eta^{-1} - I)\Sigma + CC'\sigma_x^2$. Substituting this mean and variance and following the steps above deliver expected utility.

Expected mean-variance utility. Another common form of utility is expected mean-variance:

$$U_1 = E_1\left[\rho E_2[W] - \frac{\rho^2}{2}V_2[W]\right]. \tag{7.24}$$

The optimal portfolio is identical to that with exponential (CARA) utility. After substituting in the budget constraint and the optimal portfolio, the time-1 objective function becomes

$$E[U] = \rho W_0 r + \frac{1}{2}E_1[(\hat{\mu} - pr)'\widehat{\Sigma}^{-1}(\hat{\mu} - pr)], \tag{7.25}$$

where E_1 now refers to an unconditional expectation (conditioning only on prior information) and E_2 is an expectation conditional on all information known at the time when the asset portfolio is chosen.

The second term is the mean of a non-central chi-square. The general formula for the mean of a non-central chi-square is: if $z \sim N(E[z], Var[z])$, then

$$E[z'z] = trace(Var[z]) + E[z]'E[z]. \tag{7.26}$$

To apply this formula, define $z \equiv \widehat{\Sigma}^{-1/2}(\hat{\mu} - pr)$.

In partial equilibrium, $E_1[z] = \widehat{\Sigma}^{-1/2}(\mu - pr)$ and $V_1[z] = \widehat{\Sigma}^{-1}(\Sigma - \widehat{\Sigma}) = \widehat{\Sigma}^{-1}\Sigma - I$. Substituting this mean and variance into (7.26) and multiplying by one-half yields $U_1 = \rho W_0 r + \frac{1}{2}Tr(\widehat{\Sigma}^{-1}\Sigma - I) + \frac{1}{2}E[\hat{\mu} - pr]'\widehat{\Sigma}^{-1}E[\hat{\mu} - pr]$.

In general equilibrium, $E_1[z] = -\widehat{\Sigma}^{-1/2}A$ and $V_1[z] = (\Sigma_\eta^{-1} - \widehat{\Sigma}^{-1/2})\Sigma + CC'\sigma_x^2$, as in the previous section.

7.7 APPENDIX: CORRELATED ASSETS

Let $\Sigma = \Gamma\Lambda\Gamma'$. We restrict the agent to choose signals with the same risk factor structure, which implies that the signal and the posterior belief have the same eigenvectors. Therefore, we can write the posterior belief as $\widehat{\Sigma} = \Gamma\widehat{\Lambda}\Gamma'$. The objective, after substituting in the optimal portfolio choice, is

$$\max_{\widehat{\Sigma}_i} E\left[(\hat{\mu}_i - pr)'\widehat{\Sigma}_i^{-1}(\hat{\mu}_i - pr)\right]$$

$$\max_{\widehat{\Lambda}_i} E\left[(\hat{\mu}_i - pr)'\Gamma\widehat{\Lambda}_i^{-1}\Gamma'(\hat{\mu}_i - pr)\right].$$

Realize that $\Gamma'(\hat{\mu}_i - pr)$ is an $n \times 1$ vector, $\hat{\Lambda} - i^{-1}$ is a diagonal matrix, and the whole expression is a scalar. Therefore, we can rewrite the scalar as a sum over all risk factors j:

$$\max_{\hat{\Lambda}_i(j,j)_{j=1}^n} \sum_j \frac{E\left[(\Gamma_j'(\hat{\mu}_i - pr))^2\right]}{\hat{\Lambda}_i(j,j)}, \tag{7.27}$$

where Γ_j is the jth column of the $n \times n$ matrix Γ and $\hat{\Lambda}_i(j, j)$ is the jth diagonal entry of agent i's posterior eigenvalue matrix. This is what we will use as an objective function when deciding what to learn.

Our learning constraint bounds the determinant $|\widehat{\Sigma}^{-1}|$. Since the determinant of a positive semi-definite matrix is the product of its eigenvalues, we can rewrite the constraint as $\prod_j \hat{\Lambda}(j, j)^{-1} \leq Kc$, for a constant c.

7.8 EXERCISES

1. In the Grossman and Stiglitz (1980) model, let μ, σ^2 be the prior mean and variance of the payoff and $\hat{\mu}, \hat{\sigma}^2$ be the posterior mean and variance of the payoff of an *informed* investor. What is $V[\hat{\mu}]$, the variance, conditional on prior information, of the posterior belief? In other words, how uncertain is an investor about what he will believe after he observes his signal θ?

2. In the multiple risky asset model with information choice, what are the mean and variance of the payoff from the optimal risky asset portfolio at time 2: $E_2[q'(f - pr)]$ and $V_2[q'(f - pr)]$?

3. In the multiple risky asset model with information choice, what are the mean and variance of the payoff from the optimal risky asset portfolio at time 1: $E_1[q'(f - pr)]$ and $V_1[q'(f - pr)]$?

4. Show that if agents have common prior beliefs, in the model of section 7.2, that prices still take the form $pr = A + Bf + Cx$, but that $B \neq I$.

5. In the model of section 7.2., each agent has a prior belief vector μ_i that is conditionally independent, meaning that $\mu_i - f$ is independent across agents. What if instead there is a common prior belief $f \sim \mathcal{N}(\mu, \sum)$ and conditionally independent, heterogenous signals $s_i | f \sim \mathcal{N}(f, \Phi_i)$? Derive the expression for the equilibrium price. How is it different from the one in the text?

6. Information choice with a mean-variance objective: Solve the model where utility is given by $-E_1\{\ln[F_2(\exp(-\rho W))]\}$. Assume that asset payoffs and signals are independent across assets.

(a) Start with equation (7.17) and take its natural log. The expectation of this will be the investor's objective when he chooses information.

(b) Using the last section of section 7.7, take the time-1 expectation of this objective function. The unknown variables are the posterior belief $\widehat{\mu}$ and prices p. Note that while the formula for a chi-square in section 7.7 is correct, it treats p as if it were a known variable. You need to substitute in the expression for p (7.14, 7.15) before you take the expectation.

(c) If you maximize this objective subject to a constraint on the determinant of the posterior beliefs $\widehat{\sum}$ and the no-forgetting constraint (7.20), do you get an interior solution or a corner solution?

(d) Describe the optimal attention allocation.

Chapter Eight

Returns to Scale in Information

The last few chapters have explored equilibrium models where the strategic motives in actions created the same strategic motives in information acquisition. When firms want to set prices similar to those of their competitors, they also want to acquire more information whenever their competitors acquire more. When investors prefer to buy assets that others do not demand, they want to make their information sets as different as possible from those of other investors. This chapter departs from that theme. In fact, the end of the chapter shows how returns to scale can create complementarity in information choice, even when actions exhibit substitutability.

The key idea this chapter explores is returns to scale in information. This refers to the idea that when an economy is scaled up, meaning that all its inputs or endowments are multiplied, the value of information rises. For example, information has returns to scale in a portfolio problem because it can be used to evaluate one share of an asset or many shares of an asset. When a decision maker has lots of an asset, information about the asset's payoff is more valuable.

Returns to scale makes the economics of information different from the economics of physical goods in a few important ways. First, it can create a desire for specialization in a problem where an investor can jointly choose how much information to acquire about a risky asset and how much of that risky asset to hold. Section 8.1 looks systematically at what kinds of investment and information choice problems generate increasing returns and thus corner solutions. When an investor can learn about more than one risky asset, increasing returns dictates that he should learn about a single asset (or in the case of correlated assets, a single linear combination of asset payoffs). Thus the returns to scale in information can create gains to specialization. To illustrate this, section 8.2 revisits the n-asset information and investment choice problem from the last chapter, this time in partial equilibrium. It shows that even with no strategic motives present, the investor wants to specialize by learning about one asset payoff when asset payoffs are independent.

A second form of returns to scale in information is the idea that information is expensive to discover but cheap to replicate. In an equilibrium model, this property can create complementarity in information acquisition. If the first copy of a piece of information is much more expensive than the hundredth, there is an incentive to buy information that others are buying because it is less expensive. Section 8.3 shows that when agents acquire the information that others acquire, it leads them to take similar actions. Such mimicking behavior resembles outcomes from coordination games. Yet, it arises even when there are no coordination motives in the underlying actions. Thus, returns to scale allows a model with information acquisition to produce outcomes that models with only goods production may have a hard time explaining.

Information is fundamentally different from physical goods because of its nonrival nature. It has a big fixed cost of discovery and it is cheap to replicate. This insight revitalized growth theory in the 1980s and 1990s (e.g., Romer 1990) because models with production of ideas had quite different properties from models with only goods production. The same insight can be used in models where information is acquired and produced.

8.1 RETURNS TO SCALE IN REAL INVESTMENT (ONE ASSET)

Wilson (1975) looks at a generic investment problem with a quadratic technology and shows how it can generate increasing returns to information. This is a one-agent problem; there are no strategic interactions. Rather, it uses the tools of quadratic-normal models to show how introducing information acquisition can make it impossible to construct standard competitive equilibria.

Preferences are mean-variance. Mean-variance preferences come from exponential preferences with normally distributed random variables. For example, if y is normally distributed and ρ is a parameter, $-E[\exp(-\rho y)] = -\exp(-\rho E[y] + \rho^2/2 V[y])$. Note that maximizing this objective means minimizing $E[\exp(-\rho y)]$. Furthermore, since the exponential transformation is a monotonically increasing function, minimizing the exponential of the argument is the same as minimizing the argument itself. Therefore, many settings maximize an objective that takes the form

$$U(y) = E[y] - \rho/2 \, V[y].\tag{8.1}$$

In this problem, y is output and ρ is risk aversion.

Output is produced with productivity A and an input, which we will call capital k. If not used for risky production, capital can be used in a risk-free investment at a rate of return r:

$$y = Ak - rk\tag{8.2}$$

Productivity depends on the choice of a technique α and how close that technique is to the unknown optimal one, θ:

$$A = a[1 - (\alpha - \theta)^2].\tag{8.3}$$

Agents can acquire information about θ. They are endowed with prior beliefs $\theta \sim N(\mu, \phi^{-1})$. They choose how many signals to acquire at a cost of c per signal. Those signals have distribution $s \sim N(\theta, \phi_s^{-1})$. Therefore, the posterior of an agent who observes n signals $s_1, \ldots s_n$ has mean and precision

$$\hat{\mu} = \frac{\phi\mu + \phi_s \sum_{j=1}^n s_j}{\phi + n\phi_s}\tag{8.4}$$

$$\hat{\phi} = \phi + n\phi_s.\tag{8.5}$$

Equilibrium is an α, k, and n that maximize $U(y) - nc$.

Solving the model. Start by computing the mean and variance of output for an agent who observes n signals. Then we can figure out how many signals he wants to acquire:

$$E[y] = ak[1 - E[(\alpha - \theta)^2]] - rk$$

To compute this expectation, we need to know the optimal α. The first-order condition with respect to α is $2ak(\alpha - E[\theta]) = 0$.[1] The solution is $\alpha = E[\theta]$. Therefore, the expectation term inside (8.1) is $E[(E[\theta] - \theta)^2] = Var[\theta | s_1, \ldots, s_n] = \hat{\phi}^{-1}$. Therefore,

$$E[y] = ak[1 - \hat{\phi}^{-1}] - rk. \tag{8.6}$$

Next, we compute the variance of output:

$$Var[y] = a^2 k^2 E[(\alpha - \theta)^4 - E[(\alpha - \theta)^2]^2] - 0$$

$$Var[y] = a^2 k^2 E[(E[\theta] - \theta)^4 - (\hat{\phi}^{-1})^2].$$

The first term is the fourth central moment of a normal variable. This turns out to always be three times the square of the variance:

$$Var[y] = a^2 k^2 (3\hat{\phi}^{-2} - \hat{\phi}^{-2})$$
$$Var[y] = 2a^2 k^2 \hat{\phi}^{-2}. \tag{8.7}$$

Substituting in $E[y]$ and $V[y]$, expected utility is

$$U(y) = ak[1 - \hat{\phi}^{-1}] - rk - \frac{\rho}{2} 2a^2 k^2 \hat{\phi}^{-2}. \tag{8.8}$$

Note that if information is not sufficiently precise ($\hat{\phi}^{-1}$ is too large), then positive production is not optimal. Conditional on production being optimal, note that there are no increasing returns here in either production or information. The objective (8.8) is concave in both capital k and information precision $\hat{\phi}$.

The first-order condition for the optimal scale of output is

$$a[1 - \hat{\phi}^{-1}] - r - 2\rho a^2 k \hat{\phi}^{-2} = 0.$$

$$k = \hat{\phi}^2 \frac{a - r - a\hat{\phi}^{-1}}{2\rho a^2}$$

Substituting k back into the utility U yields

$$U = \frac{1}{4\rho a^2} \left(\hat{\phi}(a - r) - a \right)^2.$$

This can be written as a function of the number of signals acquired, n, by replacing $\hat{\phi}$ with $\phi + n\phi_s$. Then, $U(y(n), n) - cn$ is the period-1 objective. Because of its quadratic form in $\hat{\phi}$, the objective is convex in n. That means that there is not an interior solution for information acquisition. Either no information is acquired or an infinite amount is.

What is happening here is a feedback between production and information acquisition. Holding production fixed, information has concave returns. Likewise,

---

[1] Note that $\partial U/\partial \alpha = \partial E[y]/\partial \alpha$ because, as we will show, $V[y]$ does not depend on α.

holding information fixed, production has concave returns. But, the more the agent learns, the more he wants to produce and the more he produces, the more valuable information becomes. The result that more production makes information more valuable is the increasing returns to scale in information. The result that acquiring more information makes additional information more valuable illustrates the convexity in the value of information. Returns to scale is key to generating the convexity. This is just one of the models Wilson (1975) explores. The rest of his work documents a series of examples where increasing returns do or do not appear. They deliver great intuition for what kinds of model assumptions can generate corner solutions like the one just presented. The essence is that either risk aversion with an additive learning technology (the example here) or risk neutrality with an entropy-based learning technology can generate increasing returns.

Wilson's conclusion is that we should worry about setting up models that deliver increasing returns to scale because convex value functions do not lend themselves to competitive outcomes. Typically, with increasing returns, one firm produces everything. But if you can place bounds on actions, a maximum feasible scale of production, for example, a competitive equilibrium outcome may still exist. The fact that this outcome is not the standard outcome with physical goods is useful because it means that the model with information choice has the potential to explain features of the data that confound standard models.

8.2 GAINS TO SPECIALIZATION (N ASSETS)

In the previous section, there was only one risk to learn about. Because of increasing returns, the investor wanted to learn either nothing or an infinite amount about that risk. This section introduces multiple risks. The investor chooses which risk or risks to learn about. Increasing returns to scale makes the value of information convex: the more the investor learns about a risk, the higher the marginal value of additional information. Thus, if an investor starts learning about a particular risk, it will become more and more valuable to learn about. So, he will keep learning about it until his capacity is exhausted. In other words, increasing returns causes the investor to specialize.

Given that the results from this one-investor model are similar to those from the equilibrium model in the previous chapter (7.3), one might wonder what the value of working out the equilibrium was. In the one-investor model, an investor who learns about an asset holds more of the asset in what appears to be an under-diversified portfolio. In equilibrium, it is possible that every investor wants to specialize in the same asset. If that were the case, investors would all end up with equally precise information about every asset. They cannot all hold more of the asset they learn about in that case. The asset demand has to equal its supply. So, the question of whether information choice rationalizes under-diversified portfolios hinges crucially on whether investors decide to learn about the same risks in an equilibrium model.

Furthermore, the logic behind specialization is different in the two models. The single investor specializes because the more he holds of an asset, the more valuable that asset is to learn about. But the more the investor learns about an asset, the lower the asset's risk and the more attractive the asset. Investing and information acquisition are mutually reinforcing activities, which create increasing returns. An investor in the equilibrium model wants to make his information set as different as possible from the average investor's information set so that he can buy lower-price assets that others are not buying. Learning as much as possible about one asset is a way of differentiating his information set as much as possible.

This single-investor, partial-equilibrium model is designed to convey the intuition of gains to specialization. Lite Van Nieuwerburgh and Veldkamp (2009), we adopt the entropy measure of information used in the rational inattention literature. Investors have a fixed amount of learning capacity (they can reduce the entropy of their beliefs by a given amount) and they choose how precise a signal to observe about each of the payoffs of N risky assets before choosing how much of each asset to invest in.

Model setup. Consider an investor who can acquire information about an exogenous $N \times 1$ vector of unknown asset payoffs f. He is endowed with a prior belief $f \sim N(\mu, \Sigma)$. At time 1, the investor chooses the precision of his signals about f. In other words, he chooses the variance of a normal distribution from which he will draw an $N \times 1$ signal vector η about asset payoffs f. At time 2, the investor observes the signals and invests. Let $E_1[\cdot]$ and $V_1[\cdot]$ denote means and variances conditional on prior beliefs alone, and let $E_2[\cdot]$ and $V_2[\cdot]$ denote means and variances conditional on period-2 information from priors and signals. Likewise, let U_1 and U_2 denote expected utility, conditional on time-1 and time-2 information sets.

A time 1, the investor chooses the variance matrix Σ_η (precision) of a signal about asset payoffs in order to maximize expected mean-variance utility over wealth W with risk aversion ρ:

$$U_1 = E_1 \left[\rho E_2[W] - \frac{\rho^2}{2} V_2[W] \right]. \tag{8.9}$$

At time 2, the investor combines his signal $\eta | f \sim N(f, \Sigma_\eta)$ and his prior belief, using Bayes' law, to get $\hat{\mu}$ and $\widehat{\Sigma}$, the posterior mean and variance of asset payoffs:

$$\hat{\mu} \equiv E_2[f] = \left(\Sigma^{-1} + \Sigma_\eta^{-1}\right)^{-1} \left(\Sigma^{-1}\mu + \Sigma_\eta^{-1}\eta\right) \tag{8.10}$$

$$\widehat{\Sigma} \equiv V_2[f] = \left(\Sigma^{-1} + \Sigma_\eta^{-1}\right)^{-1}. \tag{8.11}$$

Then the investor chooses a vector of risky asset quantities to purchase q, to maximize $U_2 = \rho E_2[W] - \frac{\rho^2}{2} V_2[W]$. For now, take this utility as a primitive. We will explore its foundations later in this section. Since the investor forms his portfolio after observing his signals, $\hat{\mu}, \widehat{\Sigma}$ are the conditional mean and variance that govern the investor's portfolio choice.

Portfolio choice. Given his information set, the investor chooses the $N \times 1$ vector $q \equiv [q_1, \ldots, q_N]'$ of quantities of each asset that he chooses to hold. The investor takes as given the risk-free return r and the $N \times 1$ vector of asset prices

$p \equiv [p_1, \ldots, p_N]'$. In making that choice, he is subject to a budget constraint

$$W = W_0 r + q'(f - pr). \tag{8.12}$$

Simplifying assumption: independent assets, independent signals. Suppose that Σ is diagonal and Σ_η is diagonal. Then their inverses are diagonal and the sum and product of these inverses are diagonal as well. Therefore, $\widehat{\Sigma}$ will also be diagonal. To solve the model with correlated assets, simply use the variance decomposition tools from section 3.8.

Information allocation choice. Since every signal variance Σ_η has a unique posterior belief variance $\widehat{\Sigma}$ associated with it (see equation [8.11]), we can economize on notation and optimize over posterior belief variance $\widehat{\Sigma}$ directly. The prior covariance matrix Σ is not random; it is given. The posterior (conditional) covariance matrix $\widehat{\Sigma}$, which measures investors' uncertainty about asset payoffs, is also not random; it is the choice variable that summarizes the investor's optimal information decision. Learning makes the conditional variance $\widehat{\Sigma}$ (uncertainty) lower than the unconditional variance Σ.

The first constraint is the *capacity constraint*. It restricts the mutual information (the reduction in conditional entropy) of prior and posterior beliefs about asset payoffs. We can rewrite the constraint in (3.4) as

$$\frac{|\Sigma|}{|\widehat{\Sigma}|} \leq e^{2K}. \tag{8.13}$$

The amount of capacity K limits how much the signal η can reduce payoff uncertainty.

The second constraint is the *no-forgetting constraint*. The variance of each signal must be non-negative. Without this constraint, the investor could erase what he knows about one asset in order to obtain a more precise signal about another without violating the capacity constraint. Ruling out increasing uncertainty implies that investors cannot choose to forget information. Using (8.11) and the independence of assets and signals, this implies that posterior variance can never exceed prior variance:

$$\widehat{\Sigma}_{ii} \leq \Sigma_{ii} \quad \forall i. \tag{8.14}$$

8.2.1 Result: Optimal Portfolio Choice

At time 2 when the portfolio choice is made, utility is simply $\rho E_2[W] - \frac{\rho^2}{2} V_2[W]$. Substituting in the budget constraint, this is $\rho W_0 r + \rho q'(\hat{\mu} - pr) - \frac{\rho^2}{2} q' \widehat{\Sigma} q$. Taking the first-order condition, with respect to q, delivers

$$q = \frac{1}{\rho} \widehat{\Sigma}^{-1} (\hat{\mu} - pr). \tag{8.15}$$

This tells us that investors buy more of assets that have high expected payoffs $\hat{\mu}$ and assets whose payoffs they are less uncertain about (high $\widehat{\Sigma}^{-1}$).

Substituting q back into the utility function tells us what the investor's expected utility is for any given posterior beliefs $\hat{\mu}$ and $\widehat{\Sigma}$:

$$U_1 = \rho W_0 r + \frac{1}{2} E_1[(\hat{\mu} - pr)' \widehat{\Sigma}^{-1}(\hat{\mu} - pr)]. \tag{8.16}$$

At time 1, the posterior mean $\hat{\mu}$ is not known. It is normally distributed: $\hat{\mu} \sim N(\mu, \Sigma - \widehat{\Sigma})$. The expectation is therefore the expectation of the sum of independent, squared normal variables. In other words, $(\hat{\mu} - pr)' \widehat{\Sigma}^{-1}(\hat{\mu} - pr)$ has a multivariate (non-central) chi-squared distribution. Section 7.6 gives the general formula for the mean of such a variable and shows that expected utility is

$$U_1 = \rho W_0 r + \frac{1}{2} Tr(\widehat{\Sigma}^{-1}\Sigma - I) + \frac{1}{2}(\mu - pr)' \widehat{\Sigma}^{-1}(\mu - pr), \tag{8.17}$$

where $Tr(\cdot)$ stands for the trace of a matrix. Because the trace of a matrix is the sum of its diagonal elements and because $\widehat{\Sigma}^{-1}$ is diagonal, we can rewrite the objective as a sum. Let Σ_{ii} denote the (i, i)th entry of any diagonal matrix Σ and let f_i denote the ith entry of any vector f. Then,

$$U_1 = \rho W_0 r + \frac{1}{2} \left\{ -N + \sum_{i=1}^{N} \widehat{\Sigma}_{ii}^{-1} \Sigma_{ii}(1 + \theta_i^2) \right\}, \tag{8.18}$$

where $\theta_i^2 \equiv \Sigma_{ii}^{-1}(\mu_i - p_i r)^2$ is the squared return per unit of prior variance. Since a Sharpe ratio is defined as the return per unit of standard deviation, θ_i^2 is the prior *squared Sharpe ratio* of asset i.

8.2.2 Result: Optimal Information Choice

The investor chooses his information precision $\{\widehat{\Sigma}_{11}, \ldots, \widehat{\Sigma}_{NN}\}$ to maximize (8.18) subject to (8.13) and (8.14). The objective is a weighted sum of the posterior precisions $\widehat{\Sigma}_{ii}^{-1}$. The entropy-based capacity constraint (8.13) bounds the determinant $|\widehat{\Sigma}^{-1}|$. Since the determinant of a diagonal matrix is the product of its entries, we can rewrite the constraint as $\prod_j \widehat{\Sigma}(j, j)^{-1} \leq \hat{K}$, where $\hat{K} = e^{2K}|\Sigma|$. So, the problem simplifies to maximizing a weighted sum, subject to a product constraint and an inequality constraint.

A simple variational argument shows that maximizing a sum subject to a product constraint generates corner solutions: both 4 times 4 and 16 times 1 yield the same product, 16. But their sums are 8 and 17. We can make the sum of two numbers arbitrarily large and keep their product the same by multiplying a very large number by a very small one. For a weighted sum, the same logic holds, except that the sum is larger if the argument with the higher weight is maximized. But the corner solution always implies that the investors should use all capacity to learn about one asset.

The following result says that the optimal information acquisition strategy uses all capacity to learn about one asset, the asset with the highest squared Sharpe ratio.

Result. *(Gains to specialization): The optimal information allocation decision takes the following form:* $\widehat{\Sigma}_k = \Sigma_k$ *for all* $k \neq i$ *and* $\widehat{\Sigma}_i < \Sigma_i$ *for one asset* i, *where* $i = \arg\max_{\ell=1,\ldots,N} \{\theta_\ell^2\}$.

To prove the existence of a corner solution formally, one needs to show that the bordered Hessian of the Lagrangian is positive definite. (See Van Nieuwerburgh and Veldkamp 2010 for the proof.) In this model, replacing $\widehat{\Sigma}(j, j)^{-1}$ with $\exp(x_j)$ and then taking the log of both sides of the constraint results in an additively separable utility function, convex in each of its arguments, subject to a sum constraint. Thus, the problem satisfies the sufficient condition for a positive bordered Hessian and, therefore, a corner solution.

This result is the same as the one for the equilibrium model in the previous chapter, except that the learning index is different. Intuitively, why does this investor want to learn only about one asset? The interaction of the learning choice and the investment choice generates gains to specialization. When choosing information, investors can acquire noisy signals about future payoffs of many assets, or they can specialize and acquire a more precise signal about one asset. Choosing to learn more about an asset makes investors expect to hold more of it because for an average signal realization, they prefer an asset they are better informed about. As expected asset holdings rise, returns to information increase; one signal applied to one share generates less benefit than the same signal applied to many shares. Specialization then arises because the more an investor holds of an asset, the more valuable it is to learn about that asset; but the more an investor learns about the asset, the more valuable that asset is to hold.

This logic shows up in the mathematical expressions for the model's solution. The value of learning about an asset is indexed by its squared Sharpe ratio $(\mu_i - p_i r)^2 \Sigma_{ii}^{-1}$. Another way to express the same quantity is as the product of two components: $(\mu_i - p_i r)$ and $(\mu_i - p_i r)/\Sigma_{ii}$, where the second expression is $\rho E[q_i]$ for an investor who has zero capacity. An investor wants to learn about an asset that has (i) high expected excess returns $(\mu_i - p_i r)$, and (ii) features prominently in his (expected) portfolio $E[q_i]$. The fact that an investor wants to invest all capacity in one asset comes from the anticipation of his future portfolio position $E[q]$. The more shares of an asset he expects to hold, the more valuable information about those shares is, and the higher the index value he assigns to learning about the asset. But as he learns more about the asset, the amount he expects to hold, $E[q_i] = (\mu_i - p_i r)/(\rho \widehat{\Sigma}_{ii})$, rises. As he learns, devoting capacity to the same asset becomes more and more valuable. This is the logic behind increasing returns to learning.

8.2.3 Indifference Results

If the investor has expected exponential utility, instead of mean-variance preferences, he will be indifferent about which risk to learn about. This is the same result as in section 7.4. Re-proving it in a one-investor model shows that indifference does not come from a failure of strategic substitutability because strategic motives are not present with only one investor. Rather, indifference arises when the desires for specialization and diversification just offset each other.

As in the previous chapter's portfolio model, preferences are exponential, $U_1 \equiv E_1[E_2[-e^{-\rho W}]]$, where ρ is risk aversion and W is final wealth. The rest of the model is the same as in the previous section. In period 2, given posterior beliefs

(8.10) and (8.11), the investor chooses his portfolio q to maximize $E_2[-e^{-\rho W}]$, subject to his budget constraint (8.12). In period 1, the investor chooses posterior beliefs $\widehat{\Sigma}$ to maximize U_1, subject to the capacity and no-forgetting constraints (8.13) and (8.14).

Substituting the budget constraint (8.12) into the objective, the first-order condition yields the optimal portfolio of risky assets:

$$q = \frac{1}{\rho}\widehat{\Sigma}^{-1}(\hat{\mu} - pr). \tag{8.19}$$

Any remaining initial wealth is invested in the risk-free asset. After substituting the optimal portfolio (8.19) into the budget constraint (8.12), substituting for wealth W in the objective U_1 and taking the time-1 expectation of $\hat{\mu}$ (see section 7.6), expected utility at time 1 is

$$U_1 = -A\left(|\Sigma|/|\widehat{\Sigma}|\right)^{-1/2}, \tag{8.20}$$

where $A \equiv \exp(-1/2(\mu - pr)\Sigma^{-1}(\mu - pr))$ is positive and exogenous.

Notice that the choice variable enters through the term $|\Sigma|/|\widehat{\Sigma}|$. Recall also that the entropy constraint is $|\Sigma|/|\widehat{\Sigma}| = K$. The solution to the information allocation problem is therefore indeterminate because the time-1 expected utility only depends on capacity K, not on how that capacity is allocated across assets. In other words, the entropy that bounds the mutual information of priors and posteriors is the *exponential utility neutral* learning technology.

Proposition 1. *Given the entropy capacity constraint $|\Sigma|/|\widehat{\Sigma}| \leq K$, an investor with expected exponential utility $E_1[E_2[-e^{-\rho W}]]$ is indifferent between any allocation of his capacity.*

A unique optimum could reemerge if we "perturbed" the learning technology to make some risks slightly easier to learn about than others. For example, if the technology bounded the product of precisions each raised to the exponent ϵ_i, arbitrarily close to one ($K = \prod_i \widehat{\Sigma}_{ii}^{-\epsilon_i}$), the investor would no longer be indifferent.

8.2.4 Preference for Early Resolution of Uncertainty

Section 8.2 breaks the indifference result using a preference for early resolution of uncertainty. Understanding the difference between the mean-variance and expected exponential objectives illuminates the reasons for indifference.

The mean-variance objective is simply the expectation of the log of exponential utility (7.16), which is equivalent to

$$U_1 = E_1\left[-\ln\left(E_2\left[\exp\left(-\rho W\right)|\hat{\mu}, \mu\right]\right)|\mu\right],$$

where $W = rW_0 + q'(f - pr)$ is the budget constraint. This formulation of utility is related to Epstein and Zin's (1989) preference for early resolution of uncertainty. These preferences are also used by Wilson (1975).

To see why the preference for early resolution of uncertainty favors specialization, consider what causes information to be valuable. The expected excess portfolio return achieved through learning depends on the covariance of q and $(f - pr)$, which is $E_1[q'(f - pr)] - E_1[q]'E_1[f - pr]$; learned information allows an investor to profit by holding a portfolio that covaries with realized payoffs. He holds a large position in assets that are likely to have a high payoff and a small (or negative) position in assets that are likely to have low payoffs. Specialized learning about one asset achieves a high covariance between the payoffs and holdings of one asset. Since the optimal portfolio loads heavily on this asset, $E_1[q'(f - pr)] - E_1[q]'E_1[f - pr]$ and thus excess portfolio returns are high. However, specialization also leads the investor to hold a portfolio q that is less predictable on the basis of time-1 information. If the investor instead learns a little bit about every asset, his holdings of every asset will deviate only slightly from his time-1 expected portfolio.

The expected exponential utility investor is averse to this time-1 portfolio uncertainty. The utility cost of higher uncertainty from specialization just offsets the utility benefit of higher portfolio returns, leading to indifference. With mean-variance utility, the investor is not averse to any risk that is resolved before time 2. Such an investor only cares about how uncertain he will be at the moment when he chooses his portfolio. For this investor, specialization is a low-risk strategy. It lowers time-2 portfolio risk by loading the portfolio heavily on an asset whose payoff risk will be substantially reduced by learning. Because specialization is a low-risk (at time 2) and high-expected-return strategy, the mean-variance investor strictly prefers it.

8.3 MARKETS FOR INFORMATION

Information is different from physical goods in two ways. First, it is non-rival. For example, we cannot all hold 50 percent of the shares of IBM. We can, however, all read a story about IBM. Second, it is cheap to replicate. Following Veldkamp (2006), this section introduces a market for information with these two features into an equilibrium investment model with one risky asset. Whereas in section 7.1, the Grossman and Stiglitz (1980) model assumed that information could be purchased at a fixed cost, this section explores the following questions: Where does this information come form? Why is this the cost? What if we model a market and a production technology for information? The answers to these questions can help explain excess volatility in asset prices.

Model setup. The model is identical to the Grossman and Stiglitz (1980) economy described in section 7.1, with one exception. The price of information is not exogenous. Instead, information can be discovered for a fixed cost χ (per capita) and can be replicated for free. There is free entry into a perfectly competitive market for this information. More specifically, firms can decide to produce information after seeing prices posted by other firms.

An equilibrium is a set of asset demands that maximize expected utility, given the realized asset prices; a set of information demands that maximize expected utility, given posted information prices; information supply and pricing choices that are a subgame perfect Nash equilbrium; and markets for information and risky assets that clear.

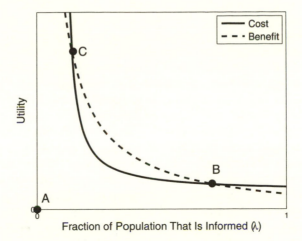

Figure 8.1 Cost and benefit of information. $B(\lambda)$ is benefit minus cost. The falling cost is
the complementarity in information acquisition. The falling benefit represents
substitutability.

Information demand. Perfect competition means that all firms must earn zero
profits. Thus, firms set the information c equal to their average cost. That average
cost is the per capita cost of information discovery χ, divided by the fraction of the
population that buys the information λ:

$$c = \chi/\lambda.$$

From solving the Grossman and Stiglitz (1980) model (equation [7.1]), we know
that the benefit of acquiring a signal about the payoff of a risky asset, net of the
information cost, is $E[U^I|p] - E[U^U|p] = \left(\sigma_e/(\sigma_e^2 + \sigma_{\theta|p}^2)^{1/2}e^{\rho c} - 1\right) E[U^U|p]$,
where σ_e is the standard deviation of the payoff conditional on the signal and $\sigma_e^2 +$
$\sigma_{\theta|p}^2$ is the payoff variance conditional on information in priors and the equilibrium
asset price. Since $E[U^U|p]$ is negative, the net benefit of information is positive if
$\sigma_e/(\sigma_e^2 + \sigma_{\theta|p}^2)^{1/2}e^{\rho c} < 1$. Therefore, an investor should buy information whenever
$B(\lambda) \geq 0$, where

$$B(\lambda) = \left(\frac{\sigma_e^2 + \sigma_{\theta|p}^2}{\sigma_e^2}\right)^{1/2} - e^{\rho\chi/\lambda}.$$

We write B as a function of the fraction of informed agents λ because it enters
in the signal cost and the benefit. Recall that there is strategic substitutability in
information acquisition in this model because more informed investors make prices
covary more with true asset payoffs ($\partial\sigma_{\theta|p}^2/\partial\lambda < 0$).

This model augments the strategic substitutability of Grossman and Stiglitz
(1980) with a strategic complementarity: the more investors buy a given signal, the
cheaper that signal becomes and the higher its net benefit. The effect of these two
competing forces can be seen in figure 8.1: as more investors become informed,

the cost of information falls (complementarity) and the benefit of information falls (substitutability).

Since all agents are ex ante identical, an equilibrium in information acquisition involves all agents buying information with non-negative net benefit ($\lambda = 1$ and $B(\lambda) \geq 0$), no agents buying information with non-positive net benefit ($\lambda = 0$ and $B(\lambda) \leq 0$), or an interior solution where agents are indifferent between being informed and uninformed. Indifference implies that the cost and benefit of information are equal ($B(\lambda) = 0$). Applying these criteria results in three points labeled A, B, and C being potential equilibria. Note that C is an unstable equilibrium. If one more investor purchased information, the net benefit of information would be positive and more investors would become informed, and vice versa for one less investor acquiring information. When a crossing point B exists, A is not an equilibrium because if no information is produced, then a firm could enter and charge slightly more than the average cost of information at B and earn a profit. Thus, the unique equilibrium in this example is B. A would be the unique equilibrium if the value of information were sufficiently low that the cost always exceeded the benefit: $B(\lambda) < 0, \forall \lambda \in (0, 1]$.

Using information complementarity to explain asset-price volatility. Every so often, demand for an asset or set of assets appears to surge in a way that is hard to explain. During such frenzies or herding episodes, it appears as if investors are buying the assets simply because others are as well. The search for the source of frenzies and herds is a search for complementarities in asset demand: how can one person buying an asset make the asset more attractive to other investors? Because assets are in fixed supply, an increase in demand must raise the market price in order for the market to clear. This is not the case for information. An increase in demand for a piece of information in a competitive market causes more information to be provided at a lower price. This can be a source of the complementarity and thus a source of large fluctuations in information provision and, in turn, fluctuations in asset prices. The following results suggest that the origin of asset market anomalies may lie in information markets, not in the asset markets themselves.

To have volatility in information demand, there must be some reason that information demand might change over time. Therefore, Veldkamp (2006) gives asset-price volatility a dynamic process. There are two assets: one risky asset with payoff u_{t+1} and one riskless asset with payoff $r > 1$. The risky asset payoff has a persistent component θ and an idiosyncratic component ϵ:

$$u_{t+1} = \theta_{t+1} + \epsilon_{t+1}.$$

The persistent component of payoffs is an AR(1) process with mean μ and proportional shocks η:

$$\theta_{t+1} = (1 - \rho)\mu + \rho\theta_t(1 + \eta_{t+1}).$$

Innovations are distributed $\epsilon \sim N(0, \sigma_\epsilon^2)$, $\eta \sim N(0, \sigma_\eta)$, independent across investors and over time.

A multiplicative shock to payoffs is a natural assumption in this setting. The proportionality of the mean and standard deviation is a feature of payoff processes

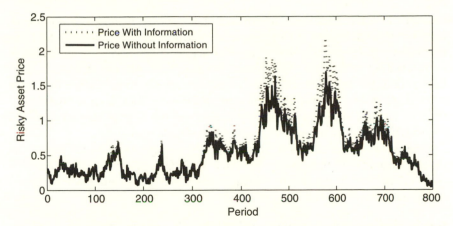

Figure 8.2 Simulated asset prices with and without information. When prices are low, no information is demanded and the two prices are identical.

shared by geometric Brownian motions, commonly used in asset pricing (see Duffie 1996). Furthermore, the assumption that payoff volatility is increasing in its level is supported in the data (see Veldkamp 2006). Note that this assumption does not make volatility procyclical. Volatility $\left(\text{var}_t \left(\frac{\Delta\theta_{t+1}}{\theta_t}\right)\right)$ is constant. The only claim here is that higher-value assets are likely to see larger absolute changes in their value. That shocks are multiplicative is important because information demand will depend on the variance of payoffs. This assumption makes the variance of expected payoff innovations $(\sigma_{\theta t})$ change over time and will cause information demand to fluctuate.

As mentioned before, one result of having complementarity in information acquisition is that small changes in state variables—in this case, payoff volatility—can have large effects on the information equilibrium and create large swings in asset prices (see figure 8.2).

The main result is that when asset fundamentals are strong, asset payoff volatility is high and information demand is high. In these periods, the asset price is higher than what a model with no information acquisition would predict. Lots of investors are buying information because information is cheap and valuable. Information reduces the residual (posterior) risk of the asset, making it more valuable for investors to hold. High demand pushes up the asset's price. In other words, information lowers risk, which lowers returns and raises prices.

8.4 BROADER THEMES

To see how the insights of this section could be applied to answer other questions, it is useful to see what the general points are.

Coordination motives versus correlated actions. One of the broader points here is that what looks like coordination may be correlation. Lots of macroeconomic outcomes look like agents are coordinating with each other (frenzies in asset markets, business cycles, etc.). Coordination is where agents want to take the same action because other agents are taking that action. Correlated behavior is when agents end up taking the same actions because they see the same or similar information. Maybe agents are not trying to coordinate actions. Instead, they learn information others are observing. Similar information leads them to take similar actions. Settings where agents take similar actions but no coordination motive is apparent are good candidates for an information-based explanation.

Other areas we might think about applying coordination versus correlation include international business cycles, cultural change, credit crunches, and currency crises. Are there really coordination motives in these settings or are agents acting similarly on the basis of similar information?

Is information a complement or a substitute? Grossman and Stiglitz (1980) say that in financial markets, information is a substitute. Yet we all watch the same news, read the same newspapers. There appears to be lots of overlap in the information people acquire. Studying how information is supplied can explain that.

Corner solutions. Specialization, the emergence of natural monopolies, or development traps are all outcomes that typify models with increasing returns. (See Romer 1990 for an in-depth discussion of the importance of returns to scale to information in economics.) If there do not appear to be increasing returns to physical production, yet such phenomena arise, perhaps increasing returns to information is an explanation.

8.5 PATHS FOR FUTURE RESEARCH

Only a small sample of possible applications of returns to scale in information have been explored in macroeconomics and finance. Section 9.2.1 uses similar insights to explain industry comovement over the business cycle. Undoubtedly, many more applications are waiting to be explored.

Development traps. The Wilson (1975) model illustrated how low levels of investment may make zero information acquisition an equilibrium. Without information, investment is too risky and falls to zero as well. This kind of model with endogenous increasing returns is a form of development trap. It could help explain why poor countries stay poor.

Income distributions. If wealthier individuals acquire more information because they have more asset value to apply that information to, they will also earn higher returns on their investments. Just like poor countries might stay poor because of a lack of incentives to acquire information, poor individuals may stay poor while the rich get richer. (See Peress 2004.)

Geographic and socioeconomic clustering: coordination motives or correlated information? The idea that people may behave similarly because they observe common information (section 8.3) could be applied to many different situations to explain behavioral similarities in geographic locations, within socioeconomic class, or within ethnic groups. They key is that each of these groups belongs to a common information market.

Learning can be easily embedded in spatial models where agents learn from the actions of others (Fogli and Veldkamp 2007) or from communicating with agents located nearby (Amador and Weill 2011). Here, the information that others have is transmitted freely by their actions to neighbors. The fact that information is generated by people's actions creates a positive information externality that causes people in a similar geographic area to behave similarly. Yet, some geographic differences persist. To keep all agents from acting identically, there needs to be a friction that prevents agents from coordinating perfectly. Imperfect information also provides this friction. If you do not know what people in other regions know, you do not know what they are doing and cannot coordinate with them. Therefore, models of local information transmission can explain geographic heterogeneity in economic transitions. Fogli and Veldkamp (2007) use this kind of model to explain geographic heterogeneity in the transition from low to high female labor force participation rates in the United States.

One way to capture changes in behavior that are concentrated among subgroups of people is to model their consumption of information. For example, perhaps areas with high female labor force participation have higher demand for information that is useful for working mothers. If local media outlets provide this information, it could make maternal labor force participation easier and encourage other nearby women to join the labor force.

This mechanism does not have to be geography specific. For example, if blue-collar workers demand information about continuing their vocational education, then publications or media programs aimed at this population should provide that information, which encourages others to seek out that kind of education as well. Such markets for information could also be ethnically fragmented. For example, if Koreans are running corner pharmacies, then providing information in Korean publications about running such a business could help other Koreans to get started in the same business.

Exchange rate instability. One way of explaining the asset-price volatility in section 8.3 is that it came from regime changes in information demand. Each level of information demand created a different relationship between the asset price and its fundamentals. Another puzzle that changing information regimes might address is the "exchange rate determination puzzle." The question is: Why don't macroeconomic fundamentals (inflation, interest rate differentials, growth rates) predict exchange rate movements? One potential explanation is that this phenomenon comes from information heterogeneity (Bacchetta and van Wincoop 2006). Another unexplored possibility comes from evidence collected by Cheung and Chinn (2001). They surveyed professional currency traders about what macroeconomic variable they believe is the most important determinant of the value of the dollar. Most traders agree on the key macroeconomic variable at any given moment in time. But the variable they name changes from year to year. From our discussion of information and covariance, recall that what information traders choose to acquire determines which macro variable will covary most highly with exchange rates. If that variable changes from year to year, there will be regime shifts in the covariance between exchange rates and fundamentals. Such regime shifts can make the exchange rate appear unpredictable.

Globalization and trade in information. Globalization has entailed both more trade in goods and services and greater cross-border information flows. People know much more about what is going on around the world than ever before. How might trade in goods and trade in information interact? There are many ways to think about this question and many open questions in trade to explore. One connection between trade and information acquisition is the logic of specialization and comparative advantage. Just like countries should each specialize in producing goods in which they have a comparative advantage, investors in financial markets should specialize in learning information they have a comparative advantage in. (See section 7.3.) But information is not identical to traded goods because of its non-rival nature. What patterns of cross-border trade in information should we see? Can predictions about information patterns help explain otherwise puzzling patterns of production and trade?

Related ideas in the finance literature. On information-based explanations for asset-price volatility, there are a few strands of literature. Herding models are included in work by Bikhchandani, Hirshleifer, and Welch (1992), Banerjee (1992), Welch (1992), Caplin and Leahy (1994), Avery and Zemsky (1998), and Chari and Kehoe (2004). Timmermann (1993) explores how investors who do not know the true data-generating process for dividends can create excess asset-price volatility through their learning. Similar to the idea of media frenzies, Yuan (2005) also uses the idea of more information when asset fundamentals are strong to generate excess volatility, as well as asymmetry in asset prices. But her information is transmitted through the price rather than through an information market.

Froot, Scharfstein, and Stein (1992) argue that there is information complementarity because investment is a strategic complement. To make investment complementary requires that investors have short trading horizons. A similar complementarity in investment model is explored by Allen, Morris, and Shin (2006) and Chamley (2006).

A new literature has revisited the idea of asset-price bubbles, where imperfect or heterogeneous information among investors plays an important role. (See Bullard, Evans, and Honkapohja 2007 and Pastor and Veronesi 2003.)

Related work on information choice. Two early works on the value of information are by Radner and Stiglitz (1984) and Wilson (1975). These authors show that the value of information generically is not concave. There is always a region with some increasing returns. (See also Keppo, Moscarini, and Smith 2005.) Furthermore, the value of information is increasing in the scale of the investment.

Turmuhambetova (2005) uses a similar setting to explore how much information an investor should acquire rather than how that information should be allocated. Peng (2005) and Peng and Xiong (2006) explore how information processing affects the dynamics of asset prices rather than the cross-section of asset demands. Their setting is a blend of the CARA utility and normal distribution setting explored in this chapter and the continuous-time portfolio literature.

In the corporate finance literature, Dow, Goldstein, and Guembel (2010) consider investors who can pay to acquire a signal about the payoff of a firm's risky real investment. After observing their signal, investors submit buy and sell orders to a market maker, as Kyle (1985) shows. The firm can observe the order flow (the sequence of buys and sells) and can partially infer what investors have learned. After observing the order flow, the firm chooses whether or not to undertake the risky investment. Like the portfolio problem explored earlier in this chapter, this model has a feedback effect. Investors prefer to acquire information on investments they expect to be profitable because if the firm decides not to undertake the investment, the information is worthless. At the same time, by acquiring information, investors make the firm's asset price more sensitive to changes in the true quality of the investment. Thus, an increase in the ex ante probability of a profitable investment can both increase the expected value of the firm's equity and prompt information acquisition, which will further increase the equity price.

8.6 EXERCISES

1. In the model in section 8.1, assume that the investor now has the following utility: $U(y) = E[y]$. All other specifications remain the same. Does this model have an interior solution for information acquisition? What are the affects caused by risk aversion in the model of Wilson (1975)? Show your results carefully.

2. In the model in section 8.2, what is the solution with the capacity constraint that is additive in precision?

3. In the model in section 8.2, suppose that the utility is given by $E[\exp(W)]$. Derive the period-1 expected utility as a function of Σ and $\widehat{\Sigma}$.

4. Solve for the partial equilibrium of the information portfolio choice model where the investor, instead of having mean-variance preferences of wealth, has logarithmic preferences over wealth.

5. In the model in section 8.2 with N assets, assume that the payoffs of the assets are correlated. Express the optimal allocation of attention, as well as asset prices as a function of eigenvalues and eigenvectors of the variance-covariance matrix.

6. In the model in section 8.3, assume now that the information producer is a monopolist. What is the price of information? How would this affect the volatility of asset prices?

Chapter Nine

Information as an Aggregate Shock

What are the shocks that drive business cycles? The dominant paradigm in the business cycle literature is that technology shocks drive cycles. Because technology progress also drives long-run growth, this paradigm has the advantage that it offers a unified framework for thinking about short-term and long-term changes in output. Yet many cyclical movements are difficult to connect with any observable change in productivity. Variables like sentiment or stock prices seem to have components, orthogonal to any measured productivity variable, that explain up to half of business-cycle fluctuations (Beaudry and Portier 2006). The models described below attempt to reconcile the productivity shock and sentiment views of business cycles. In each model, information about productivity produces economic fluctuations without a concurrent change in aggregate productivity itself. These are often called "news-driven business cycles."

While only one of these models involves information choice, the search for aggregate shocks picks up on a theme that emerged in the previous chapter: when agents observe correlated information, they behave in a coordinated way. Another way of stating the main point of the news-driven business cycle literature is in light of the "industry comovement puzzle." Across industries, output is more correlated than technology.[1] The high correlation of output across industries is what led early writers of business-cycle models to formulate models driven by aggregate shocks. Yet there does not seem to be a large aggregate component of productivity. The question then takes the form: Why do industries with different productivity processes choose similar production, creating aggregate output fluctuations?

This chapter investigates models where firms behave similarly, in part because they observe similar information. In some of the models, market-clearing prices make actions strategic substitutes. In others, firms produce complementary goods. But what all the models have in common is the feature that information, or the noise in the signal, is itself a shock to aggregate output.

Since these models are general equilibrium production economies, most have involved solution techniques that involve numerical approximation. Since such solution techniques merit a book of their own, this chapter will not endeavor to teach the solution methods. Rather, it sketches four models and describes what features of each model enable it to generate realistic news-driven business cycles. Each model is reduced to its essentials to highlight the differences in mechanisms.

---

[1] For the average industry, the correlation of its GDP with aggregate GDP is $mean_i(corr(GDP_i, GDP_{avg})) = 0.51$, while the average industry's total factor productivity has a much lower correlation with aggregate productivity: $mean_i(corr(TFP_i, TFP_{avg})) = 0.17$. See Veldkamp and Wolfers 2007.

9.1 NEWS ABOUT FUTURE PRODUCTIVITY

This chapter presents examples of two different types of news-driven business-cycle models. In the first type of model, agents observe signals ("news") about what future productivity will be. One of the key challenges such models face is getting output to rise on good news. A standard real business cycle with typical parameters predicts that when agents learn that productivity will be high in the future, they reduce their labor supply and consume more, resulting in a drop in investment and a fall in output. The good news makes agents expect higher lifetime income. This wealth effect, without any substitution effect coming from higher current productivity, makes agents increase their consumption of both goods and leisure. Since optimism about the future of the economy is typically observed in booms, this does not make for a realistic theory. To overcome this problem, each theory employs a combination of the right preferences, the right production function, and the right kind of technology shock to shut down or overwhelm the wealth effect on labor.

The second type of news-driven business-cycle model is one where agents observe noisy signals about current productivity. Section 9.2 explores such models.

9.1.1 Model 1: Cross-Industry Complementarity

Beaudry and Portier (2004) offer a model where news about future productivity can create realistic business cycles. It is a 3-sector model with strong complementarities across sectors. Although Beaudry and Portier lay out the full, decentralized economy and show that the solution to the social planner's problem coincides with the decentralized equilibrium, we will take a shortcut by examining the social planner's problem directly.

Preferences. The social planner's objective is to maximize the expected discounted sum of log consumption C_t and linear utility in leisure $(\bar{l} - l_{x,t} - l_{k,t})$:

$$U = E_0 \left[\sum_{t=0}^{\infty} \beta^t (\ln(C_t) + v_0(\bar{l} - l_{x,t} - l_{k,t})) \right]. \tag{9.1}$$

Production technology. There are three sectors: consumption C, intermediates X, and capital K. Intermediate good output depends on productivity θ_x, labor l_x, and a fixed factor m:

$$X_t = \theta_{x,t} l_{x,t}^{\alpha_x} m^{1-\alpha_x}, \tag{9.2}$$

where the diminishing-returns-to-scale parameter is $\alpha_x \in (0, 1)$. The capital stock is the capital stock from the previous period, depreciated at rate δ, plus new investment goods, which are produced with productivity $\theta_{k,t}$, labor $l_{k,t}$, and a fixed factor n:

$$K_{t+1} = (1 - \delta)K_t + \theta_{k,t} l_{k,t}^{\alpha_k} n^{1-\alpha_k}, \tag{9.3}$$

where the diminishing-returns-to-scale parameter is $\alpha_k \in (0, 1)$. Note that intermediates are non-durable while capital is durable. Labor used for intermediate goods and for investment goods must sum to less than the aggregate time endowment

$$l_{x,t} + l_{k,t} \leq \bar{l}. \tag{9.4}$$

Finally, production of consumption goods requires intermediates and capital:

$$C_t = (aX_t^{\nu} + (1-a)K_t^{\nu})^{1/\nu}.$$

The authors assume $\nu < 0$, which makes intermediate goods and capital complements. This complementarity is what causes the intermediate and investment good sectors to comove.

Information structure. The news shocks that drive business cycles will be the arrival of information about the intermediate goods sector. Productivity in the investment sector is deterministic:

$$\ln \theta_{k,t} = g_{0,k} + g_{1,k}t. \tag{9.5}$$

It is the stochastic productivity in the intermediate goods sector that agents learn about. The constant and drift components of productivity $g_{0,x}$ and $g_{1,x}$ are known, but the persistent autoregressive component $\hat{\theta}_{x,t}$ is not known:

$$
\begin{aligned}
\ln \theta_{x,t} &= g_{0,x} + g_{1,x}t + \ln \hat{\theta}_{x,t} \\
\ln \hat{\theta}_{x,t} &= \lambda \ln \hat{\theta}_{x,t-1} + \epsilon_t \quad \lambda \in (0,1).
\end{aligned}
\tag{9.6}
$$

The innovation ϵ_t can take on either a low or a high value, $-g_{1,x}$ or $g_{1,x}p(1-p)$, where p is the probability of the low state.

Signals at time t are about ϵ_{t+n} and are also binary. The signal v_t is either $-g_{1,x}$ or $g_{1,x}p(1-p)$, where the probability that the signal is correct ($v_t = \epsilon_{t+n}$) is q.

Key mechanisms in the model. Beaudry and Portier (2004) do not solve the model analytically. Instead, they calibrate and simulate the model to see how it reacts when good and bad signals are observed. The calibration uses standard values for most of its parameters. But there are four parameters specific to this model: the two parameters governing the technology and information processes (p, q), the technological parameter ν, and the number of periods n that news arrives in advance of the technology shock. Using a simulated method of moments, the authors choose these four coefficients to fit the volatilities of output, consumption, and investment, measured in two different ways. Using this calibrated model, they show that consumption, hours worked, investment, and output all rise on good news. But since their results are numerical, it is not immediately obvious why this particular model works.

The reason agents work more when good news arrives is that they will want to produce lots of intermediate goods in the future, when intermediate good productivity is high. But intermediates and capital are complements, so they will also want to have a large capital stock when the productivity shock hits. Since capital accumulates gradually, agents increase their labor supply immediately to start investing more. The alternative strategy is to wait until the productivity shock arrives to invest more. But waiting would require working more and consuming less to finance a large increase in investment and intermediates. Consumption would fall and then rebound. Since agents are averse to such consumption fluctuations, they build up capital before the shock arrives.

The key model assumptions are (1) a strong desire for consumption smoothing, (2) little desire for labor supply smoothing, and (3) having intermediates and capital be complementary inputs in the production of consumption goods. The third assumption, complementarity across sectors, is the one that addresses the comovement problem most directly. In this model, the reason that sector-specific news generates an aggregate shock to output is that sectors' goods are complements. Put together, these assumptions ensure that when good news about future intermediate productivity arrives, greater investment is driven by more labor, not less consumption. Thus, good news produces output booms.

9.1.2 Model 2: Gradual Capital Adjustment

Like the model in the previous section, Jaimovich and Rebelo (2006) also model news about future productivity. However, their mechanism for getting consumption and labor to rise on good news is different. They use adjustment costs to capital to get agents to start working in advance of the productivity shock—this time to the productivity of investment—to build up the capital stock.

Preferences. Agents have preferences over consumption C_t and hours worked N_t:

$$U = E_0 \left\{ \sum_{t=0}^{\infty} \frac{\beta^t}{1-\sigma} (C_t - \psi N_t^\theta X_t)^{1-\sigma} - 1 \right\}, \qquad (9.7)$$

where $X_t = C_t^\gamma X_{t-1}^{1-\gamma}$ and $\gamma \in (0,1)$. These preferences are a combination of two existing types of preferences: Greenwood, Hercowitz, and Huffman (1988) preferences, which are designed to shut down wealth effects on labor, and King, Plosser, and Rebelo (1988) preferences, which are designed to be consistent with balanced growth.

Production technology. Output is produced with capital services, a product of the capital stock K_t, capital utilization u_t, and labor N_t:

$$Y_t = A_t (u_t K_t)^{1-\alpha} N_t^\alpha, \qquad (9.8)$$

where A_t is total factor productivity. This output can be used for consumption C_t or investment I_t:

$$Y_t = C_t + I_t/z_t,$$

where z_t represents the productivity of investment goods.

Changing the level of investment from what it was in the previous period incurs an adjustment cost $\phi(\cdot)$, which is a function of I_t/I_{t-1}. There is no cost incurred for keeping investment constant ($\phi(1) = 0$):

$$K_{t+1} = I_t \left[1 - \phi\left(\frac{I_t}{I_{t-1}} \right) \right] + [1 - \delta(u_t)]K_t.$$

The depreciation rate of capital is assumed to be convex in capital utilization $\delta'' > 0$.

The authors explore two types of news. In both cases, they assume that the model is in a steady state and that agents learn about a one-time, permanent increase in productivity two periods before the increase takes place. The first type of news is about a change in total factor productivity A_t. The second type is about investment-specific productivity z_t.

Key mechanisms. The main result is that both types of news shocks generate a contemporaneous increase in consumption and hours worked if the news is good (unexpectedly high future productivity). The news about total factor productivity generates only a modest effect. Most of the response to the shock takes place when the shock actually changes productivity. In contrast, with the investment-specific news, most of the reaction takes place when the news is revealed, before productivity itself changes. The authors do not solve the model analytically. Instead, they calibrate and simulate to demonstrate its effects. However, their explorations of various model modifications highlight the importance of key model assumptions.

One important piece of the model is the preferences. The reason for the non-standard preferences is to minimize the wealth effect on labor. In other words, these preferences prevent agents from reducing hours worked when they learn good news that will raise their future expected income. However, there is still a wealth effect on consumption, which ensures that good news results in a consumption binge.

A second important piece is the capital adjustment cost. This is what induces agents to work more before productivity increases. They want to have a large capital stock to produce with when productivity is high. But since the adjustment cost is convex, building that capital stock up rapidly is very costly. To minimize adjustment costs, they start right away, gradually increasing investment. Higher investment requires more labor input, increasing hours worked. In contrast, if there were no adjustment cost, agents who heard good news would reduce investment in order to finance their consumption binge. They would wait until high productivity arrived to increase investment.

The capital adjustment cost alone is not enough to get labor to rise on good news. For labor inputs to rise, the marginal value of labor must rise as well. If current productivity is unchanged, then there must be additional capital for labor to complement. But the capital stock is a slow-moving variable. Variable capital utilization allows firms to quickly expand their capital stock to produce more goods. In the process, this increases the marginal utility of labor and therefore the supply of labor. In sum, to adjust the capital stock before the shock arrives, agents use their existing capital more intensively and work harder.

9.1.3 Matching Stock Market Fluctuations

Christiano et al. (2010) augment Jaimovich and Rebelo's work (2006) with pricing frictions in order to explain the role that suboptimal monetary policy plays in amplifying business cycles. In the process, they show what model features are needed to reproduce realistic features of equity markets. They consider an episode where households observe a signal that future productivity will be high and then later learn that the signal was false. In their model, such an episode produces a rise and then fall in consumption, investment, output, and stock prices.

According to Jaimovich and Rebelo, good news about future productivity triggers a fall, rather than a rise, in stock prices. The reason is that a rise in investment today, without a contemporaneous increase in the investment's productivity, drives down the price of investment goods, which is the stock price.

To correct these problems, Christiano et al. add the following ingredients to the Jaimovich-Rebelo setting. First, they introduce sticky prices. In a perfectly competitive market, only the firms offering the lowest price get revenue. To make a sticky price model work, there needs to be imperfect competition. The standard way to introduce that is to have monopolistic competition in intermediate goods. Intermediate goods generate final goods with a constant-elasticity production function: $Y_t = (\int_0^1 y_j^{1/\gamma} dj)^\gamma$. To make prices sticky, the simplest way is to use Calvo (1983) sticky prices, which means that in each period, a randomly chosen fraction ξ of firms get to adjust their price at no cost. The remaining firms cannot re-optimize their price. Specifically, Christiano et al. assume that the remaining firms set a price that is the previous period's price, adjusted for the aggregate rate of inflation.

Second, they introduce sticky wages. This requires having heterogenous (specialized) labor inputs that generate composite labor with a constant elasticity aggregator that is just like the intermediate goods aggregator. This ensures that there is some demand for the services of high-wage workers. Then households face Calvo sticky wages: a constant fraction of households can optimize their wage in each period. The remaining households increase their wage by the aggregate rate of wage inflation.

Finally, monetary policy is governed by a Taylor rule. In other words, the risk-free interest rate is a linear, increasing function of the expected inflation rate and the output gap (the ratio of final goods output to its non-stochastic steady-state level).

These modifications increase the size of the output response to a technology shock. When a positive signal about future productivity arrives and then the positive innovation does not occur, the response of output, investment, and hours is roughly three times larger than what is proposed by Jaimovich and Rebelo (2006). Furthermore, stock prices increase, then decrease, rather than the reverse. These effects stem from a suboptimal monetary policy. When the positive signal arrives, the real wage in a frictionless model would rise. Since nominal wages are sticky, an efficient monetary policy would raise real wages by letting inflation drop. The Taylor rule dictates that the monetary authority do the opposite: increase the money supply to increase inflation. The resulting real wage is too low, which encourages high employment and increases the size of the boom. Cheap labor also makes capital more valuable, which pushes up the stock price.

9.1.4 Empirical Evidence on News Shocks

There is an active debate about how to measure news about future productivity and what role this news plays in business cycles. Beaudry and Portier (2006) identify news shocks as changes in stock prices that are uncorrelated with current productivity. Subsequent work by these authors also imposed a long-run identification restriction: the news shock must also have a long-run effect of productivity. Under these identification schemes, the authors found that news about high future productivity was associated with increases in consumption, output, and hours worked. In other words, good news generates a boom.

Sims (2009) and Barsky and Sims (2009) use several forward-looking variables, including stock prices, consumer confidence, and inflation, in their vector autoregression. The "news shocks" are the component of a linear combination of these variables that are uncorrelated with current productivity. They choose the linear combination so that these news shocks best explain future productivity. Then they jointly estimate the responses of macroeconomic aggregates to this news shock. Similar to Beaudry and Portier (2006), Sims (2009) and Barsky and Sims (2009) find that positive news about future productivity is associated with an increase in consumption. But whereas Beaudry and Portier (2006) found that good news is associated with a boom in output and hours worked, Sims (2009) and Barsky and Sims (2009) find that good news is associated with a downturn, a decline in output and hours. Furthermore, Sims (2009) claims that news shocks are not a big component of business-cycle fluctuations. In particular, they fail to account for four of the six most recent recessions.

9.2 NEWS ABOUT CURRENT PRODUCTIVITY

The second type of news-driven business cycle model is one where agents learn about current period productivity. The goal of these theories is to create an environment where a public signal creates correlated errors in beliefs about productivity that induce agents to produce more (less), even if their true productivity is not high (low). While the previous theories can be representative agent economies, these rely on heterogeneous producers. There are three key challenges in producing this type of a news-driven business cycle. First is the comovement problem. With heterogeneous producers, particularly good news for one of these producers encourages him to hire more labor (or use more capital), which draws labor away from other producers and pushes down their output. The second problem is persistence. Persistence is an issue for all kinds of models that rely on asymmetric information. (This was a key point of Woodford's work (2002) from section 6.2.) If agents can achieve full information by learning what others know, what kinds of information frictions slow down learning enough to produce cycles that last for quarters or years? The third problem is amplification. Imperfect information creates beliefs that are generally less volatile than the true underlying shock that agents are learning about (see section 5.3). How do we amplify information shocks to make the resulting output fluctuations sufficiently large?

9.2.1 Model 3: Aggregate News Shocks

While sections 9.1.1 and 9.1.2 examined the effects of news about *future* productivity, the next two sections consider the effect of noisy signals about *current* productivity. Both models deal directly with the industry comovement problems. True productivity in different sectors is not highly correlated. Yet the output in these sectors is highly correlated. In both cases, the source of the additional output correlation is the noise in a signal that is informative about aggregate productivity. Lorenzoni (2009) calls this effect a "demand shock."

Veldkamp and Wolfers (2007) use coordination motives in information acquisition to generate correlated production decisions across sectors over the business cycle. The main idea is that agents who observe only aggregate information have similar beliefs and make similar decisions. A firm that only observes one aggregate shock only reacts to one aggregate shock. As in section 8.3, aggregate information is cheap because its discovery cost is shared among many purchasers. Idiosyncratic information is expensive because its discovery cost must be borne alone. The following analysis explores the simplest version of the model where there is no trade in goods or labor. Only information is traded. The model's logic extends to settings where there are goods and factor markets. The end of the section describes this richer model.

Model setup. Every agent in the economy lives on an island (just as in Lucas 1972). There is a continuum of islands, indexed by i, and a representative agent on each island. Each agent has exponential utility, with constant absolute risk aversion, ρ, and preferences defined over consumption c and labor n:

$$U_i = -E[exp\,(-\rho(c_i - \psi n_i))]. \tag{9.9}$$

For now, consider the simplest version of the model where each agent consumes only what there produces on his island. Production is linear in island-specific labor:

$$y_i = z_i n_i.$$

Labor productivity has aggregate and idiosyncratic shocks that agents can learn about ($\bar{z}$ and η_i) and an unlearnable shock e_i

$$z_i = \mu_z + \beta_i \bar{z} + \eta_i + e_i.$$

Labor's marginal product z_i is unknown (normally distributed) at the time when labor inputs must be chosen. Agents can pay to observe two types of signals. Aggregate signals reveal $s_0 = \bar{z} + e_0$. Island-specific signals reveal a combination of aggregate and island-specific productivity, $s_i = \beta_i(\bar{z} + e_0) + \eta_i$. All shocks and noise terms are independent normal variables.

Information production requires a fixed cost χ for discovery of any signal. There is zero cost to replicate the signal. Any agent can enter the market for signals at any time. However, resale of information is prohibited.

Equilibrium. Agents choose the following to maximize their objective, taking others' actions as given.

1. Information production: Each agent announces signal prices $\tilde{\tau}_{ij}$. Then each chooses whether to produce each signal at cost χ. The profit on signal j is π_j.
2. Information purchases: Each agent i chooses whether or not to purchase signal j. $L_{ij} = 1$ if agent i buys signal j and 0 otherwise.

3. Goods production: Agents choose c and n, given all observed signals, subject to the budget constraint

$$c_i = z_i n_i + \sum_j (\pi_j - \tau_j L_{ij}), \tag{9.10}$$

where τ_j is the lowest offered price of signal j, $\min_i \tilde{\tau}_{ij}$.

Key mechanism 1: The market filters out industry information. As in the investment model in section 8.3, the equilibrium information price is $\tau_j = \chi/\lambda_j$, where λ_j is the number of agents who buy signal j. For industry-specific information, the industry must pay χ because they will be the only buyer. There is a range of parameters such that the market supplies lots of aggregate information at a low price and little industry-specific information.

The value of information in this setting is the same as it is in Grossman and Stiglitz's work (1980). (See section 7.1 for a derivation of the following solution.) A firm will purchase the aggregate signal s_0 if two conditions are satisfied:

1. Buying the aggregate signal at price χ/λ yields higher utility than buying the industry signal at the higher cost χ:

$$\frac{1}{2\rho} \ln\left(\frac{Var(z_i)}{Var(z_i|s_0)}\right) - \frac{\chi}{\lambda} \geq \frac{1}{2\rho} \ln\left(\frac{Var(z_i)}{Var(z_i|s_i)}\right) - \chi.$$

2. Buying the aggregate signal yields higher utility than not purchasing any information:

$$\frac{1}{2\rho} \ln\left(\frac{Var(z_i)}{Var(z_i|s_0)}\right) - \frac{\chi}{\lambda} \geq 0.$$

Key mechanism 2: Aggregate shocks to choice variables. Firms that observe the aggregate signal (common information) have perfectly correlated beliefs about their island-specific productivity, $E[z_i|s_0]$. Labor is linear in expected island productivity, $E[z_i|s]$. To see this, substitute the budget constraint (9.10) into utility (9.9) and take the first-order condition with respect to n_i. The resulting optimal labor input on island i is $n_i = (E(z_i|s) - \psi)/(\rho Var(z_i|s))$, where the mean and variance are conditional on whatever signal s island i has chosen to observe. Therefore, labor inputs are also perfectly correlated for two islands that observe aggregate signals: $\text{corr}(n_i(s_0), n_j(s_0)) = 1$ or -1. Perfectly correlated labor inputs are what make output more correlated than productivity.

In contrast, for firms that observe the industry-specific signal (heterogeneous information), there is no excess correlation in their output with the aggregate output. It is about the same as the correlation of their industry productivity with aggregate productivity.

Extending the model: adding labor markets. The assumption that there is no trade in goods or labor is unrealistic. The problem with adding markets is that market prices and quantities reveal information. We saw this in Grossman and Stiglitz's work (1980). If there were no asset supply shocks, asset prices would perfectly reveal others' private information and no one would pay for information that others had purchased. In this case, wages and labor demand will reveal all information that other firms have learned.

In such a setting, information becomes a public good. With sufficiently many agents, free-riding collapses the information market. If any one firm purchases aggregate information, other firms know that they will be able to observe that information for free. This makes it impossible to share the cost of aggregate information, in the absence of a commitment mechanism. Without cost-sharing, aggregate information is as expensive as but less beneficial than firm-specific information. Therefore, a few large firms purchase firm-specific productivity information. The other firms observe the productivity of the large firms and use that information to make inferences about their own productivity. Thus, the signals that the large firms buy end up being public signals that introduce common expectation errors into the beliefs of the other firms. For example, if firm 1's signal indicated high productivity and firms 2 and 3 have not acquired their own information, but know that they have productivity that is positively correlated with firm 1's, they will also believe that their productivity will be high. These common shocks to beliefs make beliefs highly correlated. When all firms think they are productive at the same times, they choose highly correlated labor inputs. Thus even when market prices reveal information, news-driven business cycles persist.

9.2.2 Model 4: Confusing Private and Public News

Like the previous model, Lorenzoni's model (2009) is one of imperfect information about *current* aggregate productivity. But unlike the previous model where most or all agents observed the same information, here information heterogeneity and higher-order expectations are central. The main point of Lorenzoni's work is that noise in signals about aggregate productivity can create economic reactions that resemble demand shocks—increases in consumption and output that are not accompanied by changes in aggregate productivity.

This model is significantly more complicated than the previous two. One reason for the extra complexity is that keeping heterogeneous information from becoming common knowledge requires frictions. Bayesian learning is remarkably quick to converge to the truth. Many frictions are needed to slow that learning down and preserve belief heterogeneity. Lorenzoni does not simply adopt the strong information barriers of the Lucas (1972) model. He shows how prices of the consumption bundles that agents consume can be revealed without collapsing the information structure to common knowledge. This generates new ideas about the nature of information frictions in decentralized markets. A second reason for the added complexity is that Lorenzoni, unlike previous authors, seeks to explain facts about prices. For there to be a meaningful price level, there needs to be a medium of exchange. This part of the model allows one to discuss monetary policy. Despite its complexity, the model is analytically tractable.

Preferences. As in the previous model, every agent lives on an island. The preferences of an agent on island l are defined over his consumption bundle $C_{l,t}$ and hours worked $N_{l,t}$:

$$U = E \sum_{t=0}^{\infty} \beta^t \left(\ln(C_{l,t}) - \frac{1}{1+\xi} N_{l,t}^{1+\xi} \right).$$

The consumption bundle is

$$C_{l,t} = \left(\int_{L_{l,t}} \int_0^1 C_{j,\tilde{l},l,t}^{(\gamma-1)/\gamma} dj d\tilde{l} \right)^{\gamma/(\gamma-1)},$$

where $C_{j,\tilde{l},l,t}$ is the consumption of good j produced on island $\tilde{l}$ by the agent from island l at time t, and $L_{l,t}$ is the subset of islands that the agent from island l is allowed to shop from.

The representative agent on each island maximizes this utility subject to his budget constraint. He does this by choosing consumption, labor, and how much to hold of a one-period bond B_{t+1} that pays off one dollar in period $t+1$. These bonds are in zero net supply and have date t price Q_t. The value of bonds, plus spending on consumption goods, must equal existing financial wealth, plus labor income and firm profits on the island:

$$Q_t B_{t+1} + \int_{L_{l,t}} \int_0^1 C_{j,\tilde{l},l,t} dj d\tilde{l} = B_t + W_{l,t} N_{l,t} + \Pi_{l,t}. \qquad (9.11)$$

The role of the bonds is to serve as a numeraire good to facilitate the discussion of what happens to prices.

Production technology. Output is a linear function of labor supply. Labor productivity depends on a permanent aggregate productivity shock, x_t, and a temporary island-specific component, $\eta_{l,t}$:

$$Y_{l,t} = \exp[x_t + \eta_{l,t}] N_{l,t}. \qquad (9.12)$$

The island-specific shock is normal and independently distributed across time and islands $\eta_{l,t} \sim N(0, \sigma_\eta^2)$. The aggregate shock is a random walk:

$$x_t = x_{t-1} + \epsilon_t \quad \epsilon_t \sim N(0, \sigma_\epsilon^2).$$

Firms' price-setting. Each period, a fraction $1 - \theta$ of firms on each island is allowed to choose the price of their good. All other firms must keep their prices fixed. Total firm profits on island l are an integral of the profits of each firm j on the island:

$$\Pi_{l,t} = \int_0^1 \left(P_{j,l,t} Y_{j,l,t} - W_{l,t} N_{j,l,t} \right) dj. \qquad (9.13)$$

Without some exogenous price stickiness, news shocks would be completely absorbed by the real interest rate and would have no effect on real output. Because firms then must have heterogeneous prices, this requires there to be different varieties of goods on each island so that higher-priced goods still get some positive demand. This is the reason for carrying around the extra j subscript for indexing firms.

When the planner on each island chooses prices for the firms that can adjust prices, he maximizes not just this current period profit but the expected discounted sum of future profits in periods when the firm will not be able to adjust its price level. The discount factor the planner uses is $\beta^\tau (C_t / C_{t+\tau})$.

Given the prices firms set, there are three price indices. First, there is the local producer price index that includes all the prices of goods produced on island l:

$$P_{l,t} = \left(\int_0^1 P_{j,l,t} dj \right)^{1/(1-\gamma)}.$$

Second, there is a local consumer price index, which includes all the producer price indices on the subset of islands $L_{l,t}$ that consumers from l shop on:

$$\bar{P}_{l,t} = \left(\int_{\tilde{l} \in L_{l,t}} P_{\tilde{l},t} d\tilde{l} \right)^{1/(1-\gamma)}.$$

Finally, the aggregate price index is

$$P_t = \left(\int_0^1 P_{l,t} dl \right)^{1/(1-\gamma)}.$$

Information structure. All agents observe their labor productivity $x_t + \eta_{l,t}$, the local wage rate $W_{l,t}$, the prices of all goods in the local consumption basket $\{P_{\tilde{l},t}\}_{\tilde{l} \in L_{l,t}}$, the total sales of local firms $Y_{l,t}$, and a noisy signal about the aggregate component of productivity:

$$s_t = x_t + e_t \quad e_t \sim N(0, \sigma_e^2).$$

If agents could observe all prices set on all islands, they would be able to infer what signals others have observed and information heterogeneity would collapse; common knowledge would prevail. Yet, consumers need some price information to decide what goods to buy from other islands. One common solution to a problem like this is to insert some noise in the price level, such as an exogenous supply shock or noise traders (Grossman and Stiglitz 1980). Lorenzoni has an alternative mechanism for resolving this problem. He allows agents to shop on a subset of islands. He chooses the subset carefully so that the islands have correlated island-specific shocks. This ensures that the price index each agent observes is noisy. Specifically, assume that the selection of islands $L_{l,t}$ is such that the local consumer price index is a log-normal signal about the aggregate price level:

$$\ln(\bar{P}_{l,t}) = \ln(P_t) + \xi_{l,t} \quad \text{where } \xi_{l,t} \sim N(0, \sigma_\xi^2).$$

Key mechanisms in the model. There are four mechanisms in this model working together to produce a rich set of results. The primary mechanism is that agents cannot fully separate aggregate productivity, idiosyncratic productivity, and signal noise. Agents observe their island's labor productivity, which is a sum of island-specific and aggregate components. In addition, they get noisy signals, exogenous and from the price level, about aggregate productivity. But because of imperfect information, noise in the public signals about aggregate productivity can create aggregate shocks to beliefs about aggregate productivity that result in aggregate output fluctuations.

When agents believe that aggregate productivity is high, they work more hours and consume more. This is true, even though the average agent knows that its own productivity is not high. Yet, agents infer that if aggregate productivity is high, all other islands will produce more of their goods. Goods from the agent's own island will be relatively scarce and therefore command a high relative price. This increases the expected return to additional hours of labor and expected future income, which prompts additional consumption. This is how the model produces realistic business cycles with the right correlation between consumption, output, and labor with news shocks. This is the sense in which the model produces something that looks like a demand shock.

The second mechanism in this model that is not present in the previous models is that prices rise on demand shocks (high realization of public signal noise) and fall when supply shocks (high aggregate productivity shocks) hit. Yet, prices cannot adjust to fully undo the effect of signal noise on output because of the price stickiness assumption.

The third mechanism is that coordination motives in price-setting amplify the reactions to public signals. Generating sizable fluctuations from noisy signals is difficult because to get large reactions, the noise must be large. But if signals are very noisy, agents tend to discount them and rely more on their prior beliefs. This is a very general issue with learning models: imperfect information typically dampens volatility. The reason why this happens can be seen in the following simple decomposition. Suppose the unconditional volatility of a random variable x is σ^2. If an agent has imperfect information, his beliefs will typically be a best linear approximation to the true variable, with noise that is orthogonal to his belief: $x = \hat{x} + \epsilon$. Thus, if the volatility of the noise is σ_ϵ^2, the volatility of the belief realization over time is $\sigma^2 - \sigma_\epsilon^2$. Thus, if the agent knew the truth, his beliefs would be as volatile as the truth (σ^2). But with imperfect information, his beliefs are strictly less volatile. Lorenzoni gets around this problem using the same mechanism as Morris and Shin (2002) to generate overreactions to public information. (See section 5.1.1.)

The fourth mechanism creates persistence in the effects of news shocks. The combination of coordination motives and heterogeneous information makes the effects of noise in public information long-lived. That mechanism is similar to the one used by Woodford (2002) (see section 6.2). For Lorenzoni (2009), it is not just price-setting that agents want to coordinate on but also production. When others produce more, the marginal utility and, therefore, the relative price of one's own type of good are higher. That makes one firm want to produce more when others produce more. The same kind of persistence that showed up in Woodford's prices arises here in Lorenzoni's quantities. Quantities react aggressively to public signals because all producers know that other producers also know that information. The effects of those public signals are persistent because even if agents learn that the signal was high due to signal noise, they do not know if other agents have learned that same information yet.

Welfare consequences of dispersed information. Angeletos and La'O (2009) build on this type of model to understand its welfare consequences. They consider two versions. In one, there are private and public signals, but all information is exogenous. In other words, agents observe prices when they trade but do not use any of this information to form their beliefs. In this model, as long as all prices are flexible, allocations are efficient. In the second version when agents learn from market prices, there is an externality. Each agent fails to internalize the benefit to others of taking a more informative action. This externality makes equilibrium actions socially inefficient.

9.3 BROADER THEMES AND PATHS FOR FUTURE RESEARCH

News about future aggregate shocks and noise in signals about current shocks both introduce common shocks to agents' choices. Common shocks can make covariance in choices exceed the covariance in productivity and generate aggregate fluctuations. High comovement appears in many contexts: asset prices comove, consumers exhibit fads, speculators all sell a currency, mergers or IPOs take place in waves, and countries' business cycles comove. Comovement is a term applied to situations where agents take similar actions or aggregate variables behave similarly without an apparent motive to coordinate. What is happening in these models is that public information is introducing correlation in agents' actions across islands or in the demand for different types of goods. Public information can thus be a source of missing aggregate shocks.

Firm and price dynamics. Why do sectors choose such similar outputs and firms choose such different prices? Section 6.3 (Reis 2006) explained why firms react too little to aggregate shocks to prices that come from the money supply. In contrast, section 9.2.1 (Veldkamp and Wolfers 2007), explained why firms react too much to aggregate productivity shocks and not enough to firm- or sector-specific ones. The motivations for these two works appear to be at odds. Are the factors that matter for each of these decisions so different? Is there an information model that can reconcile the cyclical behavior of both prices and quantities?

Regime shifts in business cycles. Stock and Watson (1996) argue that there have been structural breaks in the variances and covariances of business-cycle aggregates. One example of such a structural change is the decline in business-cycle volatility, often dubbed "the great moderation." While many theories can explain a fraction of the change, few can account for it entirely.

We know that when agents observe less information about some underlying state process, they react less to changes in that state. This raises the question of what might have caused agents to acquire less information about macroeconomic (usually productivity) shocks.

One possibility is that the volatility of productivity shocks declined slightly. Since a less volatile process is more predictable, even in the absence of acquired information, additional information is less valuable. Thus, a decline in the value of information could lead agents to acquire less of it, which would amplify the original decline in volatility.

Alternatively, it could be that growth raises wages, which in turn raises the opportunity cost of processing information. If processing information takes time that could otherwise be devoted to labor, then processing information may become more expensive. As agents process less information, production reacts less to exogenous shocks. Equilibrium effects on prices could reinforce this effect. If prices become more stable because production of competing goods is less volatile, then this may provide producers a second motive to learn less about underlying shocks that previously would have affected their good's price.

Using information choice as a model selection device. Information-driven models of business cycles have mostly employed passive learning. Beaudry and Portier (2004) and Jaimovich and Rebelo (2006) explore whether news about future productivity can be a shock that explains features of business cycles. Lorenzoni (2009) argues that shocks to public information create what look like supply shocks and the shocks to private, heterogeneous signals can create an apparent demand shock. Zeira (1994, 1999) and Van Nieuwerburgh and Veldkamp (2006) focus on how information transmission alters the shape of the business cycle. None of these models involves information choice. All of them employ passive learning.

One question to pose to these theories is: Are the assumptions of these theories consistent with any theory of rational information choice? This is the kind of question that the model of chapter 7 asks of standard asset-pricing models.

Using information choice to generate more nuanced predictions. Extending these models through information choice could produce new cross-sectional and time-series predictions that would facilitate testing and quantifying their effects. When is information most valuable to acquire? How does more information in these times change the prediction of the theory? Can a time-varying information flow allow the model to match other features of business cycles that a model with a constant flow of information cannot explain? Could more information about some sectors than others explain some of the cross-sectional features of business cycles? (For an overview of what some of the big outstanding questions in the business cycle literature are, see Rebelo 2005.)

9.4 EXERCISES

1. Write the first-order conditions for the model from Beaudry and Portier 2004. Holding fixed all future actions, how would good news about *today's* productivity affect consumption and leisure? Be precise about whatever assumptions you are making in order to be able to derive closed-form comparative statics.

2. Write the first-order conditions for the model from Jaimovich and Rebelo 2006. Holding fixed all future actions, how would good news about *today's* productivity affect consumption and leisure? Be precise about whatever assumptions you are making in order to be able to derive closed-form comparative statics.

3. Write the first-order conditions for the model from Veldkamp and Wolfers 2007. Holding fixed all future actions, how would good news about *today's* productivity affect consumption and leisure? Be precise about whatever assumptions you are making in order to be able to derive closed-form comparative statics.

4. In the model of section 9.2, why do shocks to total factor productivity (TFP) have less effect than news shocks to investment?

5. In the model of section 9.3, suppose that an agent purchases a signal about the aggregate shock. What is the value of that signal (gross, i.e., before any information costs) if no other agent observes it? What if, in turn, all other producers observe it? Based on your answer, would you say that information is a complement or a substitute?

PART IV

Measurement

Chapter Ten

Testing Information Theories

As mentioned in the introduction, this book is about how to use information choice tools to explain observed real-world phenomena. That puts the models in this book squarely in the realm of applied theory. The standard of research in modern applied theory requires the author not just present a plausible explanation for a phenomenon but also offer corroborating evidence for her theory. That often presents a challenge for theories whose key variable is an inherently unobservable information set. This chapter describes a few empirical strategies for testing models of information choice. The list is by no means exhaustive; it is meant to provide ideas. The first two sections consider direct measures of information flow and beliefs. Sections 10.3 and 10.4 look at indirect measures of information. Lastly, sections 10.5 and 10.6 use theory to map observable data into information measures.

10.1 MEASURING FLOWS OF NEWS

One way to measure information flows is to look at the quantity of information being provided. For example, Graham (1999) counts the amount of coverage assets get in investment newsletters. Fang and Peress (2009) and Veldkamp (2006) count the number of stories about firms or emerging markets in the popular press. A large empirical finance literature uses analyst coverage of firms to proxy for the information investors have. On the whole, such information proxies have significant explanatory power for asset prices.

While counts of news stories from various periodicals and news wires often must be collected by hand, perhaps with the help of a news search engine such as Lexis/Nexis, analyst forecasts are collected in the I/B/E/S (Institutional Brokers' Estimate System) database. I/B/E/S catalogues individual analysts' earnings forecasts, going back as far as 1983 for U.S. companies and 1987 for international companies. Another source of earnings forecasts is FactSet Estimates.

One issue to be aware of with these measures is that information supply is endogenous. It reacts to movements in asset prices and creates movements in asset prices. Veldkamp (2006) measures the joint relationship between *Financial Times* news stories per week and emerging market prices and returns. Using a different information proxy, Hameed, Morck, and Yeung (2010) show that firm size, trade volume, and earnings predict how many analysts will cover a stock. Brennan and Hughes (1991) model a brokerage commission rate that depends on share price such that there is an incentive for brokers to produce research reports on firms with low share prices. The authors use stock splits, where prices fall dramatically without any bad news, to test the theory. These effects operate not only on individual stocks but also on mutual funds. Kaniel, Starks, and Vasudevan (2007) establish that fund characteristics predict media coverage, which in turn predicts capital flows into the fund.

Analyzing news content. While measuring the volume of news provides a proxy for the quantity of information observed, it reveals nothing about that information's content. Recent work uses linguistic quantification methods to measure the extent to which each news item is positive or negative. Tetlock, Saar-Tsechansky, and Macskassy (2008) examined all *Wall Street Journal* and Dow Jones News Service articles about individual S&P 500 firms from 1980 to 2004. Using a dictionary of negative words, they counted the fraction of negative words in each article. The main findings are that, first, these words seem to convey information because negative words forecast negative earnings. They even convey information that is not contained in analyst reports or accounting data. Second, this verbal information is incorporated into market prices for the firm's equity on the subsequent day.

Demers and Vega (2010) use a similar approach to examine corporate earnings announcements. They use textual analysis software called *Diction* to extract measures of optimism and certainty from the language in earnings announcements. Their results show that optimistic language is slowly incorporated into market prices, resulting in an upward post–earnings announcement price drift. Certainty in announcement language corresponds with low contemporaneous price volatility and predicts low future price volatility.

10.2 FORECAST PRECISION

Perhaps the most straightforward way of measuring the information agents have is to ask them what they believe will happen. There are a few sources of such forecast data.

For theories about differences in macroeconomic information over the business cycle, the Survey of Professional Forecasters (http://www.phil.frb.org/econ/liv/index.html) is a good source of data about beliefs. This is panel data. Its time series is quarterly from 1968:4. The number of analysts varies between 9 and 76 with an average of 36 per quarter. Two measures of information precision could be backed out of this data. One is the dispersion of the forecasts. Less information is generally associated with more forecast dispersion. (Although you should verify that this is true in the model you are trying to test. If your model assumes common prior beliefs, it is quite possible that more dispersion would be indicative of more private information.) A second measure is the average mean squared error or average absolute deviation of forecasts from the realization of the forecasted variable.

With I/B/E/S data on analysts' forecasts, one can construct the same kinds of information precision measures for financial assets. For example, Bae, Stulz, and Tan (2008) show that home analysts in thirty two countries make more precise earnings forecasts for home stocks than foreign analysts do. On average, the increase in precision is 8 percent. They use this finding to support the claim that the home bias in equity holdings arises because home investors know more about home assets. To further this point, they show that the size of the home analyst advantage is related to home bias. When local analysts' forecasts are more precise relative to foreigners' forecasts (more information asymmetry), foreign investors hold less of that country's assets.

10.3 USING COVARIANCES TO INFER INFORMATION SETS

One recurring theme in the book is that information choices determine how states and actions covary. This was true in strategic games (chapter 4). It appeared again in the discussions of price-setting where the reaction of producers' prices to monetary policy innovations depended on information choices (chapter 6). In chapter 8, information choices made actions highly correlated. If agents' information about some state variable is reflected in the extent to which their action correlates with that state, then correlations can be used to infer information sets and test information-based theories. There are many possible ways to do this inference. Below are four examples.

Klenow and Willis (2007) test inattentiveness models of price-setting by asking whether information revealed in past periods acts as a shock to prices in the current period. Since an inattentive agent does not know about realized shocks until he updates his information set, the shocks only affect the price he sets with a lag. They find that lagged shocks do affect current prices, consistent with the inattentiveness theory (Reis 2006) for sticky prices. In a similar exercise with asset prices, Hong, Tourous, and Valkanov (2007) find that industry information affects the market equity index value with a lag.

Hong, Stein, and Yu (2007) did a case study of Amazon equity. They found that traders writing about and trading on data about the number of clicks on Amazon's Web page suddenly shifted in 2000 to writing about and trading based on earnings announcements. They infer that traders changed the information they used because of the change in the covariance of the stock price with the announcements of earnings fundamentals.

Instead of computing a covariance, Kacperczyk and Seru (2007) use a regression R^2. They construct a measure of *reliance on public information* (RPI) to proxy for the amount of public information the fund manager uses to manage his portfolio. RPI is the R^2 of a regression of changes in fund managers' portfolio holdings on changes in analysts' forecasts. They claim that managers rely more on public information when they have less private information. This claim is supported by the fact that funds with higher RPI earn lower profits.

Similarly, Durnev et al. (2003) measure which assets' prices contain more and less information about future earnings by regressing future earnings on asset prices. The idea is that when investors have information about future earnings, they buy when earnings will be high, pushing the price of the asset up, and sell when earnings will be low, pushing the price down. Thus, when the price moves in advance of earnings announcements (in the same direction as the announcement), then investors must have information about what that announcement will be. This is used as a proxy for how informed investors are.

One potential drawback of this approach is that the covariance of the state variable and the action may be what the model is designed to explain. If that is the case, then this approach will not distinguish between competing theories all designed to explain this covariance. The researcher will need to use other indirect predictions to evaluate the model.

10.4 REALIZED PROFITS AS PROXIES FOR INFORMATION

In a rational model, more information enables an agent to choose higher-utility actions, on average. Higher utility typically means higher profit. Thus, realized profit can serve as a proxy for how much information an agent has.

For example, using CRSP data (Center for Research in Securities Prices, available 1927–2000), Biais, Bossaerts, and Spatt (2010) show that price-contingent strategies generate annual returns (Sharpe ratios) that are 3 percent (16.5 percent) higher than the indexing strategy. In other words, today's prices covary with and thus contain information about future returns. This work gives us an idea of how much information prices contain. Since prices contain information that investors know, they also reveal how much information an average market participant knows.

Oftentimes information-based theories are used to explain features of the data that more standard endowment or production economy models have a hard time explaining. Therefore, the competitor explanations for this fact may well be behavioral theories. One way to distinguish a rational from a behavioral explanation is to look at whether the behavior results in higher profits. Biases are mistakes we make in utility maximization and should lower observable measures of welfare. Information choice by agents with (noisy) rational expectations should maximize utility.

One example of using this kind of argument is in trying to distinguish rational from behavioral explanations for portfolio under-diversification. Ivkovic, Sialm, and Weisbenner (2008) find that concentrated investors outperform diversified ones by as much as 3 per cent per year. Outperformance is even higher for investments in local stocks, where natural informational asymmetries are most likely to be present (see also Coval and Moskowitz 2001; Massa and Simonov 2006; and Ivkovic and Weisbenner 2005). If fund managers have superior information about stocks in particular industries, they should outperform in these industries. Kacperczyk, Sialm, and Zheng (2005) show that funds with above-median industry concentration yield an average return that is 1.1 percent per year higher than those with below-median concentration. These findings support the hypothesis that concentration is information ariven.

10.5 INFORMATION CHOICE AS A SUBSTITUTE FOR
INFORMATION DATA

One objection to incomplete information theories is that basing theories on unobservables, like information, makes for untestable models and vacuous theory. Yet this argument highlights why theories of endogenous information are so important. It is the standard models, the ones that make stylized assumptions about information endowments, that offer no way to test these assumptions. Micro-founded theories of information transmission that deliver information sets as equilibrium outcomes are a solution to this problem. A theory in which observable fundamentals—such as production, the volatility of productivity, or the aggregate value of information—predict information patterns is testable because it begins and ends with observable economic variables. Observables predict information patterns, which, in turn, predict other observables. Thus a strength of the information choice approach is that it can bring information-based theories, previously deemed untestable, to the data.

Estimating the portfolio choice learning index. One example of using information choice to facilitate testing the model comes from work on portfolio choice (Van Nieuwerburgh and Veldkamp 2009). I go through this example in detail to illustrate more generally how one can derive testable hypotheses from such a theory.

Equation (7.21) establishes a link between observable asset characteristics, such as size and average return, and the average investor's information. The "learning index" $(\mathcal{L}_j = (\Sigma^{-1}(j)e^{2K} + \Sigma_p^{-1}(j))/(\Sigma^{-1}(j) + \Sigma_p^{-1}(j)))$ reveals which assets are most valuable to learn about. Assets with a high learning index are more likely to be learned about than assets with a low index. Since information affects how much risk an asset poses to the average investor, learning indices should predict cross-sectional asset return patterns.

Estimating $\mathcal{L}_j$ presents two big challenges. First is that we need to estimate Σ_p, the variance of the price as a signal of true payoffs. Second is that the theory falsely assumes assets are independent. When assets are correlated, investors learn about independent risk factors (synthetic assets), which are linear combinations of underlying correlated assets. Therefore, we need to compute a learning index for each risk factor.

The following algorithm could be used to estimate learning indices:

1. Transform correlated assets into independent risk factors: Compute the eigen-decomposition (principal components) of asset payoffs. Call the eigenvector matrix Γ and the diagonal eigenvalue matrix Λ, so that $\Sigma = \Gamma\Lambda\Gamma'$.
2. Rewrite the learning index for each risk factor j: In the model, the variance-covariance matrix of noise in prices has the same eigenvectors as asset payoffs. Therefore, we can write $\Sigma_p = \Gamma\Lambda_p\Gamma'$, where Λ_p is a diagonal matrix, with jth diagonal entry $\Lambda_p(j)$. Then, the risk-factor learning index becomes: $\mathcal{L}_j^{rf} = (\Lambda^{-1}(j)e^{2K} + \Lambda_p^{-1}(j))/(\Lambda^{-1}(j) + \Lambda_p^{-1}(j))$.
3. Construct risk-factor prices and payoffs: Payoffs f are the dividend paid between t and $t+1$ plus the price at $t+1$: $f_t = d_t + p_{t+1}$. Pre-multiply the $(n \times 1)$ vectors of asset prices and payoffs by the eigenvector matrix Γ' to form $(n \times 1)$ vectors of risk factor prices and payoffs.
4. Estimate the signal noise in asset prices: For stocks, the pricing equation is $p = A + Bf + Cx$ (equation [7.10]). For risk-factor prices and payoffs, this becomes $\Gamma'p = \Gamma'A + \Gamma'B\Gamma(\Gamma'f) + \Gamma'Cx$ (recall that $\Gamma\Gamma' = I$). Regress risk-factor prices $(\Gamma'p)$ on a constant and risk-factor payoffs $(\Gamma'f)$. The

asset supply shocks are the regression residual. From this set of regressions, compute an R^2 for each risk factor. $(1 - R^2)/R^2$ of the jth regression is $\Lambda_p(j)/\Lambda(j)$.[1]

5. Use $\Lambda(j)$ from step 1 and $\Lambda_p(j)$ from step 4 to construct the learning index for risk factor j. Use an estimate of K from the literature and/or vary K for robustness checks.

6. Pre-multiply the vector of risk-factor indices by the eigenvector matrix Γ. The resulting vector contains learning indices for each asset.

Alternatively, this procedure could be applied to countries or regions by using market indices for prices and returns.

Learning indices could be used to test many aspects of the theory. (1) They should predict information-related variables such as analyst coverage. (2) Countries, regions, or firms with higher learning indices should have lower returns (higher asset prices), relative to what a standard model like the CAPM predicts. This is because the average investor is less uncertain about an asset he learns more about (higher learning index) and because lower uncertainty implies a lower return. When the average investor learns more about an asset with a higher index, he reduces its risk and therefore its return. (3) Finally, a country or region's learning index should be related to the home bias of its residents' portfolios. This relationship is non-monotonic. If the learning index is near zero, no one, not even locals, learn about home risk. When all investors learn about foreign risk, there is only a small home bias that comes from initial information differences. As the home learning index grows, more home investors specialize in home risks. Information asymmetry and home bias rise. In the limit, as the home learning index grows very large, all investors study home risks. Again, the small home bias comes only from the small differences in initial information. Because home bias depends on comparative information advantage, it is strongest for an intermediate level of the learning index.

Other examples of using theory to predict information sets. Peress (2010) predicts that investors with greater risk-sharing opportunities should acquire less information. This theory complements the one described above. It explores the cross-investor heterogeneity in information values instead of just cross-asset differences. One testable prediction that comes out of this theory is that assets with a wide shareholder base have less analyst coverage.

---

[1] To derive the link between the regression R^2 and the learning index, first compute the unconditional variance of prices: $\text{var}(p) = \text{var}(A + Bf + Cx)$. Noting that A is a constant, $\text{var}(f) = \Sigma$, substituting in $B = I$, and recalling that Σ_p is the variance of payoffs, conditional on prices $(CC'\sigma_x^2)$, we get $\text{var}(p) = \Sigma + \Sigma_p$. This is the total sum of squares of prices. Since the asset supply shocks are the regression residual, the variance in prices due to supply shocks Σ_p is the unexplained sum of squares, leaving Σ as the explained sum of squares. Since a regression R^2 is the explained sum of squares divided by the total sum of squares $(\Sigma + \Sigma_p)^{-1}\Sigma$, $1 - R^2$ corresponds to $(\Sigma + \Sigma_p)^{-1}\Sigma_p$. The ratio of these two is $\Sigma^{-1}\Sigma_p$. If we follow the same set of steps to determine the sums of squares for risk-factor prices, we would get $1 - R^2/R^2 = \Lambda^{-1}(j)/\Lambda_p(j)$, for each risk factor j.

10.6 THE BID-ASK SPREAD AND PIN

One of the most commonly used measures of information in financial markets is the probability of informed trading (PIN) Easley et al. (1996) developed this empirical measure to estimate the probability that traders in a market are informed. The data required are the sequence of buy and sell orders submitted to a market-maker. Such data are available from the Nasdaq Trade and Quote database. European data are available from the Euronext database. Easley et al. (1996) show that this measure is tied to another commonly used measure of information asymmetry, the bid-ask spread. To understand the meaning of their measure requires working through a simple Bayesian model.

The PIN model. There is one risky asset and a continuum of traders. There are discrete trading days $i = 1, \dots, I$, but within each day, time is continuous and indexed by $t \in [0, T]$. The risky asset has a payoff V at the end of each period that is serially uncorrelated (this can be easily relaxed) and takes one of three values. If there is good news, which happens with probability $\alpha(1 - \delta)$, the value is $\bar{V}$. If there is bad news, which happens with probability $\alpha\delta$, the value is $\underline{V}$, and if there is no news, which happens with probability $(1 - \alpha)$, the value is V^*. Because all traders observe V at the end of the period, any information accumulated becomes irrelevant at the start of the next period.

A market-maker is an agent that stands ready to buy or sell the asset at posted bid and ask prices. Since the market-maker is risk neutral and faces competition from other potential market-makers, he earns zero expected profit by always setting the price of the asset equal to its expected value, conditional on his information set. He learns from the sequence of buy and sell orders he observes.

There are uninformed buyers and sellers, each of whom arrives according to an independent Poisson process with rate ϵ. If there is no news, no informed traders arrive. If there is either good or bad news, informed traders who know the news with certainty arrive at rate μ.

Updating probabilities. The prior probability of each of the three events at time $t = 0$ is $P_n(0) = 1 - \alpha$, $P_g(0) = \alpha(1 - \delta)$, and $P_b(0) = \delta\alpha$. With the arrival of each trader, these probabilities are updated according to Bayes' law:

$$P_n(t|sell) = \frac{P_n(t)\epsilon}{\epsilon + P_b(t)\mu}. \tag{10.1}$$

The numerator is the probability of a sale, conditional on being in the no-news state. The denominator is the probability of selling in every state: uninformed sellers arrive at rate ϵ in every state and informed sellers arrive only when the state is bad, at rate μ. The expression for the probability of being in the good state takes a similar form:

$$P_g(t|sell) = \frac{P_g(t)\epsilon}{\epsilon + P_b(t)\mu} \tag{10.2}$$

$$P_b(t|sell) = \frac{P_b(t)(\epsilon + \mu)}{\epsilon + P_b(t)\mu}. \tag{10.3}$$

The probability of being in the bad state rises when a sale is observed. That increase comes from the additional probability μ of observing sales in a bad state. Similar calculations produce symmetric expressions for $P_n(t|buy)$, $P_g(t|buy)$, and $P_b(t|buy)$.

The bid-ask spread. Given these six conditional probabilities, we can construct the price, which is the expected value of the security, conditional on a buy or a sell arriving. When a trader wants to sell the asset, the market-maker offers to buy it at a price that we will call the bid price. The price the market-maker charges if someone wants to buy is the ask price. The ask price should always exceed the bid price because the expected value of the security rises when someone wants to buy it and falls if someone wants to sell it:

$$Ask(t) = \frac{P_n(t)\epsilon V^* + P_g(t)\epsilon \bar{V} + P_b(t)(\epsilon + \mu)\underline{V}}{\epsilon + P_b(t)\mu} \tag{10.4}$$

$$Bid(t) = \frac{P_n(t)\epsilon V^* + P_g(t)(\epsilon + \mu)\bar{V} + P_b(t)\epsilon \underline{V}}{\epsilon + P_g(t)\mu}. \tag{10.5}$$

The difference between these two prices is the bid-ask spread. It turns out that this spread is the probability that the buyer is informed times the expected loss if the news is good, plus the probability that a seller is informed, times the expected loss if the news is bad.

Estimating the probability of informed trading. PIN is defined as the conditional probability that there is a news event, either good or bad ($P_g(t) + P_b(t) = 1 - P_n(t)$). That is easy to construct theoretically. But in practice, we do not know the arrival rates μ and ϵ. The solution is to estimate these parameters by maximum likelihood.

Suppose it is a no-news day. Then buyers and sellers arrive independently at Poisson rate ϵ. A Poisson process with arrival rate ϵ is defined such that the probability of N events before time T is

$$e^{\epsilon T} \frac{(\epsilon T)^N}{N!}. \tag{10.6}$$

Since buys and sells arrive independently, the probability of observing B buys and S sells is the product of two Poisson probabilities:

$$P(B, S|no\ news) = e^{\epsilon T} \frac{(\epsilon T)^B}{B!} e^{\epsilon T} \frac{(\epsilon T)^S}{S!}$$

$$= e^{2\epsilon T} \frac{(\epsilon T)^{B+S}}{B!S!}. \tag{10.7}$$

On a bad news day, buys still arrive at rate ϵ, but sells arrive at rate $\mu + \epsilon$. The likelihood of observing B buys and S sells is

$$P(B, S|bad\ news) = e^{-\epsilon T} \frac{(\epsilon T)^B}{B!} e^{-(\epsilon + \mu)T} \frac{[(\epsilon + \mu)T]^S}{S!}. \tag{10.8}$$

The first term is the probability of B arrivals of uninformed traders who buy. The second term is the probability of S arrivals of uninformed and informed traders who sell. A symmetric expression characterizes the probability of B, S if there is good news.

Of course, the econometrician does not know what the true state is each period. He must compute the unconditional probability of B buys and S sells in a period, which is

$$P(B, S) = P(B, S|no\ news)(1 - \alpha) + P(B, S|good\ news)\alpha(1 - \delta)$$
$$+ P(B, S|bad\ news)\alpha\delta.$$

Finally, since the events in each day are independent, multiply the likelihoods for each day together to get the likelihood function for the sequence of observations:

$$L(\{B_t\}_t, \{S_t\}_t) = \prod_t P(B_t, S_t).$$

Choose the parameters $(\alpha, \delta, \mu, \epsilon)$ that maximize this likelihood function.

Easley et al. (1996) use this procedure to estimate the arrival rates of informed and uninformed traders for high-and low-volume stocks. By definition, high-volume stocks have higher arrival rates overall. In the highest-volume decile of stocks in their sample, they find an arrival rate of 0.13 for informed and 0.18 for uninformed traders. For low-volume stocks (in the eighth decile), they find an arrival rate of 0.016 for informed and 0.010 for uninformed traders. Notice that the probability of traders being informed is smaller for the high-volume stocks than for the low-volume stocks. The authors use this finding to argue that the reason why low-volume stocks have higher bid-ask spreads is because trade in those assets is more likely to be information driven.

Comparing PIN to other information measures. PIN is a different kind of information measure from the ones discussed earlier because it is measuring the extent of information asymmetry between the traders and the market-maker. The previous measures are capturing total information flow to all market participants. If there is no information flow, then there is no information asymmetry and PIN will be zero. But if there is a fast rate of information flow so that all market participants know as soon as the asset value changes, PIN will also be zero. The market-maker will set the asset price equal to the true asset value, all informed traders will be indifferent between buying and selling, and order flow will have no information content. Thus the relationship between PIN and the previously discussed information flow measures is that as information flow rises, PIN rises then falls.

Chapter Eleven

Conclusions

Many of the most spectacular events in modern macroeconomics involve information and coordination. This is because outcomes of physical production processes take time, but beliefs can change in an instant. The rise of ever faster communications technology makes communication and coordination ever easier and faster. Since coordination requires some knowledge of what other actors in the economy are doing, better communication may mean more sudden movements in macro and financial markets. Thus, the same intense scrutiny that has been applied toward understanding flows of goods and services should also be applied toward understanding flows of information.

The challenge in investigating information flows is that they are usually unobservable. But models with information choice offer a way around this obstacle. These theories predict what information agents will choose to learn. In doing so, they link observable variables to information, which in turn predicts other observable variables. This makes for testable theories.

There is lots of scope for research on information choice and processing on many topics. One of the reasons for writing a book that touches on so many applied topics is to highlight differences in their methodologies and similarities in their main ideas and, consequently, to offer opportunities for the reader to take ideas and tools from one literature and bring them to another.

How does one get started working on a new information-choice-based theory? First, look for facts that are puzzles to existing theories. Behavioral economics or finance article are good sources of puzzles. Ask yourself, might information explain that? Some of the effects we have used information choice to explain include: amplification of underlying shocks, hidden complementarities, regime shifts with changing covariances, excess volatility, and inertia. Once you have a theory model, back it up with evidence. Information choice is not so widely accepted that many people will believe a theory just because a researcher solves the model. Use information measures to argue that this is the correct explanation. In pursuing your research agenda, recognize that building up a research area is a game with strategic complementarity. Many areas of economics fall into decline because the people working in those areas see success as zero-sum. This is a mistake. The more work published on information choice, the more mainstream it will become and the easier it will be to get information choice work published. Last but not least, be creative, be persistent, and good luck!

References

Abel, Andrew, Janice Eberly, and Stavros Panageas. 2007. "Optimal Inattention to the Stock Market." *American Economic Review 97(2)*, 244–49.

Admati, Anat. 1985. "A Noisy Rational Expectations Equilibrium for Multi-Asset Securities Markets." *Econometrica 53(3)*, 629–57.

Admati, Anat, and Paul Pfleiderer. 1986. "A Monopolistic Market for Information." *Journal of Economic Theory 39*, 400–438.

———. 1990. "Direct and Indirect Sale of Information." *Econometrica 58(4)*, 901–28.

Allen, Franklin, Stephen Morris, and Hyun Song Shin. 2006. "Beauty Contests and Bubbles." *Review of Financial Studies 19*, 719–52.

Amador, Manuel, and Pierre-Olivier Weill. 2009. "Learning from Prices: Public Communication and Welfare." Working paper.

———. 2011. "Learning from Private and Public Observations of Others' Actions." *Journal of Political Economy* (2011).

Angeletos, George-Marios, and Jennifer La'O. 2009. "Dispersed Information over the Business Cycle: Optimal Fiscal and Monetary Policy." Massachusetts Institute of Technology working paper.

Angeletos, George-Marios, and Alessandro Pavan. 2004. "Transparency of Information and Coordination in Economies with Investment Complementarities." *American Economic Review, Papers and Proceedings 94(2)*, 91–98.

———. 2007. "Efficient Use of Information and Social Value of Information." *Econometrica 75(4)*, 1103–42.

Angeletos, George-Marios, and Ivan Werning. 2006. "Crises and Prices: Information Aggregation, Multiplicity and Volatility." *American Economic Review 96(5)*, 1720–36.

Angeletos, George-Marios, Christian Hellwig, and Alessandro Pavan. 2007. "Dynamic Global Games of Regime Change: Learning, Multiplicity and Timing of Attacks." *Econometrica 75(3)*, 711–56.

Avery, Christopher, and Peter Zemsky. 1998. "Multidimensional Uncertainty and Herd Behavior in Financial Markets." *American Economic Review 88(4)*, 724–48.

Bacchetta, Philippe, and Eric van Wincoop. 2006. "Can Information Heterogeneity Explain the Exchange Rate Determination Puzzle?" *American Economic Review 96(3)*, 552–76.

Bae, Kee-Hong, Rene Stulz, and Hongping Tan. 2008. "Do Local Analysts Know More? A Cross-Country Study of the Performance of Local Analysts and Foreign Analysts." *Journal of Financial Economics 88(3)*, 581–606.

Ball, Laurence, and David Romer. 1990. "Real Rigidities and the Non-neutrality of Money." *Review of Economic Studies 57*, 183–203.

Banerjee, Abhjit. 1992. "A Simple Model of Herd Behavior." *Quarterly Journal of Economics 107(3)*, 797–817.

Barber, Brad, and Terrance Odean. 2008. "All That Glitters: The Effect of Attention and News on the Buying Behavior of Individual and Institutional Investors." *Review of Financial Studies 21(2)*, 785–818.

Barlevy, Gadi, and Pietro Veronesi. 2000. "Information Acquisition in Financial Markets." *Review of Economic Studies 67*, 79–90.

Barsky, Robert, and Eric Sims. 2009. "News Shocks." University of Michigan working paper.

Beaudry, Paul, and Franck Portier. 2004. "Exploring Pigou's Theory of Cycles." *Journal of Monetary Economics 51(6)*, 1183–1216.

———. 2006. "News, Stock Prices and Economic Fluctuations." *American Economic Review 96(4)*, 1293–1307.

Bernhardt, Dan, and Bart Taub. 2005. "Strategic Information Flows in Stock Markets." Working paper.

Biais, Bruno, Peter Bossaerts, and Chester Spatt. 2010. "Equilibrium Asset Pricing under Heterogenous Information." *Review of Financial Studies 23*, 1503–43.

Bikhchandani, Sushil, David Hirshleifer, and Ivo Welch. 1992. "A Theory of Fads, Fashion, Custom, and Cultural Change as Information Cascades." *Journal of Political Economy 100*, 992–1026.

Billingsley, Patrick. 1995. *Probability and Measure*. 3rd ed. John Wiley and Sons.

Bolton, Patrick, Markus Brunnermeier, and Laura Veldkamp. 2008. "Leadership, Coordination and Mission-Driven Management." NBER working paper 14339.

Brennan, Michael, and Patricia Hughes. 1991. "Stock Prices and the Supply of Information." *Journal of Finance 46(5)*, 1665–91.

Breon-Drish, Bradyn. 2011. "Asymmetric Information in Financial Markets: Anything Goes." Ph.D. thesis, University of California, Berkeley.

Brunnermeier, Markus. 2001. *Asset Pricing under Asymmetric Information: Bubbles, Crashes, Technical Analysis and Herding*. 1st ed. Oxford University Press.

Bullard, James, George Evans, and Seppo Honkapohja. 2007. "A Model of Near-Rational Exuberance." University of Oregon working paper.

Cagetti, Marco, Lars Hansen, Thomas Sargent, and Noah Williams. 2002. "Robustness and Pricing with Uncertain Growth." *Review of Financial Studies 15(2)*, 363–404.

Calvo, Guillermo. 1983. "Staggered Prices in a Utility Maximizing Framework." *Journal of Monetary Economics 12*, 383–98.

Caplin, Andrew, and John Leahy. 1994. "Business as Usual, Market Crashes, and Wisdom after the Fact." *American Economic Review 84(3)*, 548–65.

Carlsson, Hans, and Eric Van Damme. 1993. "Global Games and Equilibrium Selection." *Econometrica 61(5)*, 989–1018.

Carpenter, Seth. 2004. "Transparency and Monetary Policy: What Does the Academic Literature Tell Policy Makers?" Board of Governors of the Federal Reserve System, working paper.

Chamley, Christophe. 2004. *Rational Herds: Economics Models of Social Learning*, 1st ed. Cambridge University Press.

———. 2006. "Complementarities in Information Acquisition with Short-Term Trades." Boston Universtiy, working paper.

Chari, V. V., and Patrick Kehoe. 2004. "Financial Crises as Herds." *Journal of Economic Theory 119*, 128–50.

Cheung, Yin-Wong, and Menzie Chinn. 2001. "Currency Traders and Exchange Rate Dynamics: A Survey of the U.S. Market." *Journal of International Money and Finance 20(4)*, 439–71.

Chiang, Alpha. 1984. *Fundamental Methods of Mathematical Economics*. 3rd ed. McGraw-Hill.

Christiano, Lawrence, Cosmin Ilut, Roberto Motto, and Massimo Rostagno. 2010. "Signals: Implications for Business Cycles and Monetary Policy." Northwestern University working paper.

Cornand, Camille, and Frank Heinemann. 2008. "Optimal Degree of Public Information Dissemination." *The Economic Journal 118*, 718–42.

Coval, Joshua, and Tobias Moskowitz. 2001. "The Geography of Investment: Informed Trading and Asset Prices." *Journal of Political Economy 109(4)*, 811–41.

Cover, Thomas, and Joy Thomas. 1991. *Elements of Information Theory*. 1st ed. John Wiley and Sons.

Cukierman, Alex, and Alan Meltzer. 1986. "The Theory of Ambiguity, Credibility, and Inflation under Discretion and Asymmetric Information." *Econometrica 54(5)*, 1099–1128.

Demers, Elizabeth, and Clara Vega. 2010. "Soft Information in Earnings Announcements: News or Noise?" INSEAD working paper.

Dow, James, Itay Goldstein, and Alexander Guembel. 2010. "Incentives for Information Production in Markets Where Prices Affect Real Investment." Wharton working paper.

Duffie, Darrell, 1996. *Dynamic Asset Pricing Theory*. 2nd ed. Princeton University Press.

Duffie, Darrell, Gaston Giroux, and Gustavo Manso. 2010. "Information Percolation." *American Economics Journal: Microeconomic Theory 2*, 100–111.

Duffie, Darrell, Semyon Malamud, and Gustavo Manso. 2009. "Information Percolation with Equilibrium Search Dynamics." *Econometrica 77*, 1513–74.

———. 2010. "The Relative Contributions of Private Information Sharing and Public Information Releases to Information Aggregation." *Journal of Economic Theory, 145*, 1574–1601.

Durnev, Artyom, Randall Morck, Bernard Yeung, and Paul Zarowin. 2003. "Does Greater Firm-Specific Return Variation Mean More or Less Informed Stock Pricing?" *Journal of Accounting Research 41(5)*, 797–836.

Easley, David, Nicholas Kiefer, Maureen O'Hara, and Joseph Paperman. 1996. "Liquidity, Information and Infrequently Traded Stocks." *Journal of Finance 51(4)*, 1405–36.

Edmond, Chris. 2005. "Information Manipulation, Coordination and Regime Change." New York University working paper.

Elliott, Robert, Lakhdar Aggoun, and John Moore. 1995. *Hidden Markov Models: Estimation and Control*. 1st ed. Springer.

Epstein, Larry, and Stanley Zin. 1989. "Substitution, Risk Aversion, and the Temporal Behavior of Consumption and Asset Returns: A Theoretical Framework." *Econometrica 57*, 937–69.

Evans, George, and Seppo Honkapohja. 2001. *Learning and Expectations in Macroeconomics*. 1st ed. Princeton University Press.

Fang, Lily, and Joel Peress. 2009. "Media Coverage and the Cross-Section of Stock Returns." *Journal of Finance 64(5)*, 2023–52.

Faust, Jon, and Lars Svensson. 2002. "The Equilibrium Degree of Transparency and Control in Monetary Policy." *Journal of Money, Credit and Banking 34(2)*, 520–39.

Fogli, Alessandra, and Laura Veldkamp. 2007. "Nature or Nurture? Learning and Female Labor Force Participation." Federal Reserve Bank of Minneapolis Staff Report 386.

Froot, Kenneth, David Scharfstein, and Jeremy Stein. 1992. "Herd on the Street: Informational Inefficiencies in a Market with Short-Term Speculation." *Journal of Finance 47(4)*, 1461–84.

Gabaix, Xavier, and David Laibson. 2002. "The 6D Bias and the Equity Premium Puzzle." *NBER Macroeconomics Annual 47(4)*, 257–312.

Garcia, Diego, and Joel Vanden. 2005. "Information Acquisition and Mutual Funds." *Journal of Economic Theory 144(5)*, 1965–95.

Geraats, Petra. 2002. "Central Bank Transparency." *The Economic Journal 112*, F532–F565.

Goldstein, Itay, and Ady Pauzner. 2005. "Demand Deposit Contracts and the Probability of Bank Runs." *Journal of Finance 60(3)*, 1293–1328.

Goldstein, Itay, Emre Ozdenoren, and Kathy Yuan. 2011. "Learning and Complementarities in Speculative Attacks." *Review of Economic Studies 78(1)*, 263–92.

Golosov, Mikhail, and Robert Lucas. 2007. "Menu Costs and Phillips Curves." *Journal of Political Economy 115*, 171–99.

Golosov, Mikhail, Guido Lorenzoni, and Aleh Tsyvinski. 2008. "Decentralized Trading with Private Information." Massachusetts Institute of Technology working paper.

Gosselin, Pierre, Aileen Lotz, and Charles Wyplosz. 2008. "When Central Banks Reveal Their Interest Rate Forecats: Alignment of Expectations vs. Creative Opacity." *International Journal of Central Banking 4(3)*, 145–85.

Graham, John. 1999. "Herding among Investment Newsletters: Theory and Evidence." *Journal of Finance 54*, 1.

Greenwood, Jeremy, Zvi Hercowitz, and Gregory Huffman. 1988. "Investment, Capacity Utilization, and the Real Business Cycle." *American Economic Review 78(3)*, 402–17.

Grossman, Sanford, and Joeseph Stiglitz. 1980. "On the Impossibility of Informationally Efficient Markets." *American Economic Review 70(3)*, 393–408.

Hameed, Allaudeen, Randall Morck, and Bernard Yeung. 2010. "Information Markets, Analysts and Comovement in Stock Returns." Alberta School of Business working paper.

Hansen, Lars, and Thomas Sargent. 2003. "Robust Control of Forward Looking Models." *Journal of Monetary Economics 50(3)*, 581–604.

Hellwig, Christian. 2002. "Public Information, Private Information, and the Multiplicity of Equilibria in Coordination Games." *Journal of Economic Theory 107(2)*, 191–222.

———. 2005. "Heterogeneous Information and the Benefits of Public Information Disclosures." University of California, Los Angeles working paper.

Hellwig, Christian, and Laura Veldkamp. 2009. "Knowing What Others Know: Coordination Motives in Information Acquisition." *Review of Economic Studies 76*, 223–51.

Hellwig, Christian, Arijit Mukherji, and Aleh Tsyvinski. 2005. "Self-Fulfilling Currency Crises: The Role of Interest Rates." *American Economic Review 96(5)*, 1769–87.

Hellwig, Martin. 1980. "On the Aggregation of Information in Competitive Markets." *Journal of Economic Theory 22*, 477–98.

Hirschleifer, David, Siew-Hong Teoh, and Seongyeon Lin. 2005. "Disclosure to a Credulous Audience: The Role of Limited Attention." University of California, Irvine working paper.

Hong, Harrison, Jeremy Stein, and Jialin Yu. 2007. "Simple Forecasts and Paradigm Shifts." *Journal of Finance 62(3)*, 1207–42.

Hong, Harrison, Walter Torous, and Rossen Valkanov. 2007. "Do Industries Lead the Stock Market?" *Journal of Financial Economics 83(2)*, 367–96.

Huang, Lixin, and Hong Liu. 2007. "Rational Inattention and Portfolio Selection." *Journal of Finance 62*, 1999–2040.

Huberman, Gur, and Tomer Regev. 2001. "Contagious Speculation and a Cure for Cancer: A Nonevent That Made Stock Prices Soar." *Journal of Finance 56(1)*, 387–96.

Ivkovic, Zoran, and Scott Weisbenner. 2005. "Local Does as Local Is: Information Content and the Geography of Individual Investors' Common Stock Investments." *Journal of Finance 60*, 267–306.

Ivkovic, Zoran, Clemens Sialm, and Scott Weisbenner. 2008. "Portfolio Concentration and the Performance of Individual Investors." *Journal of Financial and Quantitative Analysis, 43(3)*, 613–56.

Jaimovich, Nir, and Sergio Rebelo. 2006. "Can News about the Future Drive the Business Cycle?" *American Economic Review 99(4)*, 1097–1118.

Kacperczyk, Marcin, and Amit Seru. 2007. "Fund Manager Use of Public Information: New Evidence on Managerial Skills." *Journal of Finance 62(2)*, 485–528.

Kacperczyk, Marcin, Clemens Sialm, and Lu Zheng. 2005. "On the Industry Concentration of Actively Managed Equity Mutual Funds." *Journal of Finance 60(4)*, 1983–2011.

Kacperczyk, Marcin, Stijn Van Nieuwerburgh, and Laura Veldkamp. 2010. "Attention Allocation over the Business Cycle." New York University working paper.

Kaniel, Ron, Laura Starks, and Vasudha Vasudevan. 2007. "Headlines and Bottom Lines: Attention and Learning Effects from Media Coverage of Mutual Funds." Duke University working paper.

Karatzas, Ioannis, and Steven Shreve. 1991. *Brownian Motion and Stochastic Calculus*. 2nd ed. Springer.

Keppo, Jussi, Giuseppe Moscarini, and Lones Smith. 2005. "The Demand for Information: More Heat than Light." *Journal of Economic Theory 138(1)*, 21–50.

King, Robert, Charles Plosser, and Sergio Rebelo. 1988. "Production, Growth and Business Cycles I: The Basic Neo-Classical Model." *Journal of Monetary Economics 2*, 195–232.

Klenow, Peter, and Jonathan Willis. 2007. "Sticky Information and Sticky Prices." *Journal of Monetary Economics 54*, 79–99.

Kyle, Albert. 1985. "Continuous Auctions and Insider Trading." *Econometrica 53*, 1315–35.

Li, Yan, and Liyan Yang. 2008. "Complementarities in Information Acquisition with Heterogeneous Investment Opportunities." University of Toronto working paper.

Lipster, Robert, and Albert Shiryaev. 2001. *Statistics of Random Processes II*. Springer.

Lorenzoni, Guido. 2009. "A Theory of Demand Shocks." *American Economic Review 99(5)*, 2050–84.

Lucas, Robert. 1972. "Expectations and the Neutrality of Money." *Journal of Economic Theory 4*, 103–124.

Luo, Yulei. 2008. "Consumption Dynamics under Information Processing Constraints." *Review of Economic Dynamics 11*, 366–85.

Maćkowiak, Bartosz, and Mirko Wiederholt. 2009a. "Business Cycle Dynamics under Rational Inattention." Northwestern University working paper.

———. 2009b. "Optimal Sticky Prices under Rational Inattention." *American Economic Review 99(3)*, 769–803.

Mankiw, Gregory, and Ricardo Reis. 2002. "Sticky Information versus Sticky Prices: A Proposal to Replace the New Keynesian Phillips Curve." *Quarterly Journal of Economics 117*, 1295–1328.

Massa, Massimo, and Andrei Simonov. 2006. "Hedging, Familiarity and Portfolio Choice." *Review of Financial Studies 19(2)*, 633–85.

Merton, Robert. 1987. "A Simple Model of Capital Market Equilibrium with Incomplete Information." *Journal of Finance 42(3)*, 483–510.

Milgrom, Paul, and Nancy Stokey. 1982. "Information, Trade and Common Knowledge." *Journal of Economic Theory 26*, 17–27.

Mondria, Jordi. 2010. "Portfolio Choice, Attention Allocation, and Price Comovement." *Journal of Economic Theory 145(5)*, 1837–64.

Morris, Stephen, and Hyun Song Shin. 1998. "Unique Equilibrium in a Model of Self-Fulfilling Currency Attacks." *American Economic Review 88(3)*, 587–97.

———. 2002. "The Social Value of Public Information." *American Economic Review 92*, 1521–34.

Moscarini, Giuseppe. 2004. "Limited Information Capacity as a Source of Inertia." *Journal of Economic Dynamics and Control 28(10)*, 2003–35.

Muendler, Marc-Andreas. 2005. "The Action Value of Information and the Natural Transparency Limit." University of California, San Diego working paper.

Myatt, David, and Chris Wallace. 2008. "On the Sources and Value of Information: Public Announcements and Macroeconomic Performance." Oxford University working paper.

———. 2009. "Endogenous Information Acquisition in Coordination Games." Oxford University working paper.

O'Hara, Maureen. 1995. *Market Microstructure Theory*. Blackwell Press.

Ozdenoren, Emre, and Kathy Yuan. 2007. "Feedback Effects and Asset Prices." *Journal of Finance 63(4)*, 1939–75.

Pastor, Lubos, and Pietro Veronesi. 2003. "Stock Valuation and Learning about Profitability." *Journal of Finance 58(5)*, 1749–89.

Peng, Lin. 2005. "Learning with Information Capacity Constraints." *Journal of Financial and Quantitative Analysis 40(2)*, 307–29.

Peng, Lin, and Wei Xiong. 2006. "Investor Attention, Overconfidence and Category Learning." *Journal of Financial Economics 80*, 563–602.

Peress, Joel. 2004. "Wealth, Information Acquisition and Portfolio Choice." *Review of Financial Studies 17(3)*, 879–914.

———. 2010. "The Tradeoff between Risk Sharing and Information Production in Financial Markets." *Journal of Economic Theory 145(1)*, 124–55.

Radner, Roy, and Joseph Stiglitz. 1984. "A Nonconcavity in the Value of Information." In M. Boyer and R. E. Kihlstrom, eds., *Bayesian Models in Economic Theory*. Elsevier Science Publishers B.V.

Radner, Roy, and Timothy Van Zandt. 2001. "Real-Time Decentralized Information Processing and Returns to Scale." *Economic Theory 17*, 497–544.

Rebelo, Sergio. 2005. "Real Business Cycle Models: Past, Present, and Future." *Scandinavian Journal of Economics 107(2)*, 217–38.

Reis, Ricardo. 2006. "Inattentive Producers." *Review of Economic Studies 73(3)*, 793–821.

Romer, Paul. 1990. "Endogenous Technological Change." *Journal of Political Economy 98*, 71–102.

Ross, Stephen. 1976. "The Arbitrage Theory of Capital Asset Pricing." *Journal of Economic Theory 13*, 341–60.

Shannon, Claude E. 1948. "Mathematical Theory of Communication." *Bell System Technology Journal 27*, 379–423, 623–56.

Sims, Christopher. 1998. "Stickiness." *Carnegie-Rochester Series on Public Policy 49(1)*, 317–56.

———. 2003. "Implications of Rational Inattention." *Journal of Monetary Economics 50(3)*, 665–90.

———. 2006. "Rational Inattention: Beyond the Linear-Quadratic Case." *American Economic Review 96(2)*, 158–63.

Sims, Eric. 2009. "Expectation Driven Business Cycles: An Empirical Evaluation." University of Notre Dame working paper.

Stock, James, and Mark Watson. 1996. "Evidence on Structural Instability in Macroeconomic Time Series Relationships." *Journal of Business and Economic Statistics 14*, 11–30.

Stromberg, David. 2001. "Mass Media and Public Policy." *European Economic Review 45*, 652–63.

Svensson, Lars. 2006. "Social Value of Public Information: Morris and Shin (2002) Is Actually Pro Transparency, Not Con." *American Economic Review 96(2)*, 448–51.

Tetlock, Paul, Maytal Saar-Tsechansky, and Sofus Macskassy. 2008. "More than Words: Quantifying Language to Measure Firms' Fundamentals." *Journal of Finance 63(3)*, 1437–67.

Timmermann, Allan. 1993. "How Learning in Financial Markets Generates Excess Volatility and Predictability in Stock Prices." *Quarterly Journal of Economics 108*, 1135–45.

Townsend, Robert M. 1983. "Forecasting the Forecasts of Others." *Journal of Political Economy 91(4)*, 546–88.

Turmuhambetova, Gauhar. 2005. "A Simple Portfolio Problem with Endogenous Information." Ph.D. thesis, University of Chicago.

Uhlig, Harald. 1990. "Costly Information Acquisition, Stock Prices and Neoclassical Growth." Ph.D. thesis, University of Minnesota.

Van Nieuwerburgh, Stijn, and Laura Veldkamp. 2006. "Learning Asymmetries in Real Business Cycles." *Journal of Monetary Economics 53(4)*, 753–72.

———. 2009. "Information Immobility and the Home Bias Puzzle." *Journal of Finance 64(3)*, 1187–1215.

———. 2010. "Information Acquisition and Portfolio Under-Diversification." *Review of Economic Studies 77(2)*, 779–805.

Veldkamp, Laura. 2006. "Media Frenzies in Markets for Financial Information." *American Economic Review 96(3)*, 577–601.

Veldkamp, Laura, and Justin Wolfers. 2007. "Aggregate Shocks or Aggregate Information? Costly Information and Business Cycle Comovement." *Journal of Monetary Economics 54*, 37–55.

Verrecchia, Robert. 1982. "Information Acquisition in a Noisy Rational Expectations Economy." *Econometrica 50(6)*, 1415–30.

Vives, Xavier. 1984. "Duopoly Information Equilibrium: Cournot and Bertrand." *Journal of Economic Theory 34(1)*, 71–94.

———. 1988. "Aggregation of Information in Large Cournot Markets." *Econometrica 56*, 851–76.

———. 2008. *Information and Learning in Markets: The Impact of Market Microstructure*. Princeton University Press.

Wang, Jiang. 1993. "A Model of Intertemporal Asset Prices under Asymmetric Information." *Review of Economic Studies 60*, 249–82.

Welch, Ivo. 1992. "Sequential Sales, Learning and Cascades." *Journal of Finance 47(2)*, 695–732.

Wilson, Robert. 1975. "Informational Economies of Scale." *Bell Journal of Economics 6*, 184–95.

Woodford, Michael. 2002. "Imperfect Common Knowledge and the Effects of Monetary Policy." In P. Aghion, R. Frydman, J. Stiglitz, and M. Woodford, eds., *Knowledge, Information, and Expectations in Modern Macroeconomics: In Honor of Edmund S. Phelps*. Princeton University Press.

————. 2008. "Information-Constrained State-Dependent Pricing." *Journal of Monetary Economics 56(1)*, S100–S124.

Yuan, Kathy. 2005. "Asymmetric Price Movements and Borrowing Constraints: A Rational Expectations Equilibrium Model of Crises." *Journal of Finance 60(1)*, 379–411.

Zeira, Joseph. 1994. "Informational Cycles." *Review of Economic Studies 61*, 31–44.

————. 1999. "Informational Overshooting, Booms and Crashes." *Journal of Monetary Economics 43*, 237–57.

Index